Constructing the (M)other

Disability Studies in Education

Susan L. Gabel and Scot Danforth
General Editors

Vol. 22

The Disability Studies in Education series is part of the Peter Lang Education list.
Every volume is peer reviewed and meets
the highest quality standards for content and production.

PETER LANG
New York • Bern • Berlin
Brussels • Vienna • Oxford • Warsaw

Constructing the (M)other

Narratives of Disability, Motherhood, and the Politics of *Normal*

Priya Lalvani, EDITOR

PETER LANG
New York • Bern • Berlin
Brussels • Vienna • Oxford • Warsaw

Library of Congress Cataloging-in-Publication Control Number: 2019014328

Bibliographic information published by **Die Deutsche Nationalbibliothek.**
Die Deutsche Nationalbibliothek lists this publication in the "Deutsche
Nationalbibliografie"; detailed bibliographic data are available
on the Internet at http://dnb.d-nb.de/.

ISSN 1548-7210
ISBN 978-1-4331-6973-1 (hardcover)
ISBN 978-1-4331-6974-8 (paperback)
ISBN 978-1-4331-6978-6 (ebook pdf)
ISBN 978-1-4331-6979-3 (epub)
ISBN 978-1-4331-6980-9 (mobi)
DOI 10.3726/b15664

The paper in this book meets the guidelines for permanence and durability
of the Committee on Production Guidelines for Book Longevity
of the Council of Library Resources.

© 2019 Peter Lang Publishing, Inc., New York
29 Broadway, 18th floor, New York, NY 10006
www.peterlang.com

Printed in the United States of America

For
Kalavati and Soona, who mothered my parents
and
Phiroza, who mothered me and told me stories.

Every time we tell a story, the world is changed.

Table OF Contents

List of Figures ix

Acknowledgments xi

Foreword: *"There was this mother, one mother..."* xiii
    Linda Ware

Introduction: Mother: The Story 1
    Priya Lalvani

Chapter One: Standard Deviation: Stigma, Surveillance,
    and the Good ~~Mother~~ Daughter 17
    Tammy Bachrach

Chapter Two: West Side Story (Down Under) 29
    Bernadette Macartney

Chapter Three: Selves-Advocacy and the Meeting Space 51
    Erin McCloskey

Chapter Four: An Unexpected Journey with My Mother 67
    Maria T. Timberlake

Chapter Five: Masculinity at the Orthopedic Preschool 83
    Elizabeth A. Wheeler

Chapter Six: Mothering While Black: Shapeshifting Amid Ableism, Racism, and Autism 93
LaChan V. Hannon

Chapter Seven: Unbecoming Mother: Selected Notes on Miscarriage and Infertility 105
Elaine Gerber

Chapter Eight: *Bad* Mother 123
María Cioè-Peña and Laura Castro Santamaría

Chapter Nine: The Strange Case of the Two Journals: Ableism, Academia, and the Birth of a Child 137
Priya Lalvani

Chapter Ten: Becoming Anahita: A Persian Mother's Pilgrimage to Autism Pride 153
Negar Irani and Negin Hosseini Goodrich

Chapter Eleven: Mothering in the Panopticon 167
Susan Baglieri

Chapter Twelve: Karma, Dogma, and the Perfect Child 179
Monika Tiwari

Chapter Thirteen: Mother Is Wise: How Disability Constructs Maternal Identity 187
Linnéa Franits

Chapter Fourteen: Typicality and the (Br)other 203
Diane Linder Berman and David J. Connor

Chapter Fifteen: Confessions of an Inept Supermom 219
Carol Rogers-Shaw

Epilogue: "Tell Me About When I Was Born": (Mostly) True Tales About How We Became a Family 233
Priya Lalvani

Contributors 243

Figures

Figure 8.1.   A letter from Mami. 133
Figure 13.1.   My sister (L) and me (R) on our parents' laps. 189
Figure 13.2.   My sister and I during her final hospitalization. 196
Figure 13.3.   Bike riding lesson. 198

Acknowledgments

Writing, whether for a book or otherwise, might appear to be a solitary activity. However, an author never writes alone; like all human endeavors, writing is an act of collaboration with one's environment. Even when we write in (physical) isolation, we feel the presence of those whose ideas influenced our work, the socio-political climate in which the work is undertaken, the audiences (real or imagined) for whom the work is intended, and all those individuals who support us along the way.

While it is impossible to enumerate every contributing factor or list each person who made this book possible, I would like to express my gratitude to those individuals who directly shaped or supported this project, as well as those who provided me with sustenance while I gestated this book from its conception to its birth.

My deepest gratitude is owed to the authors who contributed to this book—the remarkable group of scholars, teachers, teacher-educators, activists, and mothers whose paths intersected with mine as we journeyed to claim or reclaim our motherhood from the tyranny of *normal*. I am grateful for their willingness to share their complex, poignant, powerful, and, at times, ironic stories, even though doing so meant laying bare their most private experiences and revealing their most vulnerable selves. This book is a result of their deep commitment to expanding an understanding of the constructed nature of both disability and motherhood. It is my privilege that they joined me in this book project. Their stories are a gift.

I wish to acknowledge Michelle Fine and Anna Stetsenko; they were my dissertation mentors over a decade ago, but their perspectives and ideas continue to shape and propel my work. They pushed me to challenge traditional epistemologies and awakened me to new ways of thinking about the nature of human identity. Their influence on this book, my entire body of work, and my life, has been profound.

I still cannot believe my good fortune in finding a professional home among the community of scholars at the Society for Disability Studies (SDS), and another among my amazing colleagues, friends, and graduate students at Montclair State University.

Susan Gabel and Scott Danforth, your support and enthusiasm for this project is so appreciated, and thank you, also, to the team at Peter Lang for their guidance through the process of getting this book to production. Thank you, Deanna Mendez (my graduate research assistant), for your invaluable assistance with everything, at every stage of this book, and at all hours of the day!

Thank you, mom. For never tiring of telling and enjoying stories, and for instilling in me, at an early age, the importance of questioning everything. And my family – those dispersed around the globe and those back in Mumbai—for always being there for me and your acceptance of who I am.

I am grateful for the many women in my life whom I am honored to call my friends; those with whom I grew up (or at least tried to) and navigated adulthood, and those who have become "my people"—my community and kin here in Montclair. They *get* everything I wrote in this book. And everything I left out.

Norman, my husband and my love, I am indebted to you for your belief in my work and your constant support (technical or otherwise). Your commitment to working toward social justice and inclusivity in communities inspires me.

Ultimately, this book would not exist if it were not for the two beings who call me mom. They constantly inform and drive my quest to understand the meaning of childhood, disability, and motherhood. They compel me to challenge every assumption and to rethink every conclusion. Thank you, Amiel and Minal, for your trust, your love, your vibrant spirit, and for valuable lessons on being your mother.

"There was this mother, one mother..."

LINDA WARE

A recent episode of CBS Sunday Morning opens with dancers from the New York City Ballet (NYCB) as the voice-over from the reporter explains, *"Ballet is the stuff dreams are made of —the epitome of precision, grace, and beauty. What little girl hasn't dreamed of being up on that stage?"* (CBS News, 2018). The episode titled: "Ballet for Special Children" chronicles a program designed for disabled children who might otherwise be denied "the dream of dance." We meet Karen, a young girl with cerebral palsy who, speaking through her computer, expresses her enthusiasm for the program. And then there's Dr. Joseph P. Ditkowsky, a pediatric orthopedic surgeon who specializes in cerebral palsy and serves as an advisor for the program. When asked how the program came about, he was quick to explain that *"there was this one mother"* —one mother who wrote to the NYCB seeking an accessible program for her disabled daughter. At the time, there were none sponsored by the NYCB. Some four years later, a series of workshops that pair NYCB dancers with children with "disabilities of any kind" is in full operation. Children flee their wheelchairs, drop their crutches, and find friendship in the company of others for whom their difference does not signal exclusion.

"This one mother" as a motif is common in the literature on mothers, and especially mothers attempting to support their disabled children. In *Constructing the (M)other,* Priya Lalvani traces the myriad paths that lead to the persistence of particular cultural narratives that define motherhood in the context of disability. She advances an understanding of the tensions at the intersection of discourses of the *good mother* and the *desirable child.* This universal phenomenon remains one that educators and other service providers have been slow to recognize. Often, mothers' accounts contest the professional authority inscribed in the approaches empirically confirmed through traditional research and named "best practices" in the preparation of professionals. In my own teaching of the required "parent course"—a standard component in teacher preparation, I relied heavily on filmic interpretations of mothering to engage my students. It was a conscious effort to disentangle the simplistic acronym-based parent support programs from real life and the cultural narratives that too often entangle mothers. My exemplars included Cher in the role of "Rusty," the caustic mother of Rocky Dennis in the American film, *Mask* (1985). Rusty is a mom who boldly refuses the exclusion of her son from public education due to a facial impairment; she stands up to the very system purported to act in her son's best interests. I relied, as well, on more complex accounts that are often rendered by international films. The Mexican film, *Gaby: A True Story* (1987) starred Liv Ullman as a mother conflicted by her disabled daughter's caretaker who advocates for greater independence than the mother can imagine. Norma Aleandro, a celebrated Argentinean actress, won an academy award nomination for her performance as the caretaker. Years later, Aleandro would be cast as the mother in the Argentinean film, *Anita* (2009). Based on events that followed an actual terrorist bombing in Buenos Aires, the film follows a young woman with Down syndrome as she encounters episodes that seed her independence. These films are based on the real lives of disabled young people and their efforts to navigate a place in the world, and within that narrative, the lives of mothers who unflinchingly challenge normalizing ideologies.

The multicultural accounts of mothering that these films capture are uncommon in the literature for teacher educators. Too often we see textbook publishers merely substitute "Juan" for "John" and continue retelling a dominant culture narrative—shameful, but true. In contrast, *Constructing the (M)other* provides rigorous, authentic insights—an "anthology of autoethnographies about motherhood, mothering, or mothers—about the stories we inherit, and the ways in which we choose to retell them." Lalvani's contributors cut across cultures, intertwined lives, divergent settings, complicated contexts—their stories are delivered with a poignancy that is not intended to overlay onto the singular stories and simplistic plots teachers often read. Reading about the actual lives of mothers positioned within a disability studies (DS) framework will enrich understanding and strengthen the perspective that educators develop so as to join forces with mothers and their children. Such a partnership remains one of the most challenging to sustain in educational contexts. The stories, the truths, the sense-making captured in this edited collection will likely unsettle some readers, but undoubtedly assure others who recognize that complexity and dissonance need not be feared. This is a fearless collection, and one that is long overdue in education.

REFERENCES

Carnevale, M. (Producer & Director). (2009). *Anita* [Motion picture]. Argentina: Distributors Menemsha Films.

CBS News. (2018, December 23). Ballet for special children [Television broadcast]. New York, NY: Central Broadcasting Service.

Love, M. (Writer) & Mandoki, L. (Writer & Director). (1987) *Gaby: A true story* [Motion picture]. United States: TriStar Pictures.

Starger, M. (Producer) & Bogdanovich, P. (Director). (1985). *Mask* [Motion picture]. United States: Universal Pictures.

Mother

The Story

PRIYA LALVANI

In a graduate course I teach entitled *Partnerships with Families of Children with Disabilities,* I often begin with an introductory activity in which I invite my students to share something they consider unique or interesting about their own families, or to recount a family story. When it's my turn, I sometimes share a particular family story I've inherited. As far as stories go, this one is remarkably short, and I try to recount it in the same way it was narrated to me. I say:

> *My grandmother had four children. Her sister, who wanted children of her own, did not have any. So, my grandmother gave to her sister one of her own children—a son.*

This is usually followed by silence. There are some puzzled looks and expressions of skepticism. Then, inevitably, there are questions and comments such as: What kind of mother would simply give one's child as if he were a gift to be bestowed? Only a saint would be so selfless! What about the maternal bond she had already established with the child? Did she come to regret her decision? Didn't she even *care*? And so on. It seems that my story is perceived by many as being unbelievable or, at the very least, quite odd, and my grandmother's actions as representing inexplicable, detached, or non-normative maternal behavior.

In my own family, however, this story is considered neither remarkable nor unusual; in it, my grandmother is cast neither as uncaring nor as a saint. The story was narrated to me as a simple fact, with little other details to accompany it. I should emphasize here that I do not mean to suggest there *wasn't* any more to this story, nor do I claim to know how the events that unfolded were experienced by my grandmother, her sister, or my uncle generously given as a gift. (I never had the chance to hear their interpretations; all three were deceased by the time I was an adolescent.) I can only guess that there were layers of meaning-making through which each of them came to understand their experiences. All that I mean to suggest is that in this family narrative, my grandmother's actions are represented as, and generally understood to be, a reasonable act of sisterly sharing. As a young adult (and eager undergraduate student of psychology), my attempts to unpack this narrative through the lens of Western psychological models were met with puzzlement from various family members. Rejecting pathology-based frameworks and any fixed definition of motherhood, they would gently redirect me to the math: "Your grandmother had *four* children, and her sister, whom she loved very much, did not have *any.*" Thus, it seems, in the collective family interpretation, the numbers are implicated as problematic while my grandmother's actions are positioned as a matter of fairness—a numerical regrouping toward a more equitable distribution. I've come to realize that, for my family, this narrative was not merely an account of an adoption. Rather, it served to affirm the family's identity and its mutually shared understanding about kinship expectations, the parameters of normalcy, and the meaning of motherhood.

Mother is often understood in dominant discourses as a person without further identity or as existing without context; however, motherhood is a relational identity—existing only in relation to another, as well as a patriarchal institution (Rich, 1995). Motherhood is situated in individual meaning-making in the context of cultural and historical interpretations of the role of women and the normative family. In other words, how one experiences motherhood relies, to a great extent, on what motherhood is taken to be.

There are few cultural narratives as pervasive as those that pertain to motherhood. Entrenched in the collective psyche, culturally upheld and institutionally reified, are notions of the *giving* mother, unconditional love, maternal bonds, and assumptions of selflessness and patience among mothers. Simultaneously woven into the collective psyche is the problematic binary of good mother/bad mother (Blum, 2007). In dominant discourses, some kinds of mothers are elevated, others closely scrutinized, and yet others, denied access to the category of motherhood altogether. Within each of these groups, for some women the experience of motherhood is further embedded in cultural narratives which define not only the parameters of normative motherhood, but also of normative childhood. At the intersection of the patriarchal surveillance of motherhood and ableist beliefs about disability, we can locate mothers of children with disabilities. This group of women will find themselves subjected not only to the discourses of the *good mother*, but also to the discourses of the *desirable child.*

MOTHERS OF CHILDREN WITH DISABILITIES: HISTORICAL PERSPECTIVES

If mothers have always been a subject of scrutiny (Phoenix & Smith, 2011), then it can be argued that among the most scrutinized are those who have children with disabilities. Families of children with disabilities have long held the clinical gaze, rooted in the "regimes of truth" of those in positions of power and control (Foucault, 1974). Traditional psychology, with its focus on embodied deficits and its dichotomous formulations of *normal* and *abnormal* functioning (Goodley, 2011), has been a key player not only in the medicalization of disability itself, but also in the pathologizing of parents of children with disabilities.

The attributing of blame for children's conditions to their parents dates as far back as the early Greek and Roman civilizations where, when children were born with visible disabilities, it was taken as indication that their parents had offended the gods (Braddock & Parish, 2001). Based on this belief, the response of those societies to children with disabilities was infanticide. Although infanticide is no longer a dominant cultural practice in response to children with disabilities, the habit of parent-blame has endured, taking new forms and historically finding support in psychological theories that held parents—specifically mothers—responsible for children's conditions. For instance, in the mid-20th century, based in a post-Freudian psychoanalytic framework, children's troubling behaviors were explained as being caused by "psychogenic mothers" whose personality, sexuality, or emotionality made for dysfunctional parenting (Jones, 1998). Soon, the notion of the "refrigerator mother" (Bettelheim, 1967; Kanner, 1943)—a cold, rejecting mother who was unable to establish a secure bond with her child, took hold as the causal factor for autism. Based on this idea, children with autism were separated from their families and placed in institutional facilities in order to receive "treatments" now considered highly problematic or abusive (Simpson, Hanley, & Quinn, 2002). Similarly, many practices and policies pertaining to disability in modern history, from the 19th century asylums for the so-called "feebleminded" and "insane" to 20th century eugenics policies and the institutionalization of infants and children with disabilities, were rooted in theories about genetic deficits, psychological dysfunction, or incompetence among parents of children with disabilities. Thus, historically, the oppression of individuals with disabilities has been institutionally sanctioned, in part, through the pathologizing of their parents. Specifically, the disempowerment of mothers has been a device for the committing of many acts that would be otherwise unthinkable.

In contemporary contexts, mothers of children with disabilities continue to be scrutinized. In the public imagination, they are either idealized or stigmatized (Blum, 2007). On the one hand, cultural discourses center on notions about mothers of children with disabilities as "grieving" the loss of their expected child, as "saints" for raising children with disabilities, or as "special" mothers blessed with a "gift" or "chosen" to raise a "special" child (Landsman, 2009). Ironically, in cultural narratives these same mothers are often implicated as the source of the problems, through their supposed "denial" of their children's disability, their irrational, smothering, and overprotective ways, their refusal to "accept" their children's limitations, their "unrealistic expectations," or their "constant demands" for services. In a multitude of ways, these women find themselves positioned as *other*. Through the clinical lens of pathology, their mothering is questioned, their advocacy is suspect.

In the discourses and practices surrounding the birth of a child with a disability, the scrutiny of mothers intersects with ableist beliefs about life with a disability as something to be avoided at all cost. In recent decades, decisions around reproduction have become increasingly linked with issues of choice and control. Through the available technologies of prenatal genetic testing, the promise of the "normal" child has extended to expectations of the "perfect" child (Landsman, 2009). Consequently, many women who choose to continue their pregnancies to term after a prenatal diagnosis of a genetic condition perceive that they are regarded by their physicians as making an irresponsible decision, and those who choose to forgo prenatal testing altogether perceive that they are considered as being irrational (Lalvani, 2011). In cultural discourses they become implicitly (and sometimes explicitly) positioned as bearing partial blame for their children's disabilities, through their decisions to decline using the technologies developed to assist them in bearing "normal" babies.

Assumptions about the wholly negative nature of parenting a child with a disability are upheld in professional discourses that frame the birth of a child with a disability as a "tragedy" or profound loss. Through their training, professionals in fields such as counseling, nursing, and social work are explicitly indoctrinated to expect a period of mourning among parents of children with disabilities (Gallagher, Fialka, Rhodes, & Arceneaux, 2002; Lalvani, 2014). However, many mothers in this group reject dominant narratives about burden and grief as defining their familial experiences, instead positioning their motherhood as more similar to, than different from, those of mothers in general (Green, 2007; Lalvani, 2011, 2015). It is fair to say that *normative motherhood* is a highly contested and negotiated category.

The birth of a child with a disability is not the only site for the production and politics of *normal*; the gatekeepers of normalcy will find many allies among educators. In the context of schooling, notions about the "otherness" of children with disabilities are institutionally upheld and reified through the existence of the parallel systems of general and special education. Entrenched in medical model perspectives which attribute children's "failures" to deficits in individual minds and bodies, schooling practices often serve to sort and stigmatize children through language, labels, low expectations, or the segregated spaces in which they are often educated (Baglieri & Shapiro, 2012; Connor & Ferri, 2007). Within this system that seeks to categorize, not only are children with disabilities viewed as having deficits, but also their parents —usually mothers, and disproportionately impacted are those from culturally and linguistically diverse or low-income families. In education discourses, there exist many negative assumptions about parents who resist the evaluation and classification of their children for the purpose of delivering special education services, those who reject the labels ascribed to their children, or those who challenge professional recommendations for the placement of their children in segregated educational settings, advocating instead for their children's right to be educated inclusively (for a full discussion, see Lalvani & Hale, 2015). These parents are often dismissed as being "in denial" about the existence or extent of their children's disabilities, or as having unrealistic expectations of their children. In one way or another, those who question the system become positioned in malignant ways.

CONCEPTUAL FRAMEWORK OF THIS BOOK

Selves as Co-Constructed

In sociocultural psychology (Vygotsky, 1978), the concept of identity is theorized as multiple, situated in contexts, and collectively constructed. Similarly, a number of theorists and philosophers (e.g., Mead, 1934; Wittgenstein, 1953/2008) have rejected essentialist notions of identity, positing instead a view of *self as social*—existing only in relation to others, and as emerging through the reciprocal participation of individuals in culturally-mediated activities. Drawing from this idea, discursive psychology emphasizes the crucial role of meaning-making in the construction of *selves*; here, the idea is that identities develop through the constant act of negotiating and renegotiating the meaning of experiences, both by individuals and cultures (Bakhtin, 1981; Bruner, 1986, 1990). Below, I briefly outline two sociocultural approaches to the development of identity which inform the conceptual framework for this book.

Positioning Theory

Positioning theory explains that through discourses and activities, individuals position themselves in relation to others, and thus engage in meaning-making about the nature of experiences and events (Harré & Langenhove, 1999; Harré & Moghaddam, 2003). The role of *master narratives* and *counter-narratives* is key in this process. Master narratives are the culturally agreed-upon storylines, assumed to reflect normative experiences, that are reproduced in social discourses (Andrews, 2004). Through master narratives, psychological and social phenomenon are constructed and sustained, and particular interpretations of the world are collectively upheld as "truths." Individuals adopt and reaffirm the master narratives or, alternatively, they can exercise agency by producing counter-narratives that assign new meaning to their experiences, thus constructing new realities (Bamberg, 2004; May,

2004). Positioning is therefore the process through which identities are negotiated within cultural contexts; master narratives and counter-narratives are the social tools through which we uphold or resist perceived power differentials at the interpersonal and institutional level (Bamberg, 2004).

Narrative Identity

We inhabit a world of stories (McLean, 2015). Narrative theory, which offers an alternative to the traditional (and often oppressive) dogmas of mainstream psychology, puts forth a view of *self as narrated*—or the idea that through the stories we tell, we make sense of our lives and of the world around us (Bruner, 1990; McAdams, 2001, 2008). In this view, primacy is given to individuals' own interpretations of their experiences. In other words, our life stories do not merely recount events or transmit a set of existing realities; they are social devices through which meaning unfolds (Bamberg, 2004). As Bruner (1990) explained, through our narratives, we come to explain and understand who we are, and in doing so, we construct our *selves*. In narrative theory, human identity is not viewed as static. Rather than having a core identity, individuals are understood as continually constructing and reconstructing a collection of identities, which they enact in different ways in different situations (e.g., Bruner, 1987; Gergen & Gergen, 1983).

Although our narratives give insight into our identities, it is important to recognize that they do not exist in a vacuum. Life stories are psychosocial constructions and, as such, they reflect cultural values as well as power differentials in societies (McAdams, 2001). Simultaneously it should be acknowledged, we are not passively shaped by, or constrained within, our contexts. Instead we exercise agency, not only by negotiating the meaning of our own experiences but also through actively participating in the construction of social realities. For if it is true that our stories are shaped by our environments, it is equally true that the stories we tell, in turn, create new meanings and thus change our environments (McAdams & Manczak, 2015).

Disability Studies

Disability studies (DS) is an interdisciplinary field of scholarly inquiry, as well as a forum for political activism, in which disability is conceptualized as a socially constructed phenomenon (Davis, 2013; Goodley, 2017). Rejecting the notion that disability is a universal category defined by the presence of impairments, DS seeks to understand disability in relation to the ways in which societies represent and respond to it. From this perspective, the experience of disability is not viewed as fixed; instead, it is understood as situated in historical and current cultural practices and norms (Garland-Thomson, 1997). Drawing from the social model, *disability* is distinguished from *impairment;* whereas the term "impairment" is used to refer to a particular physical or sensory condition (e.g., blindness, diminished motor function, etc.), disability is understood as encompassing the political, economic, social, and attitudinal barriers that limit or marginalize people with impairments (Oliver, 1990). For example, blindness is an impairment, however, it becomes a disability only when a blind individual is denied the opportunity to participate in the community, gain employment, or form meaningful relationships due to either a lack of physical access or because of the prejudices of the nondisabled. Thus, through a DS lens, the focus is not on "fixing" people with disabilities, but instead on changing negative attitudes and removing environmental barriers that lead to their *disablement*.

Disability studies draws attention to, and aims to confront, *ableism* in society. Ableism refers to the persistent devaluing of disability, or viewpoints in which disability is understood as an inherently negative state of being (Campbell, 2009). Similar to other "isms" (e.g., racism, sexism, classism, and so on), it originates in beliefs about the inherent "goodness" of certain ways of being, and it unfolds as a system of oppression that operates at individual, cultural, and institutional levels (Rauscher & McClintock, 1997). Unlike other forms of oppression, however, ableism generally remains outside the public awareness—it is what Chodorow (1999) referred to as a "permissible prejudice." In response to this, and drawing from a social justice framework, DS scholars petition us to retract our gaze from individuals' impairments, and focus it instead on the ways in which normalcy is constructed in societies, as well as on ableist discourses and practices that result in the reification of stigmas and the marginalization of people with disabilities (Davis, 2006; Hahn, 1997; Linton, 1998).

AUTOETHNOGRAPHY AS METHOD

If stories are the ways in which humans make sense of the world (Ellis, 2004), then autoethnographies are ways of making sense of the stories. Autoethnography is a qualitative research method in which researchers use their personal stories to explore particular social issues, through a connection of the stories to broader theoretical frameworks or academic literature (Ellis, 2004; Foster, McAllister, & O'Brien, 2006). In autoethnographies, writers engage in self-reflection and systematically analyze their own experiences in an endeavor to extend an understanding of cultural, social and political phenomenon (Ellis, 2004). Thus autoethnography is both the process and the product—the *self* is conceptualized as both the storyteller and the story (McAdams, 2008). Resonant of William James' notion of the *I* and the *me*, an autoethnography can be understood as an ongoing conversation between the *I*—the researcher who interprets, and the *me*—the researchers' interpretations of the self (Rambo, 2007).

For many researchers, autoethnography is a way of highlighting problematic social issues and attempting to make social change (Renner, 2001). Autoethnographic works, by their nature, aim to contest or resist dominant views of the world. As a form of "insider research," they can provide insights into the experience of otherness and stigma. It should be noted that autoethnographies are not meant to be generalized, nor do they attempt to uncover "objective truths." Their aim is to examine particular issues, in context, from the unique vantage point of the lived experiences of the researcher.

OUR LIVES IN STORIES: ABOUT THE CHAPTERS IN THIS BOOK

In the context of a society in which disability holds a stigmatized and devalued position, how do mothers of children with disabilities make sense of their experiences, and what stories do they tell? How do they come to interpret the normalizing ideologies implicit in the technology of prenatal genetic testing and the ableist discourses of "grief" and "tragedy" surrounding the birth of their children? How do they position themselves within an educational system in which their children become positioned as *other*, through the labels they are assigned or through the segregated environments in which they are often educated? And, to what extent are all of these experiences inextricably linked with cultural and socioeconomic privilege? These are some questions which fueled my initial interest in this book project, and which frame each of the chapters in this book.

This book is a collection of autoethnographies about motherhood, mothering, or mothers—the stories we inherit and the ways in which we choose to retell them. Some of these stories focus on the ways in which women find themselves malignantly positioned in the context of motherhood, and the counter-narratives they develop in response. Others shed light on the activities in which women engage, as they navigate institutional systems to seek acceptance or inclusivity for their family members. Collectively they reveal the master narratives on normative motherhood and the *good mother*, entrenched in sociopolitical contexts and in the patriarchal systems of control that surround us. They compel us to rethink the constructed category of motherhood itself, and who may claim access to it.

This book is theoretically grounded in the notions of *self as social* and *self as narrated*. In other words, through the telling and retelling of our stories, we negotiate, claim, and construct our identities within our cultural contexts. Additionally, the autoethnographies are conceptually framed in disability studies and, as such, they aim to highlight and confront ableism in society. Each author approaches the framing questions of this book from the varied vantage points of their multiple and intersecting identities and life stages. However, as Gabel and Kotel (2018) remind us, the retelling of past events is, by necessity, done through the lens of the present. Therefore, it should be acknowledged that although the stories in this book are about our past experiences, they are interpreted by our present selves.

In the first chapter, "Standard Deviation: Stigma, Surveillance, and the Good ~~Mother~~ Daughter," Tammy Bachrach, an assistant professor of special education examines the notion of the "good mother," exposing eugenics-based cultural discourses about *who* should bear children. Through her unique vantage point as both a daughter of a mother labeled with an intellectual disability and a mother of a daughter who experienced mental illness, she reveals how her view of disability varied based on the particularities of the impairment. Describing her dual deviation from that which is considered morally "good" in families, she traces a journey in which she struggles to disentangle her identity from the stigma and social disapproval that constrained the personhood of both her mother and her daughter.

In Chapter 2, "West Side Story (Down Under)", Bernadette Macartney, a disability rights scholar and activist in Aotearoa New Zealand, creatively uses the format of a play's script to narrate a story about attempting to support her daughter's desire to participate in the annual High School musicals. Through her tongue-in-cheek vignettes about her (ultimately futile) endeavors to seek access to the performing arts for her daughter, Macartney describes how she became silenced, and her daughter marginalized, within the very space that claimed to be inclusive of *all*. Using a Foucauldian analytic lens, her piece exposes the deficit-based discourses and practices in schools that (re)create exclusion.

In Chapter 3, "Selves-Advocacy and the Meeting Space," Erin McCloskey, an associate professor of education, tells her story of "growing an Autistic self-advocate," and the ways in which her own preconceived notions about what self-advocacy looks like evolves and becomes reconceptualized. Using the IEP meeting of her son as the setting for her explorations, McCloskey shows how interpretations of autism and self-advocacy create complicated roles that are in varying states of resistance. She concludes that centering the perspective of the Autistic person is paramount to pushing back against rigid institutional practices.

In Chapter 4, "An Unexpected Journey with My Mother," Maria Timberlake, an associate professor of education, shares a poignant story about the nature of caregiving role-reversal, taking on ableism in the context of eldercare. Timberlake's accounts of navigating the culture of a nursing home after her mother receives a label of dementia give us a glimpse into the ways that "lives unravel once a system puts a person's competency under question." With irony and insight, she notes the extent to which the assumptions implicit in special education are mirrored in the institutionalized discourses and practices of eldercare. She details her efforts to resist submission, and to create community and relationships within the system.

In Chapter 5, "Masculinity at the Orthopedic Preschool," Elizabeth Wheeler, an associate professor of English, provides a view into the intersections of disability, gender conformity, and gender identity. Through a series of vignettes about raising her son with cerebral palsy, Wheeler illustrates her claim that families, not just individuals, have multiple, complex, and shifting identities. Drawing critical attention to the cisgender norms and expectations to which gender-nontraditional families are subjected, often within spaces that are accepting of other human variations like disability, this piece reveals the tensions and contradictions in the notion of inclusivity itself.

In Chapter 6, "Mothering While Black: Shapeshifting Amid Ableism, Racism, and Autism," LaChan Hannon, a doctoral student in teacher education and teacher development, furthers the conversation about intersecting family identities, detailing the ways in which she must continually negotiate and renegotiate what it means to "raise a black boy with autism." Acknowledging and examining the "racist, sexist, and ableist ways in which [her] own mothering choices often contradict each other," Hannon lays bare the gendered, racialized, and ableist norms and expectations about what it means to be a "good mother" and a compliant student.

In Chapter 7, "Unbecoming Mother: Selected Notes on Miscarriage and Infertility," Elaine Gerber, an associate professor of Anthropology, offers a "reproductive story that does not result in a birth," recounting her experiences of multiple miscarriages and infertility which shaped her own identity as a disabled woman. With raw candor and humility, Gerber interrogates broad cultural narratives in which women who experience miscarriage are considered unnatural, their losses silenced, and in which miscarrying a fetus that would have resulted in a disabled child is considered "for the best" or a "blessing." Her stories create dissonance, revealing the ableist discourses around reproduction and (in)fertility that can be implicated in the creation of disability and the process of disablement.

In Chapter 8, "*Bad* Mother," María Cioè-Peña, an educational sociolinguist and assistant professor of inclusive education, and Laura Castro Santamaría, a mother, expose the world of high stakes surveillance faced by minoritized women. Sharing their memories of an encounter with child protective services—an event that changed both of their lives, they question the rules of "good parenting" set in place by dominant groups, as well as the (differential) consequences for deviating from those standards. Together, they compel us to consider the complicity of schools in reifying and upholding the social hierarchies that continue to alienate and oppress parents of color.

In Chapter 9, "The Strange Case of the Two Journals: Ableism, Academia and the Birth of a Child," which is my own autoethnography, I examine my journaling following the birth of my daughter with a disability, and compare it to the contents of a "mock journal" I wrote as a graduate student in a special education program. The latter was an assignment which required that I imagine myself to be a new mother of a child with a disability and document my (pretend) experiences. By juxtaposing the texts contained in these two journals, I reveal master narratives about normative families and desired children, and implicate the academy for their role and complicity in the upholding of ableism.

In Chapter 10, "Becoming Anahita: A Persian Mother's Pilgrimage to Autism Pride," Negar Irani, a mother and disability awareness advocate in Tehran, Iran, and Negin Hosseini Goodrich, a journalist and doctoral candidate in Second Language Studies, tell a tale about resistance and a power unleashed through access to information. Irani traces her journey following her son's diagnosis of autism, from a place of confusion to one in which she empowers herself to seek and spread information through social media. Rejecting the shame associated with disability, she comes to find pride in having a son with autism. Hosseini Goodrich reflects on Irani's story, connecting it with disability studies perspectives and situating it in the context of the cultural norms, gender roles, and approaches to disability in traditional and contemporary Iranian society.

In Chapter 11, "Mothering in the Panopticon," Susan Baglieri, an associate professor of secondary and special education, invites us into a particular moment in the life of a parent—one in which a decision to consent (or not consent) to the evaluation of their child for the purpose of providing special education services poses imagined paths that forever shape the way parents then think about their choices. Baglieri explicates how schooling practices surrounding dis/ability operate in the manner of the metaphoric panopticon—a structure built for the purpose of surveillance, which ultimately comes to ensure compliance through self- monitoring. Exposing the privilege as well as the uncertainty and guilt that invariably accompany any parental decision that challenges or goes against professionals' recommendations, this piece complicates the idea of parental choice in educational decisions, and challenges dominant assumptions about mothers who resist the evaluation and subsequent classification of their children.

In Chapter 12, "Karma, Dogma, and the Perfect Child," Monika Tiwari, a special education teacher, reflects on the birth of her daughter with Down syndrome within a society that expects that women will avail of the technologies of prenatal genetic testing in order to produce "normal" children. Tiwari narrates, with equal measures of outrage and humor, the responses to disability within her Indian community, including the various causes to which her daughter's disability was attributed. Her recollections about her efforts to seek a meaningful education for her daughter are a scathing critique of a segregated special education system; they reveal the institutional barriers faced by parents who dare to envision inclusive education for their children labeled with intellectual disabilities.

In Chapter 13, "Mother Is Wise: How Disability Constructs Maternal Identity," Linnéa Franits, an associate professor of occupational therapy, brings the lens of a sibling to reflect on the ways in which her mother's response to her sister's disability has shaped her own identity as a mother of a son with autism. Nesting her story within that of her mother, Franits muses that her recollections of the mothering she observed, and her own mothering cannot be easily teased apart. Finding resonance and dissonance between her mother's responses to disability and her own, she illuminates stigma as the backdrop for the familial experience of disability; indeed, she notes, knowledge of stigma is what made her mother, and now herself, "wise."

In Chapter 14, "Typicality and the (Br)other," Diane Linder Berman, a teacher and an instructor of inclusive education, teams with David Connor, a professor of education. In the form of an open letter to her nondisabled son, Adam, Berman describes her initial years as a mother when her thinking was steeped in society's arbitrary definitions of normative behavior, detailing how she came to undo the "habit of comparison" and to celebrate both her children. Connor, reflecting on Berman's story and addressing some questions posed by her, discusses what educators might learn about inclusivity and community from the perspectives of the non-disabled children in schools who have had the experience of being educated in heterogeneous classrooms with regard to dis/ability.

Finally, in Chapter 15, "Confessions of an Inept Supermom," Carol Rogers-Shaw, a doctoral student in adult education considers the ways in which her own disability identity after her diagnosis of type 1 diabetes, as well as societal expectations of the ideal birthing experience and the ideal student "set her up" to feel like she was failing her daughter right from the start. Based on Joseph M. Valente's (2011) idea of the superhero who wishes to punish perpetrators with his words, she creates a "supermom" alter-ego to recount her experiences of trying to fight back against ableist schooling practices and deficit-based narratives about her daughter. Throughout, she casts herself as an "inept supermom"—conflicted, vulnerable, and unsure in the face of dominant norms.

Each chapter in this book tells a different story through the interpretative lens of the author, yet, collectively they reveal a backdrop of institutionally sanctioned systems of able-bodied and able-minded privilege against which mothering takes place. Positioned at the forefront are the ways in which we disrupt master narratives about disability and assumptions about families like our own. In contrast to the ways in which mothers of children with disabilities have been traditionally studied, and consequently pathologized, in this book the lens of scrutiny is inverted; here, the object of investigation is, ultimately, not the mothers themselves, nor their children with disabilities, but rather, the discourses and practices through which some experiences of motherhood are positioned as non-normative, and some children as *other*. Fundamentally, these are stories of resistance. They are devices through which we negotiate the parameters of normalcy and construct alternative meanings of disability and motherhood. The stories contained in this book attest to, and affirm, the power of narratives in the upholding or resisting of cultural meanings and the fashioning of selves.

REFERENCES

Andrews, M. (2004). Introduction: Counter-narratives and the power to oppose. In M. Bamberg & M. Andrews (Eds.), *Considering counter-narratives: Narrating, resisting, making sense* (pp. 1–6). Amsterdam, Netherlands: John Benjamins Publishing.

Baglieri, S., & Shapiro, A. (2012). *Disability studies and the inclusive classroom: Critical practices for creating least restrictive attitudes.* New York, NY: Routledge.

Bakhtin, M. (1981). *The dialogic imagination: Four essays.* Autisn, TX: University of Texas Press.

Bamberg, M. (2004). Considering counter-narratives. In M. Bamberg & M. Andrews (Eds.), *Considering counter-narratives: Narrating, resisting, making sense* (pp. 351–357). Amsterdam, Netherlands: John Benjamins Publishing.

Bettelheim, B. (1967). *Empty fortress: Infantile autism and the birth of the self.* New York, NY: Free Press.

Blum, L. (2007). Mother blame in the prozac nation: Raising kids with invisible disabilities. *Gender & Society, 21*(2), 202–226.

Braddock, D. L., & Parish, S. L. (2001). An institutional history of disability. In G. L. Albrecht, K. D. Seelman, & M. Bury (Eds.), *Handbook of disability studies* (pp. 11–68). Thousand Oaks, CA: Sage Publishing.

Bruner, J. (1986). *Actual minds, possible worlds.* Cambridge, MA: Harvard University Press.

Bruner, J. (1987). Life as narrative. *Social Research, 54*(1), 11–32.

Bruner, J. (1990). *Acts of meaning.* Cambridge, MA: Harvard University Press.

Campbell, F. (2009). *Contours of ableism: The production of disability and abledness.* New York, NY: Palgrave Macmillan.

Chodorow, N. (1999). Homophobia: Analysis of "permissible" prejudice. The Public Forum.

Connor, D. J., & Ferri, B. A. (2007). The conflict within: Resistance to inclusion and other paradoxes in special education. *Disability & Society, 22*(1), 63–77.

Davis, L. (2006). Constructing normalcy. In L. Davis (Ed.), *The disability studies reader* (pp. 9–28). New York, NY: Routledge.

Davis, L. (2013). Introduction: Disability, normality and power. In L. Davis (Ed.), *The disability studies reader* (pp. 1–16). New York, NY: Routledge.

Ellis, C. (2004). *The ethnographic I: A methodological novel about authoethnography.* Walnut Creek, CA: AltaMira Press.

Foster, K., McAllister, M., & O'Brien, L. (2006). Extending boundaries: Autoethnography as an emergent method in mental health nursing research. *International Journal of Mental Health Learning, 15*, 44–53.

Foucault, M. (1974). *The archaeology of knowledge.* London: Tavistock.

Gabel, S. L., & Kotel, K. (2018). Motherhood in the context of normative discourse: Birth stories of mothers of children with Down syndrome. *Journal of Medical Humanities, 39*(2), 179–193.

Gallagher, P. A., Fialka, J., Rhodes, C., & Arceneaux, C. (2002). Working with families: Rethinking denial. *Young Exceptional Children, 5*(2), 11–17.

Garland-Thomson, R. (1997). *Extraordinary bodies: Figuring physical disability in American culture and literature.* New York, NY: Columbia University Press.

Gergen, K., & Gergen, M. (1983). Narratives of the self. In T. R. Sarbin & K. E. Scheibe (Eds.), *Studies in social identity* (pp. 254–323). New York, NY: Praeger.

Green, S. E. (2007). "We're tired, not sad": Benefits and burdens of mothers of a child with a disability. *Social Science and Medicine, 64*(1), 150–163.

Goodley, D. (2011). *Disability studies: An interdisciplinary introduction.* Thousand Oaks, CA: Sage Publications.

Goodley, D. (2017). *Disability studies: An interdisciplinary introduction* (2nd ed.). Thousand Oaks, CA: Sage Publications.

Hahn, H. (1997). Advertising the acceptably employable image. In L. Davis (Ed.), *The disability studies reader* (pp. 172–186). New York, NY: Routledge.

Harré, R., & Langenhove, L. (1999). The dynamics of social episodes. In R. Harré & L. Langenhove (Eds.), *Positioning theory: Moral contexts of international action* (pp. 1–13). Hoboken, NJ: Wiley.

Harré, R., & Moghaddam, F. (2003). Introduction: The self and others in traditional psychology and in positioning theory. In R. Harré & F. Moghaddam (Eds.), *The self and others: Positioning individuals and groups in personal, political, and cultural contexts* (pp. 1–11). Westport, CT: Praeger.

Jones, K. (1998). Mother made me do it. In M. Ladd-Taylor & L. Umansky (Eds.), *"Bad" mothers* (pp. 99–124). New York, NY: New York University Press.

Kanner, L. (1943). Autistic disturbances of affective contact. *Nervous Child, 2*(3), 217–250.

Lalvani, P. (2011). Constructing the (m)other: Dominant and contested narratives on mothering a child with Down syndrome. *Narrative Inquiry, 21*(2), 276–293.

Lalvani, P. (2014). The enforcement of normalcy in schools and the disablement of families: Unpacking master narratives on parental denial. *Disability & Society, 29*(8), 1221–1233.

Lalvani, P. (2015). Disability, stigma, and otherness: Perspectives of parents and teachers. *International Journal of Disability, Development, and Education, 62*(4), 379–393.

Lalvani, P., & Hale, C. (2015). Squeaky wheels, mothers from hell, and CEOs of the IEP: Parents, privilege, and the "fight" for inclusive education. *Understanding and Dismantling Privilege, 5*(2), 21–41.

Landsman, G. (2009). *Reconstructing motherhood and disability in the age of "perfect" babies.* New York, NY: Routledge.

Linton, S. (1998). *Claiming disability: Knowledge and identity.* New York, NY: New York University Press.

May, V. (2004). Narrative identity and the reconceptualization of lone motherhood. *Narrative Inquiry, 14*(1), 169–189.

McAdams, D. P. (2001). The psychology of life stories. *Review of General Psychology, 5*(2), 100–122.

McAdams, D. P. (2008). Personal narratives and the life story. In O. John, R. Robins, & L. Pervin (Eds.), *Handbook of personality: Theory and research* (pp. 242–257). New York, NY: The Guilford Press.

McAdams, D. P., & Manczak, E. (2015). Personality and the life story. In M. Mikulincer & P. Shaver (Eds.), *APA handbook of personality and social psychology: Personality processes and individual differences* (Vol. 4, pp. 425–446). Washington, DC: American Psychological Association.

McLean, K. (2015). *The co-authored self: Family stories and the construction of personal identity.* New York, NY: Oxford University Press.

Mead, G. H. (1934). *Mind, self, and society.* Chicago, OH: University of Chicago Press.

Oliver, M. (1990). *The politics of disablement: A sociological approach.* New York, NY: St. Martin's Press.

Phoenix, C., & Smith, B. (2011). Telling a (good?) counter-story of aging: Natural bodybuilding meets the narrative of decline. *The Journals of Gerontology Series B: Psychological Sciences and Social Sciences, 66*(5), 628–639.

Rambo, C. (2007). Sketching as autoethnographic practice. *Symbolic Interaction, 30*(4), 531–542.

Rauscher, L., & McClintock, J. (1997). Ableism curriculum design. In M. Adams, L. A. Bell, & P. Griffin (Eds.), *Teaching for diversity and social justice: A sourcebook* (pp. 198–229). New York, NY: Routledge.

Renner, P. G. (2001). *Vulnerable to possibilities: A journey of self-knowing through personal narrative* (Doctoral dissertation). University of British Columbia.

Rich, A. (1995). *Of woman born: Motherhood as experience and institution.* New York, NY: W. W. Norton.

Simpson, D. E., Hanley, J. J., & Quinn, G. (2002). *Refrigerator mothers* [Documentary]. United States: PBS.

Valente, J. M. (2011). *D/Deaf and D/Dumb: A portrait of a Deaf kid as a young superhero.* New York, NY: Peter Lang Publishing.

Vygotsky, L. S. (1978). *Mind in society: The development of higher psychological processes.* Cambridge, MA: Harvard University Press.

Wittgenstein, L. (2008). *Philosophical investigations.* (G. Anscombe, Trans.). New York, NY: Macmillan. (Original work published 1953).

CHAPTER 1

Standard Deviation

Stigma, Surveillance, and the Good ~~Mother~~ Daughter

TAMMY BACHRACH

One's identity as a mother is shaped by a multitude of influences including culture, socio-economic status, religion, and one's experiences with their own mother. What it means to be a "good mother" is heavily influenced by dominant societal narratives around motherhood (Carpenter & Austin, 2007), and those who deviate from these can be judged harshly as inadequate, negligent, or a "bad mother." In most people's minds, disability disrupts what is considered "good" or "normal." As a result, mothers with disabilities as well as mothers of children with disabilities find themselves under high levels of surveillance (Booth & Booth, 1994, 2005; Hayman, 1990; Ryan & Runswick-Cole, 2008). My experiences around motherhood deviate significantly from the norm in both of these ways; I am a daughter of a mother with an intellectual disability and a mother of a daughter who experienced mental illness. These deviations, while fraught with stigmatization from those outside the immediate family, have provided me with a means of examining and challenging our cultural narratives of disability and motherhood.

Even though I did not have a disability, I shared in the stigma of my mother's disability, and because of it, my decision to become a mother was subjected to scrutiny. Social workers, genetic counselors, and even some members of my extended family expressed concern (even anxiety) that existing within my womb lurked the potential, or the probability, that I would give birth to the "wrong kind" of child. This following vignette about the day I received a rather alarming letter from my Aunt Margaret illustrates.

A LETTER FROM AUNT MARGARET

It had been a long day at work and it felt good to be home. My husband, Mark, and I had recently moved into a new apartment after securing our first post college "professional" jobs. Walking through the door, I automatically did a quick assessment of our new apartment. Luckily, the house was tidy enough that I didn't feel that annoying compulsion to clean things up when all I really wanted to do was sit down. Mark and I had finally gotten some decent furniture. The furniture we owned during our first year of marriage had all been free hand-me-downs. Mark had to convince me that we should use credit to get the new sofa and loveseat. (What were we thinking buying a white sofa?!) It did look pretty. We didn't have children yet, so it would stay white for at least a couple of years.

I grabbed the mail and flipped through it. The only thing of interest was a letter from Aunt Margaret. Besides the Florida address, I could recognize her handwriting by now. People of her age seemed to have distinctively lovely cursive writing. I hadn't had time to write her as often as I would have liked, now that I was working full-time and taking evening classes to get my teaching credential. Still, she would drop me a line every once in a while.

It would be a few hours before Mark got home and we would have to fix some dinner, so I sat down on the sofa, pulled up my legs and opened the letter. I smiled at the photo that drew my eye first. It was a photo of one of her paintings. Her inspiration and subject matter was her beautiful backyard that backed up to the Gulf of Mexico and the peacocks that preened themselves in front of her mirrored sliding glass door. My grandparents and I had visited her home in the Florida Keys when I was 13 years old, and it was one of my fondest memories of our RV travels.

Past the greeting, Aunt Margaret caught me up on her newest art adventures and where she was showing her work. She asked how Mark and I were doing and expressed her regret (for the umpteenth time) that she had not been able to attend the wedding. I certainly understood that it would have been difficult for her to travel that distance at her age; she was my mother's older sister by 22 years and was beginning to have some health issues.

Reading on in the letter, I became puzzled by the unexpected turn in the correspondence as Aunt Margaret wrote, "As a young married couple, I know that you and Mark will be considering having children, and while I can't propose to tell you what to do, I advise you to consider this issue very carefully. Indulge an old woman to give you a little family history if you will. Even as a younger woman I had some medical issues, including what my mother called the 'Glover eye,' a family condition which has caused me trouble and discomfort for my entire life. I became a teacher and, as a young woman, decided that my students would be my only children since I did not want to pass this condition on to children."

Where is she going with this, I wondered. Is she really suggesting I don't have children? I continued reading: "Your Aunt Margie has confided to me that she has recom-

mended that you get some genetic counseling since she seems to think that your brother, Timmy, has inherited his small head and disability from your father."

That is ridiculous, I muttered to myself. My dad doesn't have a small head. Yes, he had trouble in school, but he doesn't have microcephaly like Tim.

"I think it is important to consider that if you and Mark have children, they could turn out like your mom and Timmy."

What? I was baffled. I re-read the last sentence in order to make sense of what she was saying. "They could turn out like your mom and Timmy." Slowly the immensity of what she was expressing about my mom and brother sunk in. She was saying that I shouldn't have children because they could turn out like my family.

"So?" I wanted to scream. "What is wrong with that?" I knew that Aunt Margaret had already left her home when my mom was born. "Do you even know my mom," I asked her heatedly in an imagined dialogue. "Do you know Tim? My mom and brother are some of the most self-sacrificing, kind, and hardworking people I know," I yelled at her image in my mind. My anger was rising as the insult continued to seep in. "I would hope more people would turn out like them," I wanted to shout at her.

Of course, I knew that she was only considering their learning problems, but to reduce them to their learning difficulties seemed to deny their personhood; to deny any feeling she might have toward them.

I could barely return to the letter but forced myself to continue. "Of course, this is a very difficult decision that is yours and Mark's to make, but it can be very hard on a marriage to care for a mentally retarded child. Not to mention what it is like for the child. I hope you do not resent me for butting in a bit. Please just consider these things. You know I love you and want the best for you always. Aunt Margaret."

I dropped the letter next to me on the couch. I was stunned. I was so angry that she would think both her sister's and nephew's lives a tragedy to be avoided. How dare she talk like that about my mother and Tim? Furious tears fell. These were eventually followed by a numbing sadness about the way she saw my world, and a realization that this is how my family is likely to be viewed in society.

GROWING UP WITH MOM

As the daughter of a woman labeled with an intellectual disability, disability and motherhood have always been intertwined in my life. I am the only member of my immediate family without a learning impairment. My dad has a learning disability, and my mother and only sibling have labels of intellectual disabilities. As a result of growing up in my family, I believe I developed a more unusual view of what other people term "disability." As a child, I never saw my parents' inability to read or my brother's difficulty with language as a tragedy; it was simply a fact. The relationships I had within my family were rich, mutually rewarding, and mostly typical.

It was not until I matured and became exposed to the mainstream view of disability, did I even start to see a difference. I learned about disability through the world's stigmatization and discrimination of my mother. The majority of children born to parents with intellectual impairments lose custody of their children, many without any evidence of harm (Booth & Booth, 2005; Booth, McConnell, & Booth, 2006; Collings & Llewellyn, 2012; Hayman, 1990). Despite the fact that my parents never even appeared before a court, they lost legal control of their children. Unlike most families where a parent has an intellectual disability however, I was allowed to continue to live with my mother while the parental decision-making was retained by a maternal aunt. Still, my mom lived with an ever-present fear of losing her children.

People ask when I realized that my parents had learning difficulties. I don't know. Children don't have words for some things. In a million small moments, it became evident to me that my parents had no authority. They were not in charge. My Aunt Margie was in charge. While I lived with my mom and she provided the daily care, Aunt Margie decided where we lived, where I went to school, what church we went to, what clothes we wore, what toys we played with, and what friends we could visit. I don't recall questioning why this was our reality, it just was.

As I grew older, I began to recognize how much my family members suffered, not as a result of their impairments but as a result of people's biases. My aunt counseled me to not tell people about my mom's disability, instilling a sense of shame for our family differences. She frequently belittled my mom and called her an "unfit" mother. But I did not view her as unfit. In fact, even though my mom could not help me with homework and struggled with some life tasks, I believe she was a nurturing and loving mom. Her uncomplicated, selfless example of motherhood and her unconditional love for my brother and I helped to inform and prepare me for motherhood.

Most women do not expect to have a child with disabilities, and take steps to avoid this outcome (Landsman, 2005). At childbearing age, it was expected that I would avail of genetic counseling before deciding to become a mother. I considered it possible, perhaps even probable, that I would have children with learning difficulties. My husband and I would be ok with that. I understood that some people, even members of our extended family, would judge this decision as irresponsible, but I was confident in my ability to see disability as difference—a form of diversity, not as a tragedy. Despite my tendency toward social conformity, my childhood experiences with disability enabled me to avoid some aspects of what Gabel and Kotel (2018) called "the power of the trope of the good mother" and the fear of social disapproval that results from giving birth to a child with an obvious disability (p. 190). In many ways, they enabled me to reject the normative discourses around disability. Or so I thought. My experiences were limited to developmental disabilities and ultimately, the parameters of my understanding and acceptance would be challenged when disability presented itself through the unfamiliar form of mental illness in my oldest daughter, Emilie.

MOTHERING EMILIE

My daughter Emilie's personality seemed to change overnight. The smiling "typical" child, who had gotten straight A's in school, began to fail, experiment with her own self-expression, take destructive risks, and injure herself. In shocking detail, she expressed her vile contempt for her family and, ultimately, herself. I wasn't able to recognize sadness and pain when it manifested as anger and contempt. Family therapy seemed to have little effect and she was admitted to College Hospital. With a clarity birthed in immense emotions, the day I admitted my oldest child into a psychiatric hospital is seared in my mind.

"I don't care mom; it will be fun. Wait until I tell Megan I'm going to a mental hospital. It's funny," stated Emilie. Megan was Emilie's new friend.

"Cutting yourself is not funny. I want you to get the help you need," I responded in motherly fashion.

"What I need is to get away from you and dad," she retorted.

Emilie chatted with a hyperness that, in retrospect, I should have seen as bravado. "How could I be waiting to admit my daughter into a mental facility?" I wondered internally. How had we gotten here? I had followed her psychologist's directive to take her to College Hospital. She had called ahead. At the time, I believed this was more about calling Emilie's bluff than it was a legitimate fear that Emilie would kill herself.

The dusty brown hues of the carpet and furniture seemed intended to be unmemorable, to assist the patient and family to block out the memory of this family event—to enable the memory to fade. I reminded myself this is an exercise, calling her bluff. She is testing us. She is not really sick.

"How could I be here? Why am I doing this alone?" I questioned myself, internally. "Will they admit her? Will they deem the 15 or so cuts on her forearm as a self-destructive call for help?"

"They will probably just send us back home," I thought. But then what? I didn't want to go forward, not here. I didn't want to go back home. Maybe just back.

Yes, if only I could go way back—back to Emilie at age 6 or 7.

Fantasizing, I could see her face—the beautiful girl who would smile rather than snarl at me disdainfully. I wanted to figure out where I screwed up. If I could go back, would I even know what to do differently?

Hopelessly, no. I wouldn't know. Only confusion and failure reigned in my new world.

"Emilie Bachrach," the nurse called, and we entered the intake room. Questions were asked and answered. My insurance card was handed over and a transaction was made. We stood.

"Ok, they will keep her for a few days," I assured myself. "At least I know where she will be sleeping tonight. She will not run away tonight," I reasoned to myself in pitiful attempts to ease my anxiety and pain.

The nurse slid a key card over a white plastic box. Automatic sliding doors opened, and we walked through. They closed behind us with a whoosh and a locking clink.

"The doctors here will know how to help her," I reasoned internally.

Another dance with the key card, the whoosh of the door open, clink of the lock again as we walked deeper into the hospital.

The interior was so gray. Sadness seemed to have a smell. Medical personnel bustled around, and no one wanted to make eye contact.

Another locked door opened. Whoosh. Clink.

Understanding dawned. All these locks. This is not bluff-calling. They are locking her in. They are taking my daughter. Or, am I leaving my daughter? Bile rose in my throat.

After that day, a parade of experts marched through our lives seeking to uncover hidden sins and insidious causes for her pain, or to determine what parenting flaw or dysfunction had caused her depression. Carpenter and Austin (2007) stated that a common social criterion for measuring one's success as a mother is her child. As Emilie's behavior began to deviate sharply from the social and moral rules of our Christian, white, middle-class community, we began to feel intense scrutiny from the professional community and, eventually, even from those closest to us.

Locating the cause of Emilie's relatively sudden behavioral change became the focus of our family life. Family therapy sessions that had at first offered up hope, seemed to deliver only greater confusion and self-doubt. "Had she been abused," they asked. "Was there any sexual assault in her history?" Various and contradicting hypotheses abounded, all focusing on the parental environment and a behavioral cause. At times we were asked to respond to Emilie's behavior in ways that intuitively felt wrong and usually resulted in exacerbating her agitation. Only when environmental and behavioral causes had been thoroughly examined were biological and mental health issues explored. We sought a diagnosis to alleviate Emilie's pain and reduce her self-destructive behavior. However, I gradually came to realize that, similar to findings in Singh (2004), I also sought a medical diagnosis as a means of eliminating self-blame. As we laid our lives bare in family therapy, I was silenced, as Carpenter and Austin (2007) described, by professionals who misunderstood and judged our family. Some therapists concluded that we were too rigid, causing rebellion. Others proposed the opposite—that we were too permissive. The various perspectives left us uncertain. Gradually, I began to silence myself to avoid further judgement even from extended family, friends, and my church community.

Our social network revolved around our church and the broader Christian community which included the Christian school Emilie attended. In periods of Christian church history, mental illness has been linked to sin or viewed as an indication of a spiritual deficit within individuals or their families, rather than a psychological or medical problem (Stanford, 2007). Some of these attitudes toward mental illness remain today and were encountered by our family. Following Emilie's seven-day hospitalization for inflicting harm on herself, her school principal evaluated her problem as one of rebellion and sin rather than depression. Eventually Emilie was suspended from her junior high school for disobedience and, without the appropriate recommendation from her junior high, was not accepted into the local Christian high school.

Many of our friends at church were sympathetic, albeit awkwardly silent, when we shared the difficulties our family was going through. Most people in our social group found Emilie's all-black Goth attire and her sullen attitude off-putting, and we sensed a growing concern from others that her negative behavior may prove to be a bad influence on the other teenagers in the youth group. One of my closest friends, after supporting us through Emilie's hospitalization and several run-away attempts, asked if all of this suffering our family was going through could be the result of some secret sin in my husband's life. The underlying message was that "good, Christian families" don't have children who behave in this manner, so blame had to be found within. The end result was that I began to retreat, to hide, and to isolate myself and my family from those who we once considered our spiritual community.

My identity as a "good mother" was questioned both externally and internally. Like the mothers who had given birth to children with Down syndrome described in Gabel and Kotel (2018), I found myself surrounded with discourses in which able-bodied lives were associated with goodness and morality. Like some of the mothers in their study, I too had considered myself a good person and a "good mother" who initially believed that I did not deserve to have a child with *this* disability. The manifestations of Emilie's depression and mental illness were so easily linked to behavioral rebellion and immorality that it readily equated to a moral failing in me as her mother. I began to hate the expression "the apple doesn't fall far from the tree" and heard within it an indictment. My prayer life began to fluctuate between pleas for help and relief to expressions of anger and injustice: "God, why this? I understand developmental disabilities; I could handle that. I've done what I was supposed to do and been responsible. I have taken care of my mother, brother and Aunt Margie but I can't do this. I can't bear the anger and pain my daughter is expressing. You are asking too much."

Internally, I assaulted myself with accusations. I was not a "good mother" and was destined to fail all of my children. I knew that I loved Emilie but had to admit inwardly that I was relieved when she was not around. Frequently it felt like I didn't know her and that I didn't like her. Guilt tore at me. How could a good mother not like her daughter? So consuming was my sense of failure that I no longer wanted to be a mother.

Each day I went to bed weary and dreamt of destructive forces, only to awake remembering and dreading the conflict that faced each day. I feared that I couldn't protect my child as she experimented with drugs, hitch-hiked, stayed out all night, and ran away from home. The sick, sinking feeling of dread hit my stomach like a Pavlovian reaction every time the phone rang. My husband's and my own carefully guarded emotions were ripped raw, revealing our own ugly anger and vulnerability. At times we supported each other and other times we turned on each other as our responses to her illness began to differ. My "expertise" as a special education teacher no longer had any relevance. My espoused and "progressive" beliefs about disability seemed hypocritical as I struggled with the reality of Emilie's emotional suffering as well as my own.

Goffman (1963) refers to the stigma that results from a close relationship with one who bears a negative or stigmatizing characteristic as "courtesy stigma." Manago, Davis, and Goar (2017) examined the stigma that parents share with their children with disabilities and their process to resist this stigmatization. Initially I accepted this stigma, all the while hopelessly searching for assistance to aid my daughter in her emotional pain. But soon I came to acknowledge that the pain I shared with my daughter as a result of her impairment was exacerbated by the crises of identity I experienced as a mother. I realized that although the primary focus of our efforts was to keep Emilie safe, there was also a need to distance ourselves from embarrassment. This intertwining of our identities was problematic, leading me to expend precious energy trying to bring her into line with who I wanted her to be (a positive reflection on me) rather than accepting her for who she was becoming. Like a ball of multi-strained yarn, aspects of Emilie's impairment, her emerging autonomy, my identity as a mother, social expectations, religious ideology, fear and guilt became entangled into a chaotic mess. Not until each of these strands could be examined would we struggle free.

For some time, I failed to separate my daughter from the depression and anger that she was experiencing. Her anger bubbled over into personal assaults on herself and her family. I lived constantly with the full impact of her disdain for me, our family and our beliefs, trying to sort out what we had done to deserve such rage. Gradually, with the help of others, I began to see her depression as the underlying cause of her behavior. With this revelation came relief. A diagnosis, a biological cause, felt like an acquittal before the court of professional and public opinion that previously charged me as guilty of harming my own daughter through poor parenting, ignorance, neglect or even potential abuse.

This reprieve was short-lived however, as I now had to consider my daughter as *disabled*. How did this shift my understanding of disability? How did it fit within my view of disability as natural and a valued way of being? Up until then, I had believed that my experience with my mother and brother provided me an antidote to the discriminatory lens that Parens and Asch (2003) describe as "resulting when people from one group fail to imagine that people in some 'other' group lead lives as rich and complex as their own" (p. 41). Experiencing disability with Emilie challenged the "disability as diversity" position. Emilie's life was not just *different* from mine and from what I had imagined for her. By all accounts she was unhappy and, potentially, in danger. While the negative impact of my parents' disabilities seemed primarily to result *not* from their impairment but rather from social biases and the environmental limitations placed on them, Emilie's impairment led her to suffer intensely, both internally and externally as a consequence of living outside the social norms. I found it difficult to watch her suffering and to separate my emotions from hers. I hurt for her and with her, desperately seeking a cure—a reprieve for both of us. I struggled with the obvious contradiction between my approach to developmental disabilities and the emotional reality I experienced watching my daughter change and struggle with mental illness.

Initially I put my trust in the professionals and followed them down various paths even when it required me to silence a nagging internal voice of resistance. I was afraid and did not want to lose my daughter to suicide or accidental death, so I acquiesced. We followed advice that resulted in multiple medication trials, hours of family therapy, and eventual separation when we placed Emilie in a boarding school for "troubled" teens. While I still believed in the necessity and value of positive professionals who are willing to support families, I began to see that the course of treatment for mental health is one of trial and error—little more than guessing: "If this medication works, we can deduce that she has bipolar disorder. If a highly structured environment of punishments and rewards works, we will know the problem is behavioral and a result of environmental (i.e., parental) deficits and a rebellious child."

A definitive diagnosis never came, and after years of conflicting expert advice, my confidence in the expertise of professionals began to recede. With it came the realization that Emilie was not going to someday wake up instantly changed. Somehow, this knowledge empowered me. I began to reject the narratives that constrained both my daughter's unique personhood and mine as her mother. Gradually, I began to trust myself, my relationship with my daughter, and my ability to mother. I never returned to the naïve confidence that professed the knowledge "to fix" my child or had allowed me to believe that I could control the outcome of my children's lives. The ridiculous notion that I could/should take credit or blame for the outcomes of the complex human beings to whom I have given birth dissipated like mist. Why had I laid that on myself? Why does society lay it on mothers?

Only through this process of intense disequilibrium, my foundation shaken, did I begin to untangle mother from child, child from disability, and mother from societal scrutiny. Emilie was not her anger and depression, she was not me, and she could not be reduced to society's judgments of her. Thus, disentangled from dominant narratives, I could better see who she was and would become. She was a young woman who not only felt emotions intensely, she passionately held to positions and values that were different from mine. We were two distinct people. I began to see her as she is, to start to appreciate and admire her strength, and to move toward a new self. Eventually I was able to reshape my view of the "good mother" to what disability studies scholars, Parens and Asch (2003), contend is good parenting, "which is appreciating, enjoying and developing as best one can the characteristic of the child one has, not turning the child into someone that she is not or lamenting what she is not" (p. 43). My love for my daughter shifted from one that, while seemingly self-sacrificing, was compromised by my expectations and need for affirmation to a less conditional, more enduring love and admiration for my real daughter. Emilie and I have both aged and matured. These experiences have shaped our relationship, have re-molded our worldviews and forged within us greater resiliency. I no longer desire to live a scripted life. In many ways, Emilie has taught me to ask tough questions that challenged my own assumptions and to examine the dominant voices that fill our lives. The life lessons about disability, diversity and discrimination that began within my childhood experience as a daughter of a woman with an intellectual impairment, were further challenged, stretched and refined by my daughter. Today, the best that I can say is that I have landed in the humble position which acknowledges that some questions have no answers; theoretical models and professional expertise have critical limitations. Today I am content to walk through life's complexities with my daughter.

REFERENCES

Booth, T., & Booth, W. (1994). Working with parents with mental retardation: Lesson from research. *Journal of Developmental and Physical Disabilities, 6*(1), 23–41.

Booth, T., & Booth, W. (2005). Parents with learning difficulties in the learning difficulties in their child protection system. *Journal of Intellectual Disabilities, 9*(2), 109–129.

Booth, T., McConnell, D., & Booth, W. (2006). Temporal discrimination and parents with learning difficulties in the child protection system. *British Journal of Social Work, 36*(6), 997–1015.

Carpenter, L., & Austin, H. (2007). Silenced, silence, silent: Motherhood in the margins. *Qualitative Inquiry, 13*(5), 660–674.

Collings, S., & Llewellyn, G. (2012). Children of parents with intellectual disabilities: Facing poor outcomes or faring okay? *Journal of Intellectual & Developmental Disability, 37*(1), 65–82.

Gabel, S., & Kotel, K. (2018). Mothers in the context of normative discourse: Birth stories of mothers of children with Down syndrome. *Journal of Medical Humanities, 39*(2), 179–193. doi: 10.1007/s10912-015-9367-z.

Goffman, E. (1963). *Stigma: Notes on the management of spoiled identity.* Englewood Cliffs, NJ: Prentice-Hall.

Hayman, R. (1990). Resumptions of justice: Law, politics, and the mentally retarded parent. *The Harvard Law Review, 103,* 1202–1271.

Landsman, G. (2005). Mothers and models of disability. *Journal of Medical Humanities, 26*(3), 121–139. doi: 10.1007/s10912-005-2914-2

Manago, B., Davis, J., & Goar, C. (2017). Discourse in action: Parents' use of medical and social models to resist disability stigma. *Social Science & Medicine, 184,* 169–177.

Parens, E., & Asch, A. (2003). Disability rights critique of prenatal genetic testing and recommendations. *Mental Retardation and Developmental Disabilities Research Reviews, 9,* 40–47.

Ryan, S., & Runswick-Cole, K. (2008). Repositioning mothers: Mothers, disabled children and disability studies. *Disability & Society, 23*(3), 199–210. doi: 10.1080/09687590801953937.

Singh, I. (2004). Doing their jobs: Mothering with Ritalin in a culture of mother-blame. *Social Science & Medicine, 59*(6), 1193–1205.

Stanford, M. (2007). Demon or disorder: A survey of attitudes toward mental illness in the Christian church. *Mental Health, Religion & Culture, 10*(5), 445–449.

CHAPTER 2

West Side Story
(Down Under)

BERNADETTE MACARTNEY

SYNOPSIS

West Side Story (Down Under) is a narrative of my personal experiences, scripted and interpreted in the form of a two-act play. Set in Aotearoa New Zealand, the play is about my daughter, Maggie Rose's desire to participate and perform in the musicals at her high school, and my attempts to navigate access to the performing arts for her over multiple years, leading up to the high school's performance of *West Side Story*.

The classic musical, *West Side Story* is an adaptation of Shakespeare's tragedy, Romeo and Juliet. Written and set in late 1950s New York, it is a story of two rival gangs fighting for supremacy over the city streets. Like the original, my play *West Side Story (Down Under)* exposes the micro-politics and mechanics of power that divide and exclude (Foucault, 1977, 1980, 1982). It offers insights into how disablist values, beliefs, relationships, and structures combine within localised contexts and situations to (re)create exclusion.

My experiences and identity as a mother, teacher, teacher educator, disability studies in education (DSE) scholar, and disability rights activist have made me observant about the ways that different constructions of disability create or remove barriers to developing a positive identity, participating, and succeeding. In this chapter, taking creative license, I borrow some conventions from theatre and performance in order to recount my story in the form of a play's script. Woven throughout the script are "playwright's notes" where I combine DSE and Foucauldian critiques to reveal power relations in schools. I examine how Maggie, myself, and others were silenced and marginalised, and also regulated ourselves, in relation to the deficit discourses and grand narratives about disability that were circulating.

SOCIO-POLITICAL SETTING

Our story takes place in Aotearoa New Zealand, a British colonised, Pacific Island nation of 4.8 million people located over two main islands in the South Pacific. The main ethnic groups within our population are: European-Pākehā (74%), Māori (the indigenous peoples) (15%), Pacific peoples (8%), and Asian (12%) (Statistics New Zealand, 2013).[1] Indigenous people began settling here 800–1000 years ago. British governance and settlement was formalised less than 200 years ago in 1840 through the Treaty of Waitangi, an agreement between the British Crown and representatives of some indigenous tribes. The Treaty promised to recognise and respect Māori autonomy, share power, and protect Māori people, land, resources, language, culture, beliefs and practices. These promises have not been upheld by settler governments. Aotearoa New Zealand has three official languages. They are te reo Māori, English, and New Zealand Sign Language (NZSL). Te reo Māori and NZSL are not compulsory subjects or languages of tuition in most New Zealand schools. English is the predominant language in usage in most places, and most Pākeha (white) New Zealanders are monolingual. Western culture-based institutions and values dominate New Zealand's economic, social and political structures.

Education in Aotearoa New Zealand

The majority (over 90%) of Māori children and young people attend English language medium education settings. There are also total immersion early childhood education settings, schools and curriculum based within a Māori worldview, language, cultural norms and practices. An estimated 100,000 children and young people in the New Zealand school system are identified as having disabilities. New Zealand currently has a dual special/regular school system. There is a network of special schools, and there are segregated classrooms or "units" within some "regular" schools for children labelled as having special education or learning support needs throughout the country. Although over 95% of disabled/labelled children attend "regular" schools, they may experience anything from limited to full access to inclusion, participation, and learning alongside their non-disabled peers within these settings.

Institutions "for" people with intellectual disabilities were closed and replaced with community participation and housing throughout the 1980s and 1990s in New Zealand. New Zealand is a signatory to both the United Nations Convention on the Rights of Children (UNCROC) (1990) and the Convention on the Rights of Persons with Disabilities (CRPD) (2007). However, a fully inclusive education system has not yet been clearly articulated and supported by New Zealand governments or its agencies in policy, law or rhetoric, and many do not understand and/or support a fully inclusive system. The closure of special (segregated) schools, and "units" in regular schools, is a sensitive and contentious issue amongst families, disabled people, teachers, school leaders, government officials, and (special) education providers in New Zealand.

Disability in Aotearoa New Zealand

Disabled[2] people are New Zealand's largest minority group making up 24% of the total population. Disabled New Zealanders experience disproportionate negative health, employment, educational achievement, participation in tertiary education, mental health, and economic outcomes compared to the non-disabled population. Disabled people are more than twice as likely as non-disabled people to be unemployed, and unemployment is much higher among certain impairment groups (Statistics New Zealand, 2017). In 2017, the average weekly income of disabled people was just over half of what non-disabled people receive. Education complaints from, or on behalf of, disabled school students are among the most frequent received by the New Zealand Human Rights Commission each year. Common experiences for disabled students in New Zealand schools include being denied enrolment, routine exclusion from wider school activities, punitive school responses to behaviour and vulnerability to harassment, bullying and assaults (NZHRC, 2016).

CHARACTERS

Maggie Rose

Maggie is a young Pākeha (white) woman and a student at Central High School. She loves language, literature, music and performance. She sings and plays piano and electronic keyboard. She composes and records her own music using GarageBand software and her instruments. She is learning piano accordion. She loves to learn scripts and song lyrics, and is adept at memorising text. She learns and loves *te reo me nga tikanga* Māori, the language and culture of New Zealand's indigenous peoples. Maggie has had piano lessons since she was six, as well as lessons in singing, drama and choir inside and outside of school. She loves planning and being part of social occasions. Maggie loves to perform. She wants to be Maria in *West Side Story*.

Maggie is labelled as being intellectually disabled. At school, she was funded as a "high needs" student. This meant that the school received funding for teachers' aides and an additional part-time, qualified teacher to co-ordinate her teaching team. Maggie has physical and sensory impairments. She generally holds an arm or hand when she walks and can become panicked, dizzy and disoriented in some spaces and situations. Maggie requires a high level of personal care. Her family assists her with toileting, washing, grooming, dressing, eating, and her mobility.

Bernadette (Maggie's Mother)

Bernadette is a Pākeha (white) woman in her early 50's. She lives in a small city in Aotearoa New Zealand with her two daughters, Maggie Rose and Sally, and her partner, Tony. Bernadette is the primary caregiver of her children. She views parenting as her first obligation and tries to prioritise it above other things. Parenting Maggie involves being the advocate, central co-ordinator, and organiser of her access to, and participation in, education, the community, and life in general. In order to support Maggie in experiencing a meaningful, connected and satisfying life, Bernadette relies on the sustaining networks of people and resources in her community. This is time-consuming and emotional work.

Since Maggie Rose was diagnosed/labelled as "globally developmentally delayed" as a baby, Bernadette has been studying, researching, teaching, writing, and advocating for human and disability rights and inclusive education. She is a DSE scholar and has a background in early childhood teaching, research and teacher education. She is a spokesperson and lobbyist for various disability rights organizations and she contributes to various efforts at Sally and Maggie's High School to further develop an inclusive culture and practices. She doesn't get paid for any of this work. Her occasional paid work includes teaching about disability rights and inclusive education, writing resource-guides for educators, co-planning and facilitating inclusive education and disability rights events. She also does a bit of paid house-cleaning which she describes as giving her some pocket money, and a quiet time and space to think.

Tony (Maggie's Father)

Tony works as a manager of a non-governmental disability advocacy and service organisation. He was a member of the Board of Trustees at Maggie's first school for 9 years and is an awesome advocate for Maggie Rose and for social justice. In addition to his day job, he is a musician and usually has a "band on the go." The house is full of music.

Sally (Maggie's Sister)

When Maggie was 5 years old, her sister Sally was born. Sally plays piano and banjo. She loves writing, maths, science, and cooking. She especially likes to play puzzles and games, and is always keen to go shopping. She loves her sister and is very caring towards her most of the time. Sally and Maggie went to the same early childhood centre and schools.

Noel (Music Teacher, Director of Singing and Orchestra)

Noel is one of the two teachers in the Music Department team during the seven years Maggie studies music at Central High School.

Melanie (Director of Acting and Choreography, The Pyjama Game)

Melanie was also Maggie's school Drama teacher.

Clare (Director of Acting and Choreography, West Side Story)

Clare knows Bernadette and Maggie quite well from having been Maggie's Drama class teacher for several years outside of school.

Roy (Teacher's Aide)

Roy and Maggie were in the same year group as students at Central High. They studied Music for five years before Roy left school. Roy became Maggie's Music teachers' aide the year after he left school.

Paula (Learning Support Teacher)

This is Paula's first year working in the Learning Support Department at school, so she is new to her role. She believes in the right of all students to be included within wider school activities.

Stephanie (Speech and Language Therapist)

Stephanie has been working on contract at the school with Learning Support staff and individual students. She has a holistic view of education and speech language therapy.

Other Characters

Gabe (drama teacher)
Jen (Maggie's singing teacher)
Martin (deputy principal)
Emily (a parent at the show)
Rosie (Bernadette's former work colleague)
High school students
Various students are cast in the chorus or orchestra, have speaking and singing roles, or as working on sound, lighting, etc. They remain in the background, but their presence is implied throughout the play.

Prologue One: "Ten Fingers and Ten Toes"

Narrator: In this scene, Bernadette is pregnant with Maggie. She is having lunch with a colleague, Rosie. Rosie is a speech and language therapist who teaches a course in the same early childhood teacher education programme as Bernadette. After fifteen years of studying and working in early childhood education, Bernadette is really looking forward to having a baby of her own. While she feels nervous about the birth, she is feeling excited about meeting the baby, falling in love and becoming a mother.

Rosie: Do you know if your baby is a boy or a girl?

Bernadette: No we don't. I'm not having any scans unless I really need to. Just so long as it has ten fingers and ten toes, we'll be happy.

Rosie: But your baby might not have ten fingers and ten toes.

Bernadette: Pardon?

Rosie: Your baby, it might not have ten fingers and ten toes. It might be disabled.

Bernadette (thinking to herself): What a joy germ! Fancy criticising a pregnant mother for wanting a normal baby. How rude!

Bernadette: (smiling weakly): Well I hope not.

Prologue Two: Placenta Party

Narrator: Maggie Rose, Bernadette and Tony's first child is born. Bernadette is 32 and Tony, 36.

They send the following Birth notice:

> *Paine, Margaret Rose Macartney (Maggie Rose), born in a southerly storm at home in Diamond Harbour, at 1.44am on Monday May 27, 1996, 5lb 8oz and growing. Julie and Viv—your love, support, ice packs, and hot towels were perfect. Thanks to Julie Richards for her love and awesome midwifery skills, and to the Christchurch Home Birth midwives. From Tony (Dad), Bernadette (Mum), and Maggie (baby).*

Tony and Bernadette organize a placenta party—they invite their family, friends and community to gather to bury Maggie's placenta, welcome and celebrate her arrival into the family and community. It is winter when they all gather. People bring and share gifts and wishes for Maggie Rose and her life. Bernadette and Tony plan to keep these in a special box, to open and explore on Maggie's 21st birthday. Tony and Bernadette's wish is, "For Maggie to grow up strong, feel good about yourself and have things in your life that you feel passionate about."

PLAYWRIGHT'S NOTES

Throughout our lives, we are cast within, and shaped by, dominant culture. We make sense of, and construct, our Truths and our realities through the stories we tell and believe about the world (Clandinin & Connelly, 2000). Discourse(s) can be thought of as the "stories we live by" (*ibid.*, 2000). However, not all stories are equal in value, visibility and influence. Edgar and Sedgwick (2002) note that a key function of Discourse is not only what it includes but also what it *excludes;* it operates by providing the rules for what counts, and what doesn't count, as knowledge.

Foucault (1982) used the terms *bio-power* and *bio-politics* to describe cultural networks and socio-political systems of knowledge that control individuals and groups in modern society. He identified three mechanisms of bio-power through which people are objectified, sorted, controlled and regulate themselves (1977, 1980, 1982). The first mechanism are the regimes of truth'—the dominant cultural discourses and the modes of inquiry, knowledge, and practices of Western science. These are assumed to be factual and therefore, value free, benign and unproblematic (Besley & Peters, 2007; Foucault, 1980). There are unspoken rules, often taken-for-granted, that dictate what *is* and *isn't* knowledge within a particular context, *whose* knowledge and perspectives matter, and *who* will benefit from particular ways of thinking and acting. The theories, disciplines and practices of medicine, psychiatry, developmental psychology, and special education count as knowledge; within these, disability and difference is constructed as deviance from normalcy.

"Truths" about what is normal, and therefore desirable, in people and society permeate our thinking, relationships, and communities through social-cultural networks and institutions. The phrase "ten fingers and ten toes" is a common cultural expression reinforcing the message that normal bodies (and people) are more valued, preferable and desirable. Based on this Truth, I assumed that having a disabled baby would be a tragedy, and lesser than having a "normal" baby. Rosie's comment exposed my assumptions, which I only began to notice and question on a deeper and more sustained level through my relationships and experiences as Maggie's mother.

ACT ONE

Setting

Central High School is a city suburban school with 1,300 students. Students are mainly from Pākeha (white, New Zealand European), middle to upper income families. Māori, Pasifika, disabled and international students are significant minority groups within the school with around 100 students attending from each of those communities. The school has a reputation for being more liberal and inclusive than most schools in the region. Students don't wear uniforms and are encouraged to develop and express their individuality. People often refer to the school's inclusive ethos as, "the Central High way."

Central High School is also well known for its music and performing arts programmes. The teachers at the school say the musicals are open to, and inclusive of, everyone. All students are welcome to participate; auditions are held to give the students the experience of auditioning for a performance, and to cast students in roles, not for the purpose of excluding or screening out students. Students are cast in speaking and singing roles or as Chorus members. Chorus members are not required to audition. Students can also be involved in a variety of aspects of the production like sound, lighting, or playing in the orchestra.

For two years before Maggie started attending Central High School, she (and her family) went to the school's musicals. The older children of family friends were at the school and some of them performed and had main roles in the shows. Maggie looked up to these young men and women and really enjoyed these shows. Maggie's family had told her that she could be in the musicals when she went to Central High School. Maggie was excited about the prospect.

Act One, Scene One
South Pacific

Narrator: It is Maggie's second year at Central High School. She is 15 years old. She has been cast in the Chorus of the musical: South Pacific. She was given a book containing the South Pacific script, which she reads and has kept close at hand for many months. She googles South Pacific performances and songs online. She goes to rehearsals after school and on weekends, though she has missed some because Bernadette and Tony didn't know they were happening. The school staff expect students to keep track of the rehearsals and to pass information on to their families. Maggie has difficulties doing that without support.

It is the day before the first performance of South Pacific. Martin, a Deputy Principal at the school phones Bernadette at home during the day.

Martin: Hi, Bernadette, Martin from school here.

Bernadette: Hi, Martin, how are you?

Martin: Good, thanks. Hey, I'm sorry, but I have to let you know that *Maggie* can't be in the *South Pacific* show.

Bernadette (surprised): What?!

Martin: She's not ready. She didn't attend enough rehearsals or join in much with the rehearsals she was at. She's not prepared enough, or comfortable enough, to perform.

Bernadette (crying): But it's not her fault! It's the adults, myself as well, who have let her down. What am I going to tell her?!

Martin: I know, I'm sorry.

Bernadette: I'm going to go now because I'm really upset. I don't want to say anything I might regret later. Thank you. Goodbye.

Narrator: Bernadette hangs up. She keeps crying and thinking about having to tell Maggie that she can't be in the show. She feels guilty and powerless because she believes she has let Maggie down. But no one had told her there was a problem with Maggie participating at the rehearsals. The adults seemed relaxed and happy to see Maggie when Bernadette and Tony dropped her off and picked her up. There was no teachers' aide or buddy system set up to support Maggie. Bernadette feels like she should have stayed and been more involved with Maggie during rehearsals, or made sure that she knew what was happening. She feels guilty for not having supported Maggie enough. Maggie and the family don't go to the show.

PLAYWRIGHT'S NOTES

Foucault (1980) identified the second mechanism of bio-power as the "dividing practices" that diagnose, categorise, objectify, pathologize, and intervene to reduce or contain differences within "problem" populations. Here, the term "dividing practices" describes Western cultural knowledge and mechanisms that construct some groups of people in deficit terms, and then seek to discipline, control, restrict, fix, and/or cure them. Comparing, measuring, and dividing people against perceived norms creates and legitimizes spaces and conditions for the differential treatment based on perceived deviations from "the norm." During rehearsals for *South Pacific*, Maggie didn't fit into normalised expectations of students for their participation, independence, behaviour, self-care, etc. Her perceived differences were neither recognised, nor responded to, in ways that would support her involvement and success. Instead, Maggie was ignored until she was rejected from performing. A common assumption is that any barriers and obstacles to participation a disabled person experiences is caused by their "special needs" (i.e., their impairments or their differences). The beliefs, actions, and inactions of those around them are usually not considered. Locating the problem within the individual provides a rationale and pathway for exclusion, making it seem inevitable and beyond others' power, control, or responsibility.

Act One, Scene Two
Sweeney Todd

Narrator: The next year there was a musical, Sweeney Todd, and Maggie wasn't in it.

Bernadette was feeling anxious and depressed that year, and didn't have any energy to find out about the musical. She hadn't seen or heard any information about there being a musical, auditions, rehearsals, etc. until the tickets went on sale. Maggie and her family went to the performance. Maggie enjoyed the show. Her favourite parts were when the old woman ran around the audience screaming and shouting. And the singing of course.

The same year a conflict arises at an Individual Education Planning (IEP) meeting when the issue of Maggie taking Drama as a subject the next year is questioned by Gabe, a Drama teacher. Gabe has never taught Drama to Maggie. There are 10 people seated around a large table in a meeting room. They are: Tony and Bernadette, five classroom subject teachers, and three school learning support staff. Maggie isn't present. Leading up to the meeting, she has been involved in choosing what subjects she wants to take next year.

Bernadette: So, Maggie wants to carry on with Drama next year, Gabe.

Gabe: I'm afraid Maggie doesn't meet the pre-requisites for the senior NCEA[3] classes.

Bernadette: What do you mean? What pre-requisites are these?

Gabe: She doesn't have the pre-requisite skills to contribute or participate at the expected level.

Bernadette: How do you know? What skills are these?

Gabe: In senior NCEA Drama, the students often work in small groups. Their class group work is internally assessed at school. We require a high level of participation and contribution from each student because of the assessment. It wouldn't be fair to have Maggie in a group. She may alter the achievement of the other students in the group. Her assessment may also not reflect her actual achievement because of the other student's contributions being reflected in her grades. We have to act in the best interests of all students. NCEA is very important to them.

Narrator: Bernadette stands up and puts both hands on the table. As she speaks, she becomes more animated, and raises her voice. She has never let a teacher hear or see the full force of her anger and frustration at Maggie's exclusion.

Bernadette: You can stop right there, Gabe! Maggie has done Drama here for the last two years. So, she has things to learn, so what?! Isn't that the point of school?! I'm sorry that I am so angry and it probably seems out of proportion. But Maggie has a right to do Drama! It's one of her strengths and passions for god's sake! You can't take that from her! Why does it *always* have to be a competition? I'm going to go now because I'm not in a space to continue with the meeting, I'm sorry for my outburst. Carry on…

Narrator: Bernadette leaves the room, after asking Tony if he could continue with the meeting. Tony remains, and a distraught Bernadette exits.

PLAYWRIGHT'S NOTES

Due to their pervasive and taken-for-granted nature, Disablist beliefs are more often implied, than explicit. Gabe didn't need to say, "I'm not going to let Maggie do Drama because she's not normal." As in *Act One, Scene One*, the assumption that any challenges Maggie faced were due to her differences or her "special needs," rather than the expectations of those around her, made it seem okay, and even fair, that she be excluded from the curriculum and her peers. Maggie was positioned as fundamentally *other* and in competition with her "normal" peers. Constructing Maggie as a threat to others' success and achievement made it appear reasonable for Gabe to apply different rules around her access and participation, and to justify her exclusion.

Act One, Scene Three
The Pyjama Game

Narrator: It is Maggie's fourth year at Central High. A teacher's aide is assigned to attend rehearsals and support students who need it in the school's production of The Pyjama Game. Maggie is cast in the Chorus. She begins googling, watching and listening to Pyjama Game performances on-line, reading the script and attending all of the rehearsals. She is being well supported by the performance director, a teachers' aide and some friends she had known since primary school who are in the cast and Chorus. Tony and Bernadette also enjoy the relief and freedom of knowing they could leave Maggie at rehearsals and performances and that she would be happy, respected and included.

Like many of the students, Maggie is very is excited about the after- party with the cast and crew.

Students usually audition for a part in the musicals. Those who aren't given big roles are cast in the Chorus. Maggie would have liked to audition, and Bernadette had been asking teachers for information about when auditions would be, but the school hadn't responded. Maggie was cast in the Chorus without an audition. In this scene, Bernadette has a fleeting conversation with Melanie, the performance director.

Bernadette: Ooooh, while I see you Melanie! Have you got a minute to catch up about The Pyjama Game?

Melanie: Hi Bernadette! Just a wee minute, I'm off to a meeting! I've been meaning to say to you, I realise Maggie didn't have an audition but I'm still keen to make sure she gets some lines even though she hasn't got a big part.

Bernadette: Thanks Melanie, that sounds awesome, Maggie will love that! Let me know when it's sorted and I'll help her practise. Thanks!

Narrator: But Maggie wasn't given any lines. Still, Maggie's family loved going to watch the show, seeing her perform and enjoy being part of the production. After several nights of performing, the after-party happens.

Bernadette: How was the party Maggie?!

Maggie: Good! I want to do The Pyjama Game again!!!

Bernadette: You did so well Mags. We loved it! Probably not The Pyjama Game at school again, but definitely another musical. I wonder what next year's musical will be!

Maggie: Grease!

Bernadette: Maybe!

Narrator: Maggie is very much looking forward to the next musical.

ACT TWO

Act Two, Scene One
Who's In and Who's Out?

Narrator: Later in the same year as The Pyjama Game is performed, a conversation between Noel (the music teacher and musical director) and Paula (Maggie's learning support teacher) takes place in the school staffroom [4]

Paula: Hi, Noel. How's it going? Listen, I'm just checking if there's going to be a musical next year, and if you know what it is?

Noel: Yeah, sure. It's *West Side Story*.

Paula: Nice, yeah. I'll let Maggie and her mum know. Give us a yell when you've got more details. Bernadette is keen for Maggie to audition.

Noel: I'm afraid this one probably won't work for Maggie. It's too physical. Lots of dancing and action for the Chorus.

Paula: Too physical? Oh, okay. I'll let Bernadette know.

Noel: (smiling) Cheers.

Act Two, Scene Two
"It's Too Physical"

Setting: At school, after a planning meeting. Bernadette and Paula are having a cup of tea at the table in the Learning Support Department staffroom.

Paula: Oh! While I think of it. Next year's musical, *West Side Story*…

Bernadette: West Side Story! Maggie will love it!! (*Sings*) "Maria! I once knew a girl called Maria!" Let's make sure she gets to audition for a part this time!

Paula: Yeah, well, I'm afraid Noel says it won't work for Maggie because it's going to be too physical apparently.

Bernadette: He can't say no, Paula. That's not okay. The musicals are for all students. Maggie loved The Pyjama Game! They said they would give her lines, but they didn't. Next year is her last chance at being in the musical before she leaves school. She *has* to be in it. And, she *has* to have an audition! You'll have to go back and tell him he can't say no. He *has* to make it work. He sounds like he needs help!

Paula: Yeah, you're right. Okay, I'll talk to him.

PLAYWRIGHT'S NOTES

Why did Paula comply with Noel, rather than challenge him when he said Maggie wouldn't be able to participate? What mechanisms sustain and perpetuate exclusion? Part of transforming Disablist thinking, attitudes, culture, and society is being able to recognise and name how power operates and plays out at a micro level (Freire, 1997). Noel's justification that the musical would be "too physical" for Maggie is an example of thinking and practices that divide (physically able/not able) and exclude (Foucault,

1982). Paula's acceptance of Noel's reason for Maggie's exclusion is an example of conformity with dominant Truths in which disabled people are regarded as fundamentally more different from, than similar to, non-disabled people. Disabling assumptions underpinning exclusion include a view of a person's differences as their only or defining characteristic and identity. In this situation, Maggie's identity was reduced to a lack of physical ability. Her "deficit" in physical ability was understood as adequate reason for denying her access to performing in the show. The question of *how* Maggie might be supported to participate in a way that would not be physically strenuous for her was not considered. The discrimination circulating throughout was obscured.

Act Two, Scene Three
Auditions

Setting: The family's home

Narrator: Auditions come and go without Maggie's family knowing about them. Emails from Bernadette asking about auditions go unanswered. Weeks after the auditions, where major roles were decided, Maggie was cast in the Chorus.

At home Maggie has a conversation with Bernadette.

Maggie: I want to be Maria!

Bernadette: You would make a great Maria, Maggie! But someone else has got that part for this show.

Maggie: Moana is Maria. *I* want to be Maria!

Bernadette: Jen (Maggie's singing teacher) could help you learn some of Maria's songs if you like? You could still perform them at school. Would that be good?

Maggie (nodding): Yip.

Act Two, Scene Four
Rehearsal

Narrator: Maggie has started going off to rehearsals after school and on the weekends. Roy, her teachers' aide, goes too. Soon after rehearsals for the West Side Story Chorus begin, Roy starts to ring Bernadette regularly. He tells her that Maggie is upset; he wants Bernadette to come and get Maggie, which she does. Whenever she picks Maggie up, she is usually waiting with Roy outside the building or in the corridor next to the hall where the rehearsals are taking place.

One Sunday afternoon, Maggie and Bernadette arrive at rehearsal. It is in the school hall. The ceiling is high, the space vast. Voices, laughter, and noise bounce off the ceilings, walls and windows. Bernadette and Maggie push themselves in through the heavy wooden doors. Young people are milling around in groups—talking, laughing, singing. Furniture is being moved and scraped, objects dropped.

Maggie clings on to Bernadette. She looks like she wants to drop down and kneel on the floor. She grabs onto a bench seat. Bernadette notices Clare across the hall as Clare walks over to them.

Clare: Hi (looking around). Where is Roy?

Bernadette: Hi, Clare. He'll be here soon. He said he was running a few minutes late. I wanted to talk with you. About how the rehearsals are going and whether it might be good to do some rehearsing with Maggie in the theatre or foyer? She has trouble in the hall space sometimes. She seems to feel really anxious and overwhelmed there. It happens in other large spaces sometimes, too. She'll feel dizzy and anxious and want to kneel down and not move. It's not a recipe for being able to participate (smiling). Can the Chorus, or even some small groups, use the foyer or school theatre to rehearse in sometimes?

Clare (looking and sounding exasperated): Look! I've got 30 other students in the cast and it's not as easy moving things around just to suit one person. The concert band is using the theatre. I can't see how it's possible.

Bernadette (angrily, through gritted teeth): That doesn't surprise me, Clare.

Narrator: Bernadette walks out and leaves Maggie and Clare standing together.

Act Two, Scene Five
Carpark Conversation

Narrator: Bernadette is crying as she leaves the hall and walks across the carpark. She encounters Roy.

Roy (walking towards Bernadette and the building, smiling): Hi, B, how are you?

Bernadette: Not very good; I just had a run-in with Clare about Maggie. I asked if some of the kids could rehearse with her in a different space.

Roy: Yeah, Mags hates the hall.

Bernadette: Clare said she had 30 other students to think about (rolling her eyes). *They* have to stay in the hall together, which means *you* and Mags end up in the corridor, Roy. It pisses me off!

Roy: Oh no, that's so shit, Bernadette. I'm sorry that happened.

Bernadette: Ah, well. I'd better let you go in. I just left Maggie standing there and Clare's probably freaking out because she's got Maggie "on her own"! Seeya!

Roy: Okay, bye. Have a good one.

Bernadette: Will do. Thanks for being a great friend to Maggie, Roy, thanks! (Smiling, then crying all the way home in the car).

Act Two, Scene Six
Corridor Conversation

A week after Bernadette's run-in with Clare, she decides to go an hour or so early to pick Maggie up from rehearsal. Bernadette wants to hang out at rehearsal, get a feel for what is happening, work out how to support Maggie as best she can, and break the ice with Clare.

When Bernadette arrives, all of the cast except Maggie are assembled on the hall floor facing the stage. Noel is up on the stage leading the orchestra and Chorus in a song. Bernadette looks around but can't see Maggie. She approaches one of the students at the edge of the Chorus.

Bernadette (whispering): Do you know where Maggie is?

Student: (points to the door leading to the corridor outside the hall).

Narrator: Bernadette walks over to the corridor. Maggie is seated on a couch with Roy, and Paula from the Learning Support Department sitting either side. Stephanie (who Bernadette doesn't know) is standing beside the couch.

Paula: Oh! Hi, Bernadette. We weren't expecting you so early! We're just having a… (pause) This is Stephanie, she's an SLT (*speech language therapist*). She's been doing some other work at the school. I asked her to pop in and see if she can help Maggie become more involved and active in the musical. We thought she might be able to help with ideas and strategies.

Bernadette: Hi, Stephanie, nice to meet you. Hi, Magstar.

Maggie: Hi, Mum. (Bernadette and Maggie smile at each other)

Bernadette (to the adults): So what's the plan?

Stephanie: Yes. I'm wondering about Maggie working with a smaller group or one other student to practise the Chorus songs to start off with. It might be easier for her and some of the other students to get to know and feel comfortable with each other on a smaller scale and in a better space if possible.

Bernadette: Yeah, good idea.

Narrator: Bernadette feels hurt that Noel doesn't feel the need to support Maggie. Why are the 'learning support' staff the only ones assumed to be able to help include her, and how is anything going to get better with them sitting in the corridor?

After the Corridor Conversation, Bernadette and Maggie walk through the hall. Noel is on the stage still conducting the concert band and Chorus. Maggie walks up to beneath the stage, in between Noel and the Chorus who are gathered in front of the stage. She is standing, smiling, and looking up at Noel. Noel looks at Bernadette with a puzzled look on his face.

Bernadette: Maggie is wanting to say goodbye to you.

Noel keeps looking from Bernadette to Maggie while smiling quizzically. He goes back to conducting. None of the students say goodbye to Maggie. Bernadette walks up, takes Maggie by the hand and leaves the hall.

PLAYWRIGHT'S NOTES

Foucault (1972) observed that language and action are inseparable. "Micro-politics" refers to the expression of power through the language, actions, and interactions of individuals and groups (Foucault, 1980). Throughout *West Side Story (Down Under)*, Maggie was conceptually and physically distanced and removed through the actions and interactions of people. Those who valued her participation were also complicit with her removal, and with the ultimate outcome of her not performing. I absented myself from the rehearsal space and the directors because I was afraid of the emotional costs of continually advocating for Maggie; Roy took Maggie into the corridor because she wasn't coping with being in the hall and was upset. Consistent with dominant assumptions that only special education professionals can teach or support *special* students, the Learning Support Department staff acted as intermediaries between the musical directors, Maggie, and our family. This division created a buffer zone that protected the directors' beliefs, autonomy, and power within the situation.

Foucault's third mechanism of bio-power pertains to how individuals regulate and discipline themselves in compliance with dominant discourses. Foucualt (1982) describes this aspect of bio-power as "...the way a human being turns him- or herself into a *subject*" (p. 208, emphasis added). We are all enculturated and socialised into societies where particular values, beliefs, assumptions, Truths, roles, and expectations dominate. Cultural norms permeate our thinking, doing, and ways of being in the world. We tend to follow, but can also resist cultural scripts that define what is normal, expected, or acceptable within situations. Many of the characters in *West Side Story (Down Under),* at times including myself, behaved in ways that stopped short of challenging the dominant Disablist norms and assumptions that were circulating. We didn't act in more direct and potentially confronting ways that might have created better outcomes for Maggie, other students, the teachers, and the school. We regulated our behaviour to conform, even when our intentions or explicit roles were to support Maggie's inclusion.

Act Two, Scene Seven
"I want to be Maria"

Narrator: Over the next week, Bernadette worries a lot about how Maggie is going to be able to perform when she hasn't been participating in the rehearsals. The musical performance season is only weeks away. Whenever anyone asks Maggie what role she has in West Side Story, she lights up and says, "Maria!"

Bernadette can see what is going to unfold if she does nothing. She expects she will get a phone call or an email like the one from the deputy principal a few years ago. Or, she thinks, maybe they won't contact her at all. She feels angry that they haven't included Maggie.

At home, one morning, a week or so after the "Corridor Conversation," Bernadette goes into Maggie's bedroom. Maggie is sitting up in bed eating her breakfast. Bernadette sits at the end of Maggie's bed and begins to talk about how she thinks Maggie should reconsider performing in West Side Story.

Bernadette (smiling): Morning, Maggles

Maggie: Hi, Mum

Bernadette: Can we talk about the *West Side Story* show?

Maggie: I want to be Maria!

Bernadette (smiling): I know! You would make an awesome Maria, Maggles, with your lovely voice. That would be great! Jen is keen to help you learn and practice some of the songs. (Silence. A pause). You know how you haven't been liking the rehearsals or joining in very much? I don't think you're going to be able to be in the show. Do you feel ready to perform Mags?

Maggie: No

Maggie: Do you want to perform?

Maggie: No

Bernadette (crying): Sorry, Maggie. I know it's not your fault you can't be in the show and that you're not ready. You can still be Maria, though! You can learn some of Maria's songs with Roy and Melanie (Maggie's singing teacher) and perform them. Would that be good?

Maggie (nodding): Yeah. Are you sad, mummy?

Bernadette: I feel sad about you not being in the show.

Maggie: Can I go to the after party?

Bernadette: I don't think so, Maggie.

Maggie: I want to go to the Show.

Bernadette: Okay, I'll get us some tickets. You don't need to go to rehearsals now.

Narrator: Bernadette texts Roy to say that Maggie is pulling out of the show, and to thank him for going to rehearsals with her. Bernadette assumes Roy will pass the message on to the other staff. She doesn't feel like talking with them about it. She figures it is way too late to change the outcome for Maggie.

Act Two, Scene Eight
West Side Story

Narrator: Tony, Maggie, Sally, and Bernadette go to the West Side Story performance at school. Bernadette doesn't want to go, however, Maggie does. Bernadette wants to acknowledge all of the energy Maggie has put into reading the script, learning the songs, and going to rehearsals, so Bernadette goes along too.

During the performance, the Chorus often move around quickly. Maria, the lead female character, sometimes struggles to hit the high notes and sing in key. Bernadette thinks that it could have worked for Maggie to have sung alongside Maria in one or more of the songs. It would have been a perfect way for Maggie to perform in the show and it would have worked for "Maria" too.

The lights go up for intermission.

Bernadette (to Maggie): Are you enjoying the show?

Maggie (smiling widely): Yeah!

Bernadette (smiling): That's great, Maggie!

Maggie: I want to be Maria!

Bernadette (smiling): I know, Maggie. You would make a great Maria, Maggie!

Act Two, Scene Nine
"Another great Central High performance!"

Narrator: After the show, as Maggie and her family get up from their seats to leave, Bernadette sees Emily, another parent from school.

Emily (smiling): Hi, Bernadette. Hi, Maggie, How are you? Wasn't that great?!

Maggie: (Nodding and smiling)

Bernadette: Hi, Emily. It sure was! Another great Central High performance!

Emily: And it's so good to see how inclusive it was! Gretta and Simone performed wonderfully!

Narrator: Gretta and Simone are two students who have the label of intellectual disability. They are more physically able and have less complex needs for support than Maggie.

Bernadette: Yeah, they did really well. I loved watching Gretta dance!

Emily: Nice to see you.

Bernadette: Nice to see you too, Emily, bye.

THE END

(CURTAIN FALLS)

PLAYWRIGHT'S NOTES

Experiences of exclusion are invisible to most people. My conversation with Emily highlights that a veneer or mirage of inclusion can be accepted as the "real thing." The reach and dominance of bio-power and exclusionary discourses is multi-layered and diffuse. Conscious and unconscious acts of exclusion are explained away. The performing arts program at Central High School was touted as being inclusive of *all*, yet, in its musicals, only students who could, or would, comply with pre-determined expectations for participation, behaviour, and communication, i.e., those who "fit the mould," were allowed to belong and succeed. Differences were accommodated and/or tolerated only when they did not cause much discomfort for the able-bodied students or require any significant restructuring of existing ways of doing things by the staff. Although during the year of *The Pyjama Game* there were elements that were problematic, it was a huge improvement from Maggie's earlier experiences of trying to participate in school musicals. We had assumed that this positive experience would be built upon during future musicals at school. Gretta and Simone's participation in *West Side Story* was viewed by Emily, and presumably others, as evidence of Central High's inclusiveness. Perhaps Maggie's attendance at the show was also interpreted as a sign of an inclusive school and community. The boundaries of inclusion, the rules of *who is in and who is out*, are seldom examined. I am left with many questions. In what ways could we have acted and reacted to interrupt, challenge, and replace the disablist thinking and practices causing Maggie's exclusion? How could it have become a transformative story with the happy ending that Emily had assumed it already was for all students?'

CONCLUDING NOTES

Advocacy is an aspect of parenting that is more necessary to parents of marginalized children. Without mothers and other family members acting as advocates, many more disabled students would be excluded from various aspects of school and community life. Advocacy is time-consuming, frustrating, adversarial, and emotional work. It is never easy for family members to challenge institutional powers, especially on their own. Additionally, we sometimes share the experiences of marginalization alongside our family members; this is life-long, personal, and constant.

Families often act in isolation from one another, but resistance to regimes of exclusion needs to be conscious, deliberate, collaborative, and sustained. Learning to recognise and name Disablism within our contexts and our spheres of influence is a starting place for removing barriers to belonging or succeeding. If there is any lesson here, perhaps it is that, to be transformative and effective, resistance to Disablism and other regimes of exclusion require a connected, cohesive, and deliberate approach from staff, students, families, and other allies. Rather than acting as buffers, staff within a school who are supportive of inclusive education must make it their role to lead, challenge, and mentor for inclusion. We need to name and dismantle the grand narratives and bio-politics that restrict us and through which we restrict ourselves. The alternative is continuing to defer to narratives that cast and reject some of us as "unfortunate," "special," "needy" individuals with "problems" and "deficits." Re-framing this requires turning up the volume on counter-narratives about disability and difference as a form of human diversity, underpinned by a view of inclusive education as being about human rights, belongingness, and the value of every person and group in society.

NOTES

1. The total adds up to more than 100 percent due to some people identifying as having more than one ethnicity.
2. The use of the term 'disabled person' reflects Social Model and Disability Studies perspectives that view disability as an identity, and as a result of discrimination against people with impairments or differences; that is, people are disabled by society, not by their differences or impairments.
3. National Certificate in Educational Achievement
4. This scene is based on Paula's narrative of the conversation she had with Noel about next year's musical.

REFERENCES

Besley, T., & Peters, M. (2007). *Subjectivity & truth: Foucault, education and the culture of self.* New York, NY: Peter Lang

Clandinin, J., & Connelly, F. (2000). *Narrative inquiry: Experience and story in qualitative research.* San Francisco, CA: Jossey-Bass.

Edgar, A., & Sedgwick, P. (Eds.). (2002). *Key concepts in cultural theory.* London, England: Routledge.

Foucault, M. (1972). *The archaeology of knowledge.* New York, NY: Routledge, Random House.

Foucault, M. (1977). *Discipline and punish: The birth of the prison.* New York, NY: Vintage Books, Random House.

Foucault, M. (1980). Truth & power. In C. Gordon (Ed.), *Michel Foucault: Power/ knowledge: Selected interviews and other writings 1972–1977* (pp. 109–133). Sussex, England: The Harvester Press.

Foucault, M. (1982). Afterword: The subject and power. In H. R. Dreyfus, P. Rabinow (Eds.), *Michel Foucault: Beyond structuralism and hermeneutics: With an afterword by and an interview with Michel Foucault* (pp. 208–226). Brighton, England: The Harvester Press.

Freire, P. (1997). *Pedagogy of hope: Reliving pedagogy of the oppressed.* New York, NY: The Continuum Publishing.

New Zealand Human Rights Commission (NZHRC). (2016). *Article 24: The right to an inclusive education.* New Zealand: Independent Monitoring Mechanism on the rights of persons with disabilities.

Statistics New Zealand. (2013). *2013 Census quick stats about culture and identity.* Retrieved May 2018. http://archive.stats.govt.nz/Census/2013-census/profile-and-summary-reports/quickstats-culture-identity/ethnic-groups-NZ.aspx

Statistics New Zealand. (2017). *Labour market statistics (disability) June 2017 quarter.* Retrieved May 2018. http://archive.stats.govt.nz/browse_for_stats/income-and-work/employment_and_unemployment/LabourMarketStatisticsDisability_MRJun17qtr.aspx

CHAPTER 3

Selves-Advocacy AND THE Meeting Space

ERIN MCCLOSKEY

We walk into the meeting space and everyone else is already there, settled and casually chatting. Two empty seats are on the opposite side of the long oval table, and my son, Wyatt, and I make our way to the chairs, undoing our winter coats on this particularly frigid January day. Dr. Rich[1], the special education administrator running this meeting, and the only stranger in the room, stands and points at the empty chairs with a smile. The door closes behind us. Wyatt and I fall into the tall, cushioned office chairs that move with us, rolling back and reclining under our body weight. I notice that my fourteen-year-old Autistic[2] son has that school picture smile on his face; not a natural state of happiness but rather a performance for the setting, and I become aware that I am wearing that smile too. I realize the other adults in the room are trying to put us at ease. I remember being the special education teacher in the room and trying to accomplish this same feat.

There is life-work that we do every day and then there are those moments where we get some idea about how we're doing with this work. This meeting is one of those touchstone moments when I hope the Autistic pride and self-advocacy skills I worked to instill in my son would shield him from the medicalized perspective people often assert when talking about autism. Wyatt has a strong sense of self and embraces his Autistic identity. He has participated in meetings about his special education placement before, but this one is going to be different. Wyatt's teachers have been recommending special education services since he entered school. I refrained from allowing him to be tested until the fourth grade when mandated state testing began. Then, Wyatt received a Section 504 plan that afforded testing accommodations and so he could be provided with an iPad to use in school. He received no specialized services from a special education teacher. At the start of junior high, I requested that Wyatt be tested for eligibility for special education services. He qualified and received resource room services to help him manage the anxiety of moving so quickly from class to class, to help him stay organized, and to be provided with additional instruction in writing. This level of assistance was working.

The meeting that is discussed here was being held in preparation for Wyatt's entry to high school. Unlike the junior high school he attended, the high school had a program designed for Autistic students. This program, called CASA (Communication and Social Assistance), provided academic assistance along with a component that taught social skills—the kind of instruction that used "scripts" and, in my mind, lacked the celebratory concept of Autistic pride by teaching Autistic folks that they should act in neurotypical ways to appease neurotypical people. I had spent many years pushing back against suggestions to use "proven" methods of behavior management such as Applied Behavioral Analysis (ABA), designed to "recover" my child from autism (Broderick, 2009). The endgame of these treatment plans was always to move forward an ableist agenda of making my son indistinguishable from his neurotypical peers. The abusive history (Silberman, 2015), and present-day atrocities (Davies, 2014) of these approaches were topics I addressed in my college classes, and I felt strongly that viewing autism as something that needed to be fixed was dangerous.

Having spent many years involved in special education and then having an Autistic child meant that, in some ways, I could envision the path he would be on with regard to his public school education. During his kindergarten screening, before he was even officially enrolled in school, it was recommended to me that he be moved from the placement to which he was originally assigned—a "traditional" kindergarten class, to a class that was "inclusive"—meaning that the class was taught by a teacher who was certified in both special and general education, had a teaching assistant, and enrolled larger numbers of students who were already classified as students with disabilities. After a ten-minute screening, despite his ability to complete all of the academic tasks, decisions were being made about what classroom was "right" for him. I remember the teacher who was conducting the screening probed for information about "what I had done" about his rocking. I had done nothing and felt ashamed. I took him to a developmental pediatrician, and she gave him a ball to squeeze and instructed him to squeeze rather than rock. The message was, and continued to be, that we needed to manage Wyatt's movements so that he did not appear Autistic. There were so many of these seemingly small moments that would creep into discussions in the spaces of schools, offices and meetings that would require me to explain my beliefs about raising an Autistic child, and that would make me feel guilty about accepting Wyatt rather than working to change him. What was it about these spaces that made me acquiesce to approaches I didn't believe in? In my own college classroom, I was the expert explaining the repercussions of this way of thinking. Why was I not the expert in these spaces?

As Wyatt's mother, I was continually being told what mothering an Autistic child should look like. The pressure to be a "good" mother seemed to mean compromising my beliefs to appease others. A good mother, after all, obtained services for her disabled child based on the recommendations of the professionals. It is not completely surprising that I went against my own instincts about what was right for my child, since I am part of the "legacy of a historical positioning of families of children with disabilities as the source of the problem" (Lalvani, 2014, p. 1223). Additionally, as Lalvani (2014) details, when mothers object to the recommendations made by professionals, we are positioned as being in denial or as holding unrealistic expectations for our disabled children. And so, like the mothers who have come before me, I succumbed to the "experts," those who have, historically, called us "refrigerator mothers"- cold parents who failed to attach to our children, coerced us to institutionalize our children, and prescribed harmful therapies to "fix" our children. When Wyatt's developmental pediatrician recommended that he be enrolled in social skills classes, I acquiesced even though I had doubts about what was being taught there. When a speech and language therapist included him in one of her groups in second grade, even though he wasn't a "classified" special education student, I wasn't completely comfortable with allowing it, but I did. There was a constant push to be doing something, and I complied, even when my actions went against my own instincts about what was right for my son.

Zoe Gross (2012), an Autistic woman and a student in one of my classes, pushed me to listen carefully to the *real* experts, the Autistic folks who had received therapies to "fix" them and who had parents who were taught to "disregard the priorities and perspectives of Autistic people themselves" (p. 268). As a researcher, I advocated for inclusive environments and for the voices of people who were given labels to have a say in the field of special education. As a researcher, I could often be "preachy" about what I wanted to see happen in the field of special education. As a mother, my advocacy was more complicated, less preachy, more doubting, and more unsure about how to proceed against the voices that called out to me to fix my son, change him, medicate him, and normalize him. I turned to folks like Winter (2012) who wrote about the process of trying to normalize Autistic students to make neurotypical people happy. She stated,

> An autistic child who grows up knowing that something which is that intrinsic to their very selves is so hated and loathed by those around them, who has those same adults demand that they suppress, deny and "get rid of" all evidence of it, is not going to grow up feeling good about themselves. They will likely grow to hate their Autism, and themselves with it. (p. 116)

The goals I was supposed to have for my Autistic son were taught to me by doctors, therapists, and the media. Simply stated, mothers of Autistic children were expected to work at changing their Autistic children, not celebrating them.

Teacher, advocate, researcher, and mother required different ways of being. I felt split into different "selves." This has, over time, happened both consciously and unconsciously, but it has made me uneasy, confused and doubtful. I am assertive in my beliefs when it is just my family. One time, in the car with my children, we hear a radio commercial for a residential school designed for Autistic people. In it, a mother shares why she made the difficult decision to place her Autistic son in residential care, a therapist discusses how autism dramatically affects all members of the family, and a teacher discusses how she uses specific techniques to teach her students skills and how to behave socially. These seemingly innocuous testimonies would be moments that Wyatt would describe as "sad." My researcher-self interrogates the commercial by pointing out that everyone else but the Autistic child was represented in this commercial, and I model a critical stance by questioning the difference between teaching children "skills" and honoring the way they interact with the world. A week later, we hear the same commercial and my younger son plays my role and questions the absence of the Autistic voice. My mother-self is proud. I congratulate myself on teaching my kids how to critique these dominant narratives about autism. There is parity between my work as a teacher, researcher and mother. I try to teach Wyatt to do this when confronted with ableist ideas. I model the critique of these ideas hoping that he will own this behavior. I want it to be his voice that objects. In a sense, I want Wyatt to do the work in the meeting space that I cannot seem to do.

Student voices are underrepresented in the IEP meeting and, as Test, Hughes, Konrad, Neale, and Wood (2004) explain, teaching students to advocate for what they desire in the school meeting space can be thought to generalize to post-secondary environments. My own desire to hear the voices of the students who were at the center of these meetings stemmed from a project I was working on at this same time that explored parents' experiences negotiating special education programs and services for their children. I had spent one school year following different families as they negotiated with their districts to allow their children to stay in inclusive classrooms, to not be moved to segregated special education schools, and to receive services that would allow them to have full access to the general education curriculum. The children, who were in first, fourth, and tenth grade were not present for any of these meetings, and the absence of their voices was pronounced. I explained to my son that I wanted to include us in this project and, with his consent, I set out to expand my methods for data collection, using institutional autoethnography (IE) as a framework. IE, as developed and discussed by Smith (2005) looks at the everyday experiences of people in an institution and investigates how policies, texts, social processes and discourse allows access to, or limits, power. Smith advocates working from a person's "standpoint" in order to gain insight into their experiences. For this research project, I took the standpoint of parents, working from their perspective to understand how decisions were made about their children. Then, I chose to stand in my own shoes and next to my son, to understand how this experience felt to me as a parent and to gain insight into how a student understands and experiences these meetings.

The emotional work of mothering, particularly around my son's disability and how people view him, is visceral. I had worked to prepare my son to advocate for his needs and desires, and here was an instance where those teachings might be put into play. I was interested, as both a researcher and a mother, to see how my son would navigate this setting. I hoped I had prepared my son to position himself as someone who could advocate for his needs and desires.

THE MEETING

We are one of over 6 million school-age families who meet with school officials to discuss the placement, services, and goals of our child with a disability (National Center for Education Statistics, 2013). I enter this meeting space knowing that the IEP that is developed at this meeting will be its focal point (Zeitlin & Curcic, 2013), that my experiences will be less favorable than those of the special education teachers in the room (Zeitlin & Curcic, 2013), and that student participation in IEP meetings increases the value of these meetings for all members, but particularly parents (Martin, Marshall, & Sale, 2004). I am armed with my own experiences as a teacher, with the perspective I have gained from the families with whom I have spent the last year, and with the copious amounts of reading I have been doing about these very meetings.

I first sat at the meeting table as a special education teacher in 1992. I was prepared and ready to discuss my students with other teachers, service providers, and with the parents who attended. I quickly noticed that the work of the meeting room fell to mothers. Almost always, mothers were in attendance, and only sometimes, fathers. In my first meeting, and every meeting that followed, I took note of how mothers were sometimes positioned by meeting members even before they stepped foot in the room: some described as caring, some as overbearing, and some as neglectful. I noticed that when parents were not there, the meeting unfolded very differently. Without parents, meetings proceeded without the formal presentation of the testing or the sharing of classroom artifacts. Basically, a recommendation was made and if it seemed reasonable, it was written into the individualized education program (IEP).

Being in the role of mother was more unsettling than I had expected. I found myself wondering what they had said about me before I entered the meeting room.

Would I be able to actively work against the constructed version of who I was supposed to be in this space? Pulling together the different strands of my identity-the special education teacher, the researcher who studies disability, the mother who is involved (but not too involved), the professor at a small college who teaches about special education to pre-service teachers—turned out to be an overwhelming task. This one, unified "self" that I had hoped would emerge didn't. Instead, many different *selves* stepped forward and back as they negotiated the meeting room.

Positioning Selves in Preparing for the Meeting Space

The parents I interviewed talked about the process of preparing for the annual review meeting. We do many things prior to the meeting; we prepare for the process by pulling out old report cards, reviewing testing information, consulting people we know for advice, calling advocates, reviewing programs and services the school district can offer, talking with special education teachers and service providers to get the inside scoop on how the district administrators will run the meeting, and rolling over in our heads the responses we might have to any issues that arise. For many of us, this preparation comes from a place of privilege; knowing how to prepare for these meetings means we possess the cultural and economic capital that is necessary to engage these institutional forces. It is these responses that will be used to craft a concept of who we are as the mother. How we negotiate the meeting will be used to define us as parents. If we disagree with a recommendation, we might be seen as uncooperative, and if we have an emotional reaction to how our child is defined, we might be seen as unreasonable or hysterical. We all try to prepare for the unknown of the meeting space. Now, it was time to try to prepare Wyatt.

I pulled out my son's IEP, and we sat together to review the document. Wyatt had never read this document. When it had first arrived in the mail, I asked him if he wanted to read it over. He replied, "Nah, I'm good." I skimmed the document, threw it in a drawer, and hadn't looked at it since. Now, I let Wyatt take the lead on this discussion and overall, he thought the document was fine but at one point, he had an objection. Under the section entitled "physical development" it stated,

> Wyatt tends to rock when sitting or standing. This rocking gets worse when Wyatt is anxious about anything. Although his peers are accustomed to this habit, in some social situations this might bring negative attention to Wyatt.

"Whaaaat?" Wyatt asked when he read this section aloud. "I don't think that's true" he continued. I asked,

Erin: Ok, so how should we change it? You believe this part is true though, when you're anxious?

Wyatt: Yeah, yeah, that's true, but, but drawing negative attention to me, seriously? No, that's not true at all.

Erin: Ok, so we'll cross that out. Have you ever had anyone say anything like that to you in middle school?

Wyatt: They usually ask me why I rock and then I answer and they're ok with it. It doesn't bother them that much and it doesn't certainly draw any negative attention to me!

Erin: What do you tell them when they ask?

Wyatt: I tell them I rock because I like it and they're like, "Ok, whatever."

Erin: (laughing) On to the next thing?

Wyatt: (laughing) Yes.

My mom-self is proud of Wyatt. I experience a bit of joy when he speaks back to this document that tried to depict his movement as distracting to others, as though he needed to be someone different, and that others' needs were more important than his. I also appreciate the succinct description he has for why he rocks and his acknowledgement that his anxiousness is represented in a very physical way. He speaks back to the document that has been created to describe him, to create him, and to pathologize him. It is this voice that I have been missing. The day-to-day reality of Wyatt's life is that his peers are curious, and they ask *him* about it. It's a passing conversation and not one that defines his worth or what class he will be placed in.

As I re-listen to the recorded conversation I had with Wyatt, I realize that this conversation is easy. There are both "what a silly document that looks to depict who I am" and "it helps me to have extra time on tests" moments. I wonder if this would be the same for the other students who were talked about in my study but whose voices are missing. The translation of an individual's needs to a written document, so taken for granted in the field of special education, is complicated and convoluted. To think that any of us can be depicted as isolated categories that operate separately from each other, that our emotional needs can be objectified and measured, that there are individuals looking to change who we are, all seems absurd. And still, we plan for this meeting, and I suspect that this is exactly what is to unfold.

I had multiple conversations through email and by phone with my son's special education teacher, Ms. Douglas, before the onset of this meeting. She relayed the personality of the administrator, Dr. Rich ("she talks a lot"), and how she believed Dr. Rich would push for a program at the high school that was designed for Autistic kids, the CASA program. Ms. Douglas shared that she believed that Wyatt's one period of resource room was more appropriate. She said that Wyatt's content area teachers agreed, and she asked me to share my opinion of this plan. Wyatt had a tricky transition to junior high school, and he has worked really hard to manage the demands of a rigid schedule where learning starts and stops every 43 minutes. He has worked hard to manage multiple binders, planners, his iPad, and the varying personalities of his teachers. He would move to the high school with all of this learning under his belt, and I believed that the support of the resource room teacher was, for him, the best plan forward. I told Wyatt about this conversation and asked him to share his thoughts. He agreed that resource room had been helpful, and that he would like to continue to have this class in his schedule as he moved on to high school.

We finished looking over Wyatt's current IEP and he admitted that he was a little nervous about the meeting. I admitted that I was a little nervous, too.

Negotiating "Normal" in the Meeting Space

Dr. Rich introduced herself and explained that she "runs the special education programs at the high school." She explained to Wyatt that she was conducting this meeting because they were planning for high school. Wyatt responded, "Yeah, I'm really excited about that." Ms. Douglas said, "He *is* really excited. He would go tomorrow if we let him." Everyone laughed. Dr. Rich set the agenda for the meeting. She said to Wyatt, one of the few times that she addressed him directly, that she was going to hear from all of the people around the table that knew him, and they were going to discuss his strengths and his learning needs. "Together" she stated, "we will come up with a plan, and you are going to be a part of that discussion. If you have questions at any point, about what people are recommending, or you feel that there is something that is really important that we didn't touch on, you can let me know and we'll stop and answer your question because this is really important. It's about you." Wyatt nodded confidently and I felt myself relax a little bit.

This meeting lasted about an hour. Ms. Douglas was given the floor first, and she talked for 12 minutes. In sum, she stated that she "loved to see the growth he has shown." After she concluded, Dr. Rich asked Wyatt to recap what Ms. Douglas had just said. I was confused by this "test" but I kept quiet. Recapping her 12-minute talk, Wyatt said, "She loved my growth throughout the past year. I still need a bit of help on organization." Then, Wyatt's social studies teacher took the floor. She talked for 4 minutes. She concluded by saying how proud she was of Wyatt, and that he had a grade of 94 in her class.

The bulk of the meeting, over 40 minutes, was spent assigning value to Wyatt's "stimming." Dr. Rich shared that, "Wyatt, sitting here before me…seems more like a CASA kid than a traditional resource kid at the high school." She described CASA as a program for students "on the spectrum." On the school district's website, there is a visual representation of all of the special education programs offered at the high school. The programs are organized in a line, much like a timeline or a continuum. On the extreme left side of the line is resource room, and all the way to the right is the CASA program. In between these two programs are a number of self-contained special education programs described in terms of the ratio of number of students to teacher to aides. One of these programs is described as "life skills," and one is described as "behavior management." The last program simply says "CASA," and that it is a 12:1:1 with a ratio of twelve students, one teacher, and one aide. The district has provided this visual as a way to show they have many special education programs that can serve as the continuum of alternative placements. The continuum of alternative placements is a structure that, by law, must be in place to ensure that students with disabilities are educated in the least restrictive environment (LRE). The option of education with full supports in the general education classroom which, as per the laws, must necessarily be the first consideration on this continuum, and which is the least restrictive environment, was noticeably absent from the visual depiction on the school's website. As Taylor (2001, 2004) has critiqued, in order for a disabled person to be "allowed" access to environments that are least restrictive, they must somehow *prove* they are ready to be in that integrated setting. All school districts must have a continuum that spans maximum contacts with nondisabled peers to full time placement in a segregated school. Ableism is embedded in these legal requirements because the LRE is often based on the comfort of the nondisabled. How decisions get made about these two policy requirements has been a major focal point in my research with parents (McCloskey, 2016). As Kurth (2014) discovered, educational placement decisions vary by state rather than by child-specific factors such as test scores or interpretations of behavior. Discrepancies between states can be so pronounced that geography is likely to be more predictive of where students might be placed with regard to restrictive environments than these test scores or behavioral reports. Kurth showed that students with autism in New York State, the state I live in, are consistently placed in restrictive placements, and that while discussions about the LRE on the micro level tend to focus on the child, state residence and funding formulas play significant roles in determining the placement of students with autism. So, even though the law states that "to the maximum extent" children with disabilities must be taught alongside their nondisabled peers, large numbers of children are being educated in segregated settings. When programs specifically designed for Autistic individuals exists, like the CASA program, school districts must find bodies to fill them, regardless of whether this is the best setting for that child. When the choices are narrow, there is discursive maneuvering to describe how "certain kids" need "certain placements," and that some kids are, in their entirety, the sum of what neurotypical people see as their behaviors (McCloskey, 2018). Students who are described as learning disabled become their reading level, students who are labeled as intellectually disabled become their IQ scores, and as I show here, Wyatt becomes his stimming.

The shift from including Wyatt in these conversations that are taking place about him, to him to being addressed in the third person, happens about five minutes into the conversation about what program will suit his needs. Dr. Rich no longer addressed Wyatt directly but rather, she stated,

He has moved entirely throughout the entire time we've sat here, so I don't know how self-aware Wyatt is about that.

It's just a very evident thing to talk about, but my thought about it was really leaning more towards social relationships and social skills because that, I would anticipate, it would have an impact on other learners. You [Ms. Douglas], with your relationship with Wyatt can stop him [from rocking] but a 14-year-old next to him may not feel comfortable doing that.

I don't know that he is necessarily aware of, you know, the theory of mind stuff, you know, how is he perceived by other people.

So, Wyatt sitting here before me and everything you've shared here with me about him sounds much more similar to a CASA kid than a traditional resource kid at the high school. And some of the things that you [Ms. Douglas] do for kids in the resource room at the junior high, our high school resource teachers are probably not going to do. It's kind of not part of their-the way they usually function in resource room there.

These statements come crashing down over me, and I find that I cannot talk. I know I need to push back against this privileging of the neurotypical perspective, this medicalized language and theory of mind bullshit, this "he might inconvenience the teacher" because that's not how they function, but the blood was pulsing in my ears and I stammered out, "I think that the way we've raised Wyatt is to be proud of being Autistic. He will oftentimes tell people he's Autistic and that's why he rocks. He has actually been somebody who helps other children with autism kind of come into being proud about that. I would say that in terms of putting him in a separate program to learn these skills to pass as normal is not really a concern—"

Dr. Rich: It's not about passing as normal.
Erin: Well, I think in some ways it might be—
Dr. Rich: Well, I don't like the word normal because I see learning in terms of learning differences generally, that would have been my framework.

I am overcome with emotion, and I don't even know where to start to refute this idea that the whole special education system isn't based on conceptions of normality. Ms. Douglas stepped in and went a few rounds with Dr. Rich. Wyatt's social studies teacher backed Ms. Douglas. For ten minutes, they pushed for resource room while Dr. Rich advocated for CASA. I tell my mother-self to fade to the background and let the researcher-self have at it. I notice how the only person in the room, who has *never* worked with my son, heck, who just met him moments ago, talked the most. I noticed Wyatt looking down at the table at the tape recorder we set up before the meeting. The researcher-self told the mother-self to relax, it was almost over. Only consent to resource room. Dr. Rich ended this discussion by stating that she would record resource room as Wyatt's placement for next year but that she would continue to monitor him for possible placement in the CASA program. Handshakes all around and promises to see us next year at the annual meeting. Cringing, smiling, self-loathing, pride, disgust.

Reconstructing Selves After the Meeting

I try to figure out what happened but I cannot seem to pull it all together. How could I let Dr. Rich silence me so easily? We all knew what we were there to do, what we believed, and we had the words and the strength to construct our identities but the feeling of failure I experienced was strong. It will be months before I listen to the tape of the meeting but I know that I must move the ball forward and at least engage my research participant, Wyatt, in a conversation about the meeting so that he can verify and support my analysis of what occurred. My researcher-self will utilize the qualitative method to enhance the validity known as member checking to assure that my account of the situation is accurate (Glesne, 1999; Merriam, 2001).

We sat down, four days after the meeting took place and I asked him how he thought things went. He said, "The meeting was a good way for the teachers to express their feelings about me and how I perform in classes, and it was interesting to see what I would do when I go to high school." I thought to myself that perhaps he did not quite get what the discussion about CASA was about so I showed him the district visual of the continuum of alternative placements and how CASA was on the really restrictive side and resource was on the complete opposite side, and I asked him what he thought about Dr. Rich proposing that he go all the way to the restrictive side while everyone else felt like resource room would be the best spot. And Wyatt said, "I think that it's okay if she wants to talk. It's her opinion."

Is this self-advocacy? Johnson (1999) wrote, "people with disabilities must become students of power and leadership" (p. 14), but Baggs (2012) reminds us that "When a non-disabled person gets full of ideas about what disabled people should be saying and thinking about our lives, and holds us lockstep in his control while pretending to teach us all these revolutionary ideas, that is not self-advocacy" (p. 327). As I reviewed the data from my own experiences, looked at the special education paperwork developed to define Wyatt and attended these meetings with him, I realized that my vision of self-advocacy was different from his. I thought I saw self-advocacy when a situation or comment evoked anger but, as Baggs reminded me, my desire to promote self-advocacy skills in Wyatt was trying to hold him in lockstep to my ideas about what self-advocacy looked and sounded like. In response to anger, I hoped my son would advocate for a different interpretation or perspective. I saw this when he pushed back against the wording in his IEP that depicted his rocking as behavior that drew negative attention from his peers. "This," I thought then, "was self-advocacy." Through the standpoint of my son however, I realized he was a self-advocate in other ways, and I needed to stop defining self-advocacy as both a mother and a researcher in order to see his vision.

Self-advocacy for me was a single story (Adichie, 2009), with one way to be a self-advocate; I believed that I knew it when I saw it, and that it came from a place of anger and/or frustration. To me, it meant parents advocating for themselves when they faced unfair decisions by school officials, and when their children's capabilities were diminished by others, or when adult Autistic self-advocates fought back against unjust legislation, unfair media representation, and more. This meeting, and my and Wyatt's inclusion in this research project, allowed me to expand that single story and to see our own self-advocacy methods as more than reactions to unjust situations.

I wondered for the past year, what the voices of the students whose parents attended meetings about their educational futures might say if they were in the room. As the meeting opened, Wyatt is engaged as an active participant who should stop the meeting if he has any questions. By the end of the meeting, he is talked about in the third person. I would not describe Wyatt as shy, and I believe that if he had something he wanted to say, he would have said it. As Wyatt reflected on the meeting and the transcript, he stated that next time he wanted to be better at "public speaking." He went on to say, "There are portions where I don't say anything, talking to a person I haven't met before. I'm just trying to listen carefully and process all of this in my brain."

I found it disturbing when Dr. Rich made assumptions about Wyatt based only on his rocking behaviors. As his parent, I wanted Dr. Rich to acknowledge his incredible personhood independent of what she saw when she looked at him. As a researcher, I am deeply disturbed by the positioning of Autistic children's behavior as devoid of meaning and an inconvenience to their general education peers. My reflections, however, are not Wyatt's. Wyatt did not see Dr. Rich's discussion of his rocking as a malevolent act, but rather as an area where she was uninformed, perhaps because she was an adult, and perhaps because she was neurotypical. Wyatt was used to adults interpreting his rocking as a sign of deficits in his cognitive ability, his ability to engage socially, and at times, when people speak to him in an exceptionally loud voice, his ability to hear. He was used to being asked questions, providing explanations, and moving forward with his life. In fact, when we discussed this, he stated that he actually preferred when people talked to him about autism. He said that he doesn't mind answering questions, and that it makes him feel like he is helping people understand.

My mother-self believed, very much, that self-advocacy was about my son acting independently and engaging in discussions about his autism in order to fight for the services and supports that he wanted and needed. My researcher-self believed that this was what was missing from the meetings that I had attended; not just the voices of the students but the voices that I imagined the students to have. I was a non-disabled person who was full of ideas of what self-advocacy was, much like Dr. Rich was a non-disabled person who was full of ideas about how

Autistic individuals interacted in mainstream settings. The commonality between Dr. Rich and myself was that we both held expectations about Autistic individuals that were driving our actions. Dr. Rich believed that Wyatt's rocking was somehow connected to his academic and social performance in school, and I believed that Wyatt's self-advocacy skills only showed themselves when he was discursively pushing back against conceptions of autism that I found upsetting.

Wyatt's statement about trying to process all that is being said reminded me that I can respond to the issues he raised through *his* method of self-advocacy. My role can be to slow down the talk, ask for some time to connect with him-just me and him-to see if he has questions, and make space for his voice. I knew, and proved, that the neurotypical perspective was privileged. Having the presence of the Autistic individual in the meeting space can teach neurotypical people lessons that they might not even know they are there to learn but we will need to privilege that perspective.

I walked by the bench in the hallway where my sons keep their backpacks. Both bags were overflowing with binders and papers. I told myself to remind them to organize these bags (I could already hear them groaning) when one paper in particular caught my eye. It was titled, "Temple Grandin Reaction." I remember how Wyatt told me that his science teacher was absent, and he had the substitute teacher show the movie *Temple Grandin* in which Claire Danes portrays Dr. Grandin and her experiences growing up with autism (Jackson, "Temple Grandin," 2010). He was angry that his classmates weren't behaving, and they were reacting "like fools" to the movie's content. Wyatt told me that when his science teacher returned to class the next day, he had them write a summary and review of the movie. On top of the paper was a check-plus written in red pen—the only mark on the paper. I read through Wyatt's paper. I end this chapter by sharing his words, which reflect his self-advocacy, and his Autistic pride. He wrote,

> What I really like about this movie is the theme of Temple having autism and how, with a few setbacks, she succeeded in her goals. This movie was really inspiring to me because I have autism and usually rock because it calms me down just like how Temple never liked to be touched and how she used her squeezing machine to do the hugging for her. To me, this movie is not just another movie. This movie is a breakthrough in my life and I think Temple Grandin will be one of my role models forever.

NOTES

1. All names and identifying information other than my son's and my own name are pseudonyms. Wyatt has given his permission to have his real name used.
2. I use identity-first language throughout this chapter because I have raised my son consistent with the belief that autism "is an inherent part of an individual's identity" (Brown, 2011, August 4).

REFERENCES

Adichie, C. N. (2009). The danger of a single story. *TEDGlobal 2009*. Retrieved from https://www.ted. com/talks/chimamanda_adichie_the_danger_of_a_single_story/transcript?language=en

Baggs, A. (2012). The meaning of self-advocacy. In J. Bascom (Ed.), *Loud hands: Autistic people, speaking* (pp. 315–319). Washington, DC: The Autistic Press.

Broderick, A. A. (2009). Autism, "recovery (to normalcy)," and the politics of hope. *Intellectual and Developmental Disabilities, 47*(4), 263–281.

Brown, L. (2011, August 4). The significance of semantics: Person-first language: Why it matters. Retrieved from http://www.autistichoya.com/2011/08/significance-of-semantics-person-first. html

Davies, Q. (2014, August 9). "Prisoners of the apparatus": The judge rotenberg center. Retrieved from http://autisticadvocacy.org/2014/08/prisoners-of-the-apparatus/

Glesne, C. (1999). *Becoming qualitative researchers: An introduction*. New York, NY: Longman.

Gross, Z. (2012). Metaphor stole my autism: The social construction of autism as separable from personhood, and its effect on policy, funding, and perception. In J. Bascom (Ed.), *Loud hands: Autistic people, speaking* (pp. 258–247). Washington, DC: The Autistic Press.

Jackson, M. (Director). (2010). *Temple Grandin* [Motion Picture]. United States: HBO Films.

Johnson, J. R. (1999). Leadership and self-determination. *Focus on Autism and Other Developmental Disabilities, 14*(1), 4–16.

Kurth, J. A. (2014). Educational placement of students with autism: The impact of state of residence. *Focus on Autism and Other Developmental Disabilities, 30*(4), 249–256. https://doi. org/10.1177/1088357614547891

Lalvani, P. (2014). The enforcement of normalcy in schools and the disablement of families: Unpacking master narratives on parental denial. *Disability & Society, 29*(8), 1221–1233. doi:10.1080/0968 7599.2014.923748

Martin, J. E., Marshall, L. H., & Sale, P. (2004). A 3-year study of middle, junior high, and high school IEP meetings. *Exceptional Children, 70*(3), 285–297.

McCloskey, E. (2013). An open letter to Wyatt. In P. Smith (Ed.), *Both sides of the table: Autoethnographies of educators learning and teaching with/in [dis]ability* (pp. 185–198). New York, NY: Peter Lang.

McCloskey, E. (2016). To the maximum extent appropriate: Determining success and the least restrictive environment for a student with autism spectrum disorder. *International Journal of Inclusive Education, 20*(11), 1204–1222. doi:10.1080/13603116.2016.1155667

McCloskey, E. (2018). Ratio profiling: The discursive construction of the continuum of alternative placements. *Disability & Society, 33*(5), 763–782. doi:10.1080/09687599.2018.1453784

Merriam, S. (2001). *Qualitative research and case study applications in education*. San Francisco, CA: Jossey-Bass.

National Center for Education Statistics. (2013). Digest of education statistics. Retrieved from http:// nces.ed.gov/fastfacts/display.asp?id=64

Silberman, S. (2015). *Neurotribes: The legacy of autism and the future of neurodiversity*. New York, NY: Penguin Random House, LLC.

Smith, D. E. (2005). *Institutional ethnography: A sociology for people*. Lanham, MD: AltaMira Press.

Taylor, S. J. (2001). The continuum and current controversies in the USA. *Journal of Intellectual & Developmental Disability, 26*(1), 15–33.

Taylor, S. J. (2004). Caught in the continuum: A critical analysis of the principle of the least restrictive environment. *Research & Practice for Persons with Severe Disabilities, 29*(4), 218–230.

Test, D. W., Hughes, C., Konrad, M., Neale, M., & Wood, W. M. (2004). Student involvement in individualized education program meetings. *Exceptional Children, 70*(4), 391–412.

Winter, P. (2012). Loud hands & loud voices. In J. Bascom (Ed.), *Loud hands: Autistic people, speaking* (pp. 115–128). Washington, DC: The Autistic Press.

Zeitlin, V. M., & Curcic, S. (2013). Parental voices on individualized education programs: "Oh, IEP meeting tomorrow? Rum tonight!." *Disability & Society, 29*(3), 373–387. doi:10.1080/0968759 9.2013.776493

CHAPTER 4

An Unexpected Journey
WITH My Mother

MARIA T. TIMBERLAKE

My mother and I used to go on small outings together. When she was in her 70s and retired from the telephone company, we developed a routine with a specific sequence of activities. We would meet half way between our respective towns and have lunch in a local restaurant, go for a walk, then browse in a bookstore. We savored every little decision; we discussed all the menu choices before selecting, then repeated the process as the afternoon continued and we narrowed down our choices in the bookstore—our rule was "just one." Choosing just one was not easy but the challenge was a pleasurable part of the process. My mother had diabetes, so later, when we inevitably found ourselves in front of a display of chocolates (part of the routine!) we followed our "just one" rule. She would thoughtfully consider the options, then choose one sugar-free chocolate and savor it while I did the same with the most decadent-looking piece of dark chocolate available. We were aware of the privilege of choice—having the time to ponder, having an array of palatable options, and knowing that the end result of the choice would always be just fine. When we said goodbye at the end of the afternoon, she'd say things like "that was fun" and "I really enjoyed that!" and list what she appreciated about the day. Even when it had been pouring rain or lunch had not really been that good, as far as she was concerned, the overall experience was delightful.

Life had made my mother brave, strong and independent. She raised four children alone in an era where single parents were still an anomaly. She did shift-work when we were kids, leaving for a few hours of work when we left for school, and then returning to her job for a few hours at night. She was unable to manifest her dream of being a fashion designer, but used her talent and sewing machine to create outfits for me and my siblings, which I now recall with fondness, but at the time thought to be embarrassingly coordinated. Her life was structured due to her circumstances but she retained a spirit for exploration. When I was an adult, she would often come along when I traveled to professional conferences, and while I was confined to the hotels, she would explore cities like Boston, Baltimore and Chicago. Her first order of business was to find a church, as daily mass was a necessity, and then after a day of discovery, she would report back to me and my colleagues about where the good restaurants and bookstores were. As a senior citizen, she finally had the freedom to choose how to spend her day and she relished the experience. I was lucky; as an adult, I enjoyed my mother's company and our excursions are precious memories.

Our last journey however, was not planned; we did not choose our options, nor delight in the things we discovered. Instead, we found ourselves navigating a nursing home and the world of institutional care after she was given the label of dementia. My mother had a traumatic health incident and was admitted to a nursing home for what I had believed would be two weeks of rehabilitation. Before I understood what was happening, her situation was permanent. A vivid memory from those first confusing days is of the physician giving my mother a worksheet with an empty circle and asking her to draw a clock face. I could not understand how assessing her drawing skills would help us figure out what was happening, and felt panicky sensing that her inability to draw a clock was sealing her fate in some way. I've subsequently learned that the clock face is a screening tool for dementia. Being unable to draw a clock face apparently signals a cognitive impairment, but at the time it seemed ridiculous, perhaps because I could not separate the assessment from the context. I remember standing by anxiously while strangers asked my mother to do this task with no explanation, and she looked around at these new people in this new room and merely sat without complying. The test was administered, the diagnosis verified and the change in status from "outpatient rehab" to "resident" was confirmed. Thus, we found ourselves in a bureaucratic system with labels, rules, specialized deficit-based vocabulary, and assessments that seemed to serve no purpose other than to uphold the system itself. I would soon come to learn that neither my professional history nor my deep love for my mother would be any match against the power of ableism in a context of medicalized labels and bureaucratically organized care. My story of my mother's acquiring the label of dementia reveals a glimpse of the extraordinary way lives unravel once a system puts a person's competency and independent functioning under question. Although we unexpectedly found ourselves in this new setting, I slowly came to recognize it as similar to another structure with which I was quite familiar—the American special education system; indeed, the treatment of adults labeled with dementia can be compared to the discourses and practices pertaining to schooling for students labeled as "intellectually disabled." In this chapter, I recount several vignettes from our last journey, to illustrate the uncanny ways in which eldercare can mirror many of the troubling aspects of special education, and reflect on the implications of these insights.

Prior to this journey, I would have assured everyone, especially myself, that my mother would never go into an institutional setting. I knew about community living, had studied choice and participant direction (Gross, Wallace, Blue-Banning, Summers, & Turnbull, 2012; Timberlake, Leutz, Warfield, & Chiri, 2014) and had advocated for inclusive education for decades. I valued community, rejected institutionalization, and was alert to medicalized and deficit-based explanations for segregation. Nevertheless, my mother and I found ourselves on a complicated journey for which I was unprepared. I instinctively collected data, searching for insights, echoing what led Ellis, and myself, to autoethnography:

> I write about experiences that knock me for a loop and challenge the construction of meaning I have put together for myself. I write when my world falls apart or the meaning I have constructed for myself is in danger of doing so. (Adams, Jones, & Ellis, 2015, p. 39)

Autoethnography is reflective and personal, allowing the researcher to "balance intellectual and methodological rigor, emotion and creativity" (Adams *et al.*, 2015, p. 2). My multiple identities which include, among many others, critical special educator, disability studies scholar, female, mother, White, and oldest daughter intersect in my interpretation of what I experienced, and of the data (personal journals, medical reports, meetings notes, photos, and videos) I collected. One role of autoethnography is to understand and critique cultural norms (Adams *et al.*, 2015). To this end, publicly interrogating my experiences with caregiving, mothering, and navigating a nursing home is my way of offering a deeper look into the concepts of "normality," and ableism.

LABELS AND THE CONSTRUCTION OF COGNITIVE IMPAIRMENT

The power of my mother's label (dementia) was extraordinary; the suggestion of impaired cognition compromised her autonomy and dignity, and took away most of her opportunity to make independent choices. Although I had little exposure to the systems of Medicare and nursing homes, I immediately became aware of the same norms of compliance and medicalization that I recognized from traditional special education. Just as parents wrestle with placing their children with disabilities in the hands of even the most well-meaning "experts," I also struggled to balance assertiveness with acquiescence. Both my mother and I had to learn the futility of trying to maintain autonomy in a system that required deference and passivity. This following story about trying to use the bathroom illustrates a point in our journey where my mother and I learned our first lesson in compliance.

A simple request—to use the restroom—was significant in cementing my mother's label as cognitively impaired and my own label of being "in denial" about my mother's disability. My mother was able to communicate verbally, but due to a series of small strokes, her speech would come and go and was sometimes unintelligible for long periods of time. However, she was frequently able to communicate to me that she needed to go to the bathroom and I would try to take her. Her mobility was very compromised[1] and I needed help to lift her but the staff were few in number, stretched thin, and often not available. I would go in search of someone and be assured that they would come as soon as they could. No one ever said "No, I can't help you." But, eventually I learned that "I'll come as soon as I can" meant "No." We had not yet learned how to behave when "the system" had determined one's capacity and what that designation actually meant in reality.

After multiple instances of agonizing over my mother's discomfort, searching the entire floor of the building looking for help, explaining the need to anyone I could find, I realized that independence and dignity in this area were no longer possible. I held my mother's hand, looked into her eyes and gently explained that, as hard as it was, she needed to urinate in in her pants and that the staff had put a garment on her for that purpose. We looked at each other for a long time as we both understood and accepted that she had to become incontinent to survive and find peace. Later, I would be informed at meetings that her incontinence was further evidence of her dementia and cognitive impairment.

This story is resonant of institutional systems in which labels influence expectations, and subsequently, labeled people's responses to their situations confirm their labels. I worked in a sheltered workshop as a college student many years ago where the individuals considered to have developmental disabilities sorted plastic combs by size and color. When they finished sorting an immense quantity of combs, the staff would dump the combs into a barrel and then the individuals would be given a supply from the same barrel to begin again. Periodically, out of likely (and understandable) frustration, one of the disabled individuals would tip over the table, sending the combs, buckets and furniture flying. I was told by the experienced staff that I must learn techniques of physical restraint in order to control such aggressive behavior. It seemed clear to me that the expectations of the environment elicited the seemingly aggressive reactions, but the experts saw it differently, identifying the undesirable behaviors as evidence of the workers' cognitive limitations.

Students in my college courses often ask for information about the 13 categories of disability (that determine eligibility for special education) because of the same belief that the label provides an explanation. In reality, each label forms a metaphorical box within which there are limited acceptable responses. The exam copies of textbooks I receive as a teacher educator introduce these limiting expectations to aspiring teachers early. For example, "Students with intellectual disabilities have limited cognitive functioning…these students have slower rates of learning and are particularly challenged by complex and abstract tasks" (Vaughn, Bos, & Schumm, 2014, p. 252). Gargiulo (2015) cautions that intelligence is a "construct or theoretical abstraction…" (p 163) but then provides a chart listing the characteristics of individuals with intellectual disabilities with each item beginning with terms such as "diminished," "deficits in," "inefficient," or "difficulty with" (p. 181). Thus, the labels prepare future educators to expect little and to approach their students with preconceived beliefs that they will be "slow."

The label of dementia felt very similar to the label of intellectual disability; both serve to nullify evidence of competency and neither is associated with strength or worth. There are numerous manifestations of dementia (National Institute on Aging)—it is an umbrella term that conveys deficits while covering a wide range of possible characteristics. The social construction of both labels is overshadowed by the medicalized diagnosis that is created and maintained through testing.

Assessments played a central role in maintaining the belief in cognitive impairment and helped to rationalize the tedium of my mother's days. Tests were administered quarterly, and one indicator of cognition was being able to accurately tell the day and date. All of my mother's routines and familiar activities were gone, there were no calendars posted on the walls, but nevertheless, she was repeatedly asked, and repeatedly, she failed this test. Pointing out the limitation of asking someone the day when their indicators for time are no longer there, or have radically changed, merely served to highlight my apparent denial and naiveté to the medical experts.

Well-meaning educators enact this in schools as they look for evidence of competency so we can "move ahead" into more complex academics and interactions. Testing defines the deficits which are then interpreted to mean that students cannot learn complex content. My years of teaching followed by my academic research on curricular access and the Alternate Assessment (Timberlake, 2016; in press) had shown me how the myriad decisions around assessment not only influenced what was taught but also served to legitimize segregation. However, even the most persuasive rationales for limiting access to knowledge and inclusive environments are unconvincing. All students can learn academics, regardless of perceived ability, if we know how to teach it (Knight, Browder, Agnello, & Lee, 2010; Nelson, 2014; Wakeman, Karvonen, & Ahumada, 2013). However, I repeatedly witnessed how testing remained foundational for entire human service systems. If professionals and family members could be reassured that individuals with dementia or students labeled with intellectual disabilities were "cognitively impaired" then the exclusion, tedium, boredom, and the custodial routines of institutional life were justified—there is no pressing or rational need to change a system that is perceived to be working.

A DAUGHTER "IN DENIAL"

My inability to comply with institutional expectations, to view my mother as a patient—a person with little capacity for rational thought, soon earned me a label of my own—the daughter "in denial." Where others saw incompetence, the daughter in me saw my mother's abilities. Where I saw humor, a clever remark, an astute observation, others saw coincidence—for them, the label defined what was realistic and what was possible. Resonant of the literature which highlights that parents of children with disabilities are routinely perceived as being in denial about their child's competency (Lalvani, 2014; Lalvani & Hale, 2015; Ryan & Runswick-Cole, 2008), I heard many familiar, yet problematic, narratives from the medical experts such as:

> "It is difficult for you to accept her limitations but you need to be realistic."
> "We understand you want what's best for her but we deal with this all the time and we know what we're doing."

One aspect of the popular narrative on parental "denial" of disability in children is the belief that eventually, parents will come to accept "reality" (Lalvani, 2017). One physician addressed my denial early on by asking me to sign *Do Not Resuscitate* paperwork when I was trying to ask how my mother's diabetes would be managed and inquire about the plan for eventual discharge. I vividly recall my shock at the conversation, as it now appeared that the experts believed my mother's death to be immenent. It wasn't—but apparently my being in denial about her capacity had to be addressed. I had become the equivalent of the "difficult parent" in the education world. I was the family member who did not accept (or willfully refused to understand) the label, who insisted on their fantasy where their loved one had unique strengths and capacities.

The uncanny parallels between schools' and nursing homes' responses to impairment highlight the ubiquity of ableism across the lifespan within helping systems. Lalvani (2014, 2015) documented the universality and invisible power of the denial narrative; that family caregivers "deny" seems to be without question. Moreover, their denial is not generally considered a virtue; we rarely hear mothers being lauded for their insistence on interpretations of their loved one that differ from the expert opinion. At the core of assumptions about denial, whether it is that of a mother or a daughter, is the rejection of the family members' perception of their loved one. The one difference that I found between children and elders is in the impact of the denial. While Lalvani's work revealed that professionals feared parental denial could interfere with the child's best interests, I experienced a concern from professionals that my denial was interfering with *my* best interest. I needed to be in close relationship with my mother, meaning long car trips across state lines to visit, hours sitting at the nursing home and conversing with residents and staff, and weekly Skype sessions. While I saw myself being connected to someone I love, others lamented that my denial kept me from "living my life."

As often occurs with parents of children in the special education system, the intimacy and deep knowledge I had of my mother was considered to be problematic instead of infinitely valuable. Despite the positionality of my time and place, the parallels between the two systems, education and nursing, are undeniable.

"KIDNEY STONES" AND THE CONUNDRUM OF "PRESUMING COMPETENCE"

One day I arrived on my mother's floor and there was a new aide working. My reaction was to immediately get to know her. Strangers were threatening to me. My mission was to make everyone know, and get to like, my mother and me, because I theorized that if I made things personal, they would take better care of my mother when I was not around. McKeever & Miller (2004) found a similar fear among parents of children with disabilities; parents worried that if they did not "play by the rules" and temper their demands or modify their reactions, their children might not be treated as well (p. 1183). Mothers worked desperately hard to pay attention to details, to advocate and assert, while also keeping the peace and not angering the people who cared for their child (Lalvani, 2014; Lalvani & Hale, 2015; Ryan & Runswick-Cole, 2008; Valle, 2011). As my mother's advocate, I embodied what Lalvani & Hale (2015) called "constant vigilance" (p. 7), so a stranger meant I needed to get to work. I greeted my mother and the other residents and sat at the table with them in an open, airy, dining room. I pulled out the chocolate ice cream that was part of our new routine, replacing the nostalgic pleasure of choosing chocolates in the past. Although her speech was often unintelligible, my mother always recognized me. She would see me coming across the room and smile, often proclaiming, "that's my daughter!" On this day, as she ate her ice cream, I made small talk and rubbed her back. She was talking to me but most of the words were not coherent. Then, in the middle of a sentence, she said "kidney stones," and looked at the aide. I made a mental note because, as the daughter in denial, I continued to believe in the relevance of her communication. I said hello to the aide, Sue[2], and lingered near her as she served lunch. I was constantly engaged in a dance of needing to be close without seeming too needy or off-putting. I needed Sue's attention and wanted to engage her so she would care about my mother when I was absent. I didn't want to take Sue's attention away from other residents who needed help but I was also on a mission to convert her to the invisible club I was creating—my mother's allies. Then I got lucky! Sue came to our table to help Lorraine eat her lunch. Sue began to spoon a thick liquid formula into Lorraine's mouth while we talked. With a silent apology to Lorraine (for taking away some of the attention that should have been directed solely to her), I asked Sue about herself and she willingly began to talk. As I learned about her commute, her previous jobs, her marriage and finally, her children, she told a story about her daughter missing a month of school because she had kidney stones. Kidney stones! My mother must have heard this story before, remembered it, and tried to tell me. She associated it with Sue and told me when I arrived. This was our nursing home version of "What's new mom?" "Well, Sue's daughter had a kidney stone." However, everyone I told about this brushed it off as coincidence. I am as unable to believe the interaction was a coincidence as others are to believe it was anything else.

Throughout my professional educational career, "presume competence" (Biklen & Burke, 2006; Jorgensen, McSheehan, & Sonnenmeier, 2007) was a concept I had enthusiastically embraced, but within the context of my mother's care I came to feel increasing discomfort about it. I understood the presumption of competence to mean that if educators perceived students as understanding more, as capable of learning more and rejecting the textbook assertions of "slowness" and ineptitude, their schooling would improve. To me, presuming competence was a mindset, an instinctive response to any person considered deficient or less capable than the so-called norm. But this interaction, and others like it, caused me to interrogate my conception of "presuming competence"—I now found the words taunting me, creating frustration and despair. Why did my presumptions and assertions of competence leave everyone around me unmoved?

My presumption of my mother's competence meant very little when I was unable to counter the implicit deficit-based narrative and convince others of her abilities. In fact, it was seen as further evidence of my denial of her cognitive impairment. In addition to the ubiquity of ableism, the false dichotomy, or the "all or nothing" of competence masked the uncomfortable complexity of such a critically important concept. Helping systems (nursing homes and schools) seem unable to handle competency in a nuanced way. Intellect is viewed as a binary– either you have it or you don't; seeing competence as fluctuating and unpredictable is simply too messy when a system is expected to run smoothly.

Additionally, helping systems are not designed to handle uncertainty. For teachers, labels and concepts such as IQ scores and "life skills" designations provide a false belief that we know what to expect. Similarly, it was believed, a woman with dementia could not be understanding everything that was said around her on one day and very little the next. Fluid competency, or what I have come to call "nuanced competency" is complicated, requires continual adaptability, and challenges the orderliness of teaching, nursing and other forms of support. In the same way that teachers reported that labels were helpful and did not consider them stigmatizing (Lalvani, 2015), many nurses, physicians, and therapists in my story had internalized assumptions that labels provided objective information. When systems (classrooms, schools, nursing homes) are designed to function efficiently, a person cannot be competent at different times and in different ways—an *either-or* is required to simplify and manitain order. Ideologically, it is certainly preferable to embrace rather than reject the enjoinder to "presume competence," but it risks becoming a catchy slogan without a substantive foundation or follow through. My story is an urgent call to reject the simplicity of competence as *there* or *not there*. Both can be true, and holding both dialectical truths, rather than one or the other, is critically important.

CREATING A SELF-SERVING COMMUNITY

After my mother had resided in the nursing home for a year and I was regularly commuting long distance to be physically present, I worried about the impersonal nature of the institutional setting and how I could make my mother's care more than a chore on someone's "to do" list. I reflected in my journal, "…we seem to be in a place where it's less about me being with her and more about the relationships I've cultivated with the people who ARE in her life every day." So, a significant aspect of my journey involved my deliberate attempts at creating a community that I could trust when I was not present. I call my behavior in these next vignettes the act of creating a "self-serving community."

I methodically created a community around my mother by intentionally and painstakingly cultivating relationships with staff, treating other residents as her friends, and modeling what I hoped was inclusive behavior—such as inviting other residents to form a circle together after dinner and have conversations. Occasionally I brought treats for everyone and created impromptu "ice cream socials." I brought picture books of cats and would invite others to join us in cooing over them and debating which cat was cutest. I deliberately blurred the line between staff and resident in these activities by addressing everyone the same way, whether it was offering ice cream or remarking on the weather. I hoped that if the relationship with me was personal, then when I was not there, not only would the care for my mother be personal but the climate of the ward would be more personal too.

I got to know the staff for a purpose that was calculated to make my mother's life better. I was frightened by how her experiences during the day (and night) rested on the shoulders of overburdened, minimum-wage receiving caregivers. I was worried about the impersonal nature of the institution and wondered, "what if she's nobody special to them?" But I also found myself asking, "what if they're nobody special to me?" I interrogated my own need and ability to manipulate the environment, to use whatever power I had to surround my mother with a feeling of community. Here, the parallels to special education cannot be overstated.

At the beginning of this journey, I could not have predicted the depth of my relationships with the staff. I recall, on the day my mother was first admitted, I was in the elevator on my way out of the nursing home after a discouraging meeting. One of the staff (I later got to know as Naomi) attempted to allay my distress and assured me, "don't worry, we will love her." I can't remember if there was more to the sentence. My brain stopped at the phrase "we will love her." I was screaming inside because this well-intentioned and supposedly kind statement was the most horrifying thing she could have said. The absurdity of being told by a stranger, who'd just met my mother, that she would "love" my mother led to angst and deep reflection.

I remained silent in that moment and the "friendship circles" from my early days in special education flashed through my mind (Falvey, Forest, Pearpoint & Rosenberg, 1997). Decades ago, I'd learned to facilitate circles where the name of the student with a disability was written in the center of the circle and names of people in relationship to the student were listed on rings around the diameter. The more intimate relationships were close to the student while the acquaintances moved outward. School teams could see how the outer rim of the circle was filled with people who were paid to be in the student's life. This was supposed to be a concern that dedicated educators would address—filling the circle with new genuine friends and social activities.

I felt newly appreciative of the clear distinction between provider, friend and family, in the designated places in the circle. How many times have similarly well-meaning educators assured parents that the staff love their child? If Naomi had said "We will do our best" or "I'll keep an eye on your mom for you," it would have been less disturbing. I should note that, although my relationship with Naomi started off with great uncertainty and a lack of trust, our future interactions built a relationship that is a testament to the power of resisting prescribed deficit-oriented roles and the value of community.

Ferguson and Ferguson (2016), Ryan and Runswick-Cole (2008) and Lalvani (2015) all noted that there are limiting ideas of what "family involvement" means. The privilege of my education and ability to understand and use my social capital helped me to define my own "family involvement." For example, I was able to create a weekly phone call ritual with two different nurses. In the late afternoon every Saturday, before dinner and medication administration, I would speak with Mona or Donna, whomever was on duty that weekend. Both kept me informed about my mother's moods and emotional status, asked the other staff for anecdotes to relay and kept me updated on her medical standing. My mother did not enjoy telephone calls at this point and hearing my disembodied voice caused her to become very agitated and dismayed instead of content. The nurses were my link to my mother and these calls strengthened my relationship with them to the point where I remain long distance friends with Mona.

Another example of creating "involvement" also includes Naomi (from the elevator), who was the staff assigned to set up the skype connection and sit with my mother on their end during our calls. At first, Naomi brought her paperwork and tried to work while my mother and I "visited." However, because we needed some facilitation, Naomi was drawn into the conversation with me, as my mother sat silently for a bit, disoriented by the computer and my voice. Before long, Naomi left her paperwork behind, and a new routine was established where she brought two cups of coffee (one for herself and one for my mother) and then connected the technology. I brought my own mug and our early conversations about the weather evolved into sincere interest in each other's lives. Surprisingly, our situation seemed to be novel, as no other families had apparently requested this kind of communication. Sometimes, however, as Ferguson and Ferguson (2016) remind us, what looks like a lack of family involvement may be due to multiple factors, including being intimidated by the setting and procedures, or being unable to attend meetings at the time or in the way professionals expect. I'm unable to know- perhaps other families attended meetings when invited and created their own forms of involvement, but I expect that they were not immune to the norms of ableism that prescribed their participation. I saw that some of the individuals working within the system were as hungry for connection as I was, but the bureaucratic structure limited their roles as much as it did my mother's and my own. In rejecting what the system defined as involvement (primarily signing forms and coming to meetings), I was able to receive, and to construct, acts of caring and love as I acclimated to the setting.

As a former special educator, I also brought a certain awareness of regulations and procedural safeguards which gave me social capital, or what autoethnographers call "insider knowledge" (Adams *et al.*, 2015). Insider knowledge of titles and roles enabled me, not only to request things like weekly skype meetings, but also to question the evaluations and conclusions as well as to explicate the functioning of systems and areas for resistance. My questions and requests for every piece of documentation were an exercise of my power, in part granted by my label of PhD. There were times when my power was an asset, but invisible institutional norms were often stronger than the power in my credentials. Again, this mirrored special education practices where parents are provided with information on legal safeguards, but enacting those rights takes time, confidence, emotional and financial resources. The structures of special education law in the U.S. created individualized forms of advocacy whereby parents theoretically co-create the IEP with educators. However, as Lalvani and Hale (2015) noted, although this may help children whose parents have the capital to advocate, it does not address systemic barriers nor help those whose parents are unable to engage productively at the same level. My "self-serving commnuity" started as a way to advocate for my mother, and although it made an impression on other individuals at the time, I recognize my responsibility to continue to work for systemic change.

A "NORMAL" LIFE: DISCOURSES OF HEROISM

I was complemented by colleagues, neighbors and extended family members for going "above and beyond" and "doing so much." The supposed complements are reminiscent of "it takes a special person" to be a special educator. Lalvani (2015) noted the existence of master narratives on families of children with disabilities "that focus on the 'tragedy'" of having a child with a disability and on perceptions of ongoing grief and hardship (p. 379) related to this experience. We were a mother and child whose roles had switched; while once she had held and protected me, I now held her hand, brought her favorite ice cream and spooned it into her mouth, and we flipped through picture books of cats for her enjoyment. I felt neither heroic nor admirable. The underlying assumption implicit in the discourses of heroism was that one of us was a burden and the other a martyr, when in reality, caring and advocating for my mother was a complicated mixture of emotions but it was never a hierarchy—I received as much as I gave and her presence enhanced the setting and everyone around her.

A disability studies perspective has the potential to legitimate different sources of knowledge about mothering (Fritsch, 2017; Lalvani, 2015, 2017; Maybee, 2011). And, although my story is about one mother and daughter, the parallels to mothering by other scholars are undeniable and suggest broader application across the age span. Fritsch (2017) argues that disability, within current political and economic neoliberalism makes "systemic barriers out to be individual problems that can be solved…" (p. 244) and illustrates how the narratives around "good mothering" and "good disabled mothering" rely on the same ableist individual construction of "good." Maybee (2011) analyzed her responses to her daughter's becoming disabled and interrogates the political and social implications of her situation and her complicated emotions. Although my mother was elderly when I experienced the labeling and resulting medicalization of her body and her life, the struggle with the social judgements of "goodness" or heroism resonates. The institutional setting most certainly created the context for much of the trauma, dehumanization and assault on my mother's dignity. However, even if my mother had lived in a less restrictive setting, she would have been seen as diminished, and me as heroic, because the devalued status of dependence and disability crosses boundaries of facilities, classrooms, schools and hospitals.

CONCLUSION

Despite numerous frustrating interactions and painful realizations along this last journey with my mother, I developed new insights on human dignity, competence, and autonomy that renewed, and also humbled, my work on inclusive education, showing me the urgent need for cooperative advocacy across education, community living and eldercare. My professional history in inclusive education and identification, first with critical special education (Brantlinger, 2005; Gallagher, 2005; Skrtic, 1991), and then with disability studies in education (Danforth & Gabel, 2016; Davis, 2013; Valle & Connor, 2011), undoubtedly influenced my perceptions of our situation. As a current teacher-educator I already recognized that laws and policies, including special education regulations, that protected the rights of students with disabilities, also marginalized and infantilized disabled people. Although some children have benefitted from aspects of special education, labeling has also produced societal segregation and low expectations. Through this journey, I discovered that parallel perceptions apply to the elderly. If they (elderly) cannot be "fixed," they can be removed from society "for their own good" and this way, the family can "have a life too." I joined disability studies scholars in critiquing restrictive notions of normal (Baglieri & Shapiro, 2017; Gallagher, Connor, & Ferri, 2014), but personally and painfully faced how deeply "normal" mattered. The implications of ableism extend across age and policies—from insurance regulations that support institutionalization, to norms of care, to perceptions that if one isn't independent then they are a drain on those around them. I found similarities in the rationales and excuses between institutional settings for the elderly and self-contained classrooms, unwritten rules about family involvement, and the level of deference and compliance required to survive in a helping system. I also found opportunities for resistance, and new insights into familiar concepts. Ultimately, I found ways to create community and relationships, and I found unexpected receptivity and appreciation. Relationships, community and love were possible, and my story closes with a call for broader interdisciplinary theorizing about families, supports, advocacy, and care.

A few weeks before my mother died, we had an unusual visit. She was sleepy and quiet. I held the spoon to her lips offering the ice cream but she had lost interest in that small pleasure. She dozed and I sat for hours with my arm around her shoulders, occasionally rubbing her hands gently. I interacted with the residents and staff as usual, but in a quieter voice and less deliberately animated manner. However, as the afternoon wore on, she straightened, looked around and asked "senior?" I interpreted this as a question; remaining "in denial," I believed she was asking if she was in a nursing home. I said something inadequate about her being sick and the doctors trying to help her, but trailed off and told her the truth. I admitted, "yes, this is a nursing home." She replied "I'm in pain." "I hurt everywhere." Then after a pause, "It's been a hard year." It had chronologically been longer than one year but she was absolutely correct. She also looked into my eyes and said clearly and distinctly "I love you so much." I will always be grateful for my "denial," proud to have earned that label and committed to dismantling the concept.

On a winter morning shortly thereafter, I received a call from the nursing home suggesting I come, and I made the eight-hour drive in record time. When I arrived, my mother had not been responsive since the night before. I said, "It's Maria," and her eyes flew open and then closed again. Our last unexpected and tumultuous journey ended as I sat by her side, whispering in her ear of our memories and travels, and assuring her that it was ok to take this next journey without me.

NOTES

1. Ironically, my mother's physical health declined as she lived in an environment of 24-hour nursing care. She was walking when she was admitted, using a walker within a week and ceased all independent mobility after several months.
2. All names are pseudonyms.

REFERENCES

Adams, T., Jones, S. H., & Ellis, C. (2015). *Autoethnography*. New York, NY: Oxford University Press.

Baglieri, S., & Shapiro, A. (2017). *Disability studies and the inclusive classroom: Critical practices for embracing diversity in education*. New York, NY: Routledge.

Biklen, D., & Burke, J. (2006). Presuming competence. *Equity & Excellence in Education, 39*(2), 166–175. https://doi.org/10.1080/10665680500540376

Brantlinger, E. (2005). Slippery Shibboleths: The shady side of truisms in special education. In S. Gabel (Ed.), *Disability studies in education: Readings in theory and method* (pp. 125–138). New York, NY: Peter Lang Publishing.

Danforth, S., & Gabel, S. L. (Eds.). (2016). *Vital questions facing disabilty studies in education*. (2nd ed.). New York, NY: Peter Lang.

Davis, L. J. (2013). *The disability studies reader* (4th ed.). New York, NY: Routledge.

Falvey, M., Forest, M., Pearpoint, J., & Rosenberg, R. (1997). *All my life's a circle. Using the tools– Circles, MAPS and PATH* (2nd ed.). Toronto, ON: Inclusion Press.

Ferguson, P., & Ferguson, D. L. (2016). Finding the proper attitude: The potential of disability studies to reframe family/school linkages. In S. Danforth & S. L. Gabel (Eds.), *Vital questions facing disability studies in education* (2nd ed; pp. 231–247). New York, NY: Peter Lang.

Fritsch, K. (2017). Contesting the neoliberal affects of disabled parenting: Towards a relational emergence of disability. In M. Rembis (Ed.), *Disabling domesticity* (pp. 243–268). New York, NY: Palgrave Macmillan.

Gallagher, D. (2005). Searching for something outside of ourselves. In S. Gabel (Ed.), *Disability studies in education: Readings in theory and method* (pp. 139–154). New York, NY: Peter Lang Publishing.

Gallagher, D. J., Connor, D. J., & Ferri, B. A. (2014). Beyond the far too incessant schism:Special education and the social model of disability. *International Journal of Inclusive Education, 18*(11), 1120–1142. https://doi.org/10.1080/13603116.2013.875599

Gargiulo, R. M. (2015). *Special education in contemporary society: An introduction to exceptionality* (5th ed.). Thousand Oakes, CA: Sage Publications.

Gross, J. M. S., Wallace, L., Blue-Banning, M., Summers, J. A., & Turnbull, A. (2012). Examining the experiences and decisions of parents/guardians: Participant directing the supports and services of adults with significant intellectual and developmental disabilities. *Journal of Disability Policy Studies, 24*(2), 88–101. doi:10.1177/1044207312439102.

Jorgensen, C. M., McSheehan, M., & Sonnenmeier, R. M. (2007). Presumed competence reflected in the educational programs of students with IDD before and after the beyond access professional development intervention. *Journal of Intellectual and Developmental Disability, 32*(4), 248–262.

Knight, V., Browder, D., Agnello, B., & Lee, A. (2010). Academic instruction for students with severe disabilities. *Focus on Exceptional Children, 42*(7), 2–14.

Lalvani, P. (2014). The enforcement of normalcy in schools and the disablement of families: Unpacking master narratives on parental denial. *Disability & Society, 29*(8), 1221–1233. https://doi.org/10.1080/09687599.2014.923748

Lalvani, P. (2015). Disability, stigma and otherness: Perspectives of parents and teachers. *International Journal of Disability, Development and Education, 62*(4), 379–393. http://dx.doi.org/10.1080/1034912X.2015.1029877

Lalvani, P. (2017). Gatekeepers of normalcy: The disablement of families in the master narratives of psychology. In M. Rembis (Ed.), *Disabling domesticity* (287–308). New York, NY: Palgrave Macmillan.

Lalvani, P., & Hale, C. (2015). Squeaky wheels, mothers from hell and CEOs of the IEP: Parents, privilege and the fight for inclusive education. *Understanding and Dismantling White Privilege, 5*(2), 21–41.

Maybee, J. E. (2011). The political is personal: Mothering at the intersection of acquired disability, gender, and race. In C. Lewiecki-Wilson & J. Cellio (Eds.), *Disability and mothering: Liminal spaces of embodied knowledge* (245–259). Syracuse, NY: Syracuse University Press.

McKeever, P., & Miller, K. L. (2004). Mothering children who have disabilities: A Bourdieusian interpretation of maternal practices. *Social Science & Medicine, 59*(6), 1177–1191.

National Institute on Aging. (2017). *What is dementia? Basics of alzheimer's disease and dementia.* National Institute of Health, U.S. Department of Health and Human Services. Retrieved from https://www.nia.nih.gov/health/what-dementia

Nelson, L. L. (2014). *Design and deliver: Planning and teaching using universal design for learning.* Baltimore, MD: Paul H. Brookes Publishing.

Ryan, S., & Runswick-Cole, K. (2008). Repositioning mothers: Mothers, disabled children and disability studies. *Disability & Society, 23*(3), 199–210.

Skrtic, T. (1991). The special education paradox: Equity as the way to excellence. *The Harvard Educational Review, 61*(2), 148–207.https://doi.org/10.17763/haer.61.2.0q702751580h0617

Timberlake, M. T. (2016). The path to academic access for students with significant cognitive disabilities. *The Journal of Special Education, 49*(4),199–208. https://doi.org/10.1177/0022466914554296

Timberlake, M. T. (in press). PAAP Season: A new rationale for segregation. In G. Conchas, K. Guitierrez, & B. Hinga (Eds.), *The complex web of inequality: How educational policies further push minoritized youth to the margin.* Routlege Research in Educational Equality and Diversity.

Timberlake, M. T., Leutz, W., Warfield, M., & Chiri, G. (2014). "In the driver's seat": Parent perceptions of choice in a participant-directed Medicaid waiver program for young children with autism. *Journal of Autism and Developmental Disorders, 44*(4), 903–914. doi: 10.1007/s10803-013-1942-4.

Valle, J. (2011). Down the rabbit hole: A commentary about research on parents and special education. *Learning Disability Quarterly, 34*(3), 183–190. doi: 10.1177/0731948711417555.

Valle, J., & Connor, D. (2011). *Rethinking disability: A disability studies approach to inclusive practices.* New York, NY: McGraw-Hill.

Vaughn, S. R., Bos, C. S., & Schumm, J. S. (2014). *Teaching students who are exceptional, diverse, and at risk in the general education classroom* (6th ed.). Upper Saddle River, NJ: Pearson Education.

Wakeman, S., Karvonen, M., & Ahumada, A. (2013). Changing instruction to increase achievement for students with moderate to severe intellectual disabilities. *Teaching Exceptional Children, 46*(2), 6–13.

CHAPTER 5

Masculinity AT THE Orthopedic Preschool

ELIZABETH A. WHEELER

Once there was a paradise by the inelegant name of the Orthopedically Impaired Preschool. It didn't look like much from the outside, just a classroom in an unused corner of a tired, brown school in Eugene, Oregon. What happened inside, however, was rare and enchanted. It was Camelot. It was "HandiLand," the imaginary kingdom my friend Cyndi and I dreamed up: a magical place with all the features to welcome and embrace our sons, who have cerebral palsy. Funded by the state of Oregon, the Orthopedically Impaired (OI) Preschool epitomized what I call *the prosthetic community*—a cluster of living beings, ideas, resources, and objects that enable full inclusion. Here, our kids with disabilities mingled and learned together with children who had no diagnoses at all. The preschool's staff members were a dream team who could troubleshoot at lightning speed. I've never seen people work together as well as those four did. Meg, the head teacher, was also a speech therapist, Jane was a physical therapist, Laurie was an occupational therapist, and Dianna Lee, the instructional aide, had the best lap in the world for comforting a homesick child.[1] Half the students had cerebral palsy and half of them were able-bodied playmates whose families paid a minimal fee. In that classroom there was scant difference between the two groups in the activities they did or the friendships they made.

The OI preschool came close to the vision of perfect inclusion that philosopher Susan Wendell describes: "I imagine a fully accessible society, [with] universal recognition that all structures have to be built and all activities have to be organized for the widest practical range of human abilities…everyone who is not disabled now can participate in sports or games or make art, and that sort of general ability should be the goal" (1996, pp. 55–56). With their endless creativity and homemade gadgets, the four teachers devised ways for every child to cut out valentines, paint at easels, and play the hokey pokey. At recess, Meg held a tiny swing in one hand and a tiny sandbox in the other, so a child could indicate her choice of playground activity with the slightest head nod. The preschool owned a wheelchair swing—a big steel platform on heavy chains the teachers hooked on the swing set. A kid could roll onto it to swing without even leaving his wheelchair. My son, Kevin, and Cyndi's son, Jaymason, raced down the play structure ramp in their walkers, yelling and shrieking.

The OI preschool had the widest possible range of physical ability. Children with and without disabilities learned how to play together, equipping them for such interactions in their future lives (Odom, 2000, pp. 20–22). The kids with cerebral palsy displayed a full rainbow spectrum of differences within the same impairment. It was like a United Nations of Cerebral Palsy (CP). Elia's very mild CP showed itself only in her left eye and slight jumpiness. Kevin was right in the middle of the spectrum, able by now to kneel, crawl, use a walker, and speak in sentences. Joy had a gentle spirit and limited motion, and spoke with her eyes rather than words. She spent morning free time in the vertical stander, taking a break from her wheelchair. Each morning Kevin asked me to lift him into the high Tripp Trapp chair facing Joy. Her stander had a tray attached to the front, and Kevin arranged blocks and zoomed cars across the tray while Joy smiled on him with her big blue eyes.

The swift and easy inclusion of the OI Preschool stood in sharp contrast to the barriers my husband John and I encountered as Kevin grew from birth to age three. For one thing, we had started to feel like misfits in our social circle. We knew several families with children the same age, but many of these friendships came unglued when their babies learned to walk and ours didn't. The kids we knew from the neighborhood and our birth group began to roam and climb all over the place while Kevin remained a non-toddling toddler. For him to play sitting up, one of us had to sit behind him, encircle his waist with our hands, and use our thumbs to prompt his sense of balance. He could take some steps if we bent over and held him up under his arms, so that's what we did if he wanted to go down a playground slide or climb a play structure. Day by day, John and I learned the tricks and tools of inclusion, but we didn't find many social spaces beyond the family that seemed to understand. One Saturday morning I entered a friend's house for a playdate, holding Kevin on my right hip and looking around for a place to set him down and prop him up. Our hostess gestured toward the far corner of the living room and said, "Over there are some toys *Kevin* can play with."

We also belonged to a neighborhood playgroup that threw everyone's body assumptions into sharp relief. During this time in our lives, John was home with Kevin while I was working full time, so the two of them went to this Wednesday playgroup, at my insistence. I wanted Kevin to make friends in the neighborhood, and I hate to miss a party, even vicariously. I came home from work one Wednesday and asked John how the playgroup had gone.

"This group really doesn't work for us," he said. "You know what makes me mad? They've decided to meet at a different playground every week, so I have to troubleshoot and adapt to each place all over again every time."

"Did you talk to them about it?"

"Yes."

"What did they say?"

"They didn't say anything. But then, there are only one or two moms in the group who will talk to me at all."

I chalked these complaints up to John's introvert personality until the first time I took Kevin to the playgroup. While I was contorting my back helping Kevin climb up a mini jungle gym, the other moms sat on benches yards—whole yards!—away from their children, chatting with each other and drinking coffee. They looked at Kevin and me as if we were from the moon. No one came near us. I wondered what they thought of me. Did they think I was a helicopter mom hovering unnecessarily over my kid? I would have been very glad to land my helicopter on that park bench, but I didn't have the option. I let John quit the playgroup.

In retrospect, I wonder at my own initial insistence on sticking with it. At the time, there were many things I hadn't yet grasped about our family's relationship to the world outside our home. I know now that the activity has to work for us as a family. It has to work for the kid, but it has to work for the parents, too. We can't do things for the sake of fitting in, because regardless, we're not going to fit in. As a Korean American who grew up in both countries and belonged in neither, John had given up on fitting in while still a child. I'm a middle-class white woman whose American ancestry goes back centuries. Moving back and forth across the country all my life, I strive to put down roots as if I've always belonged. "A misfit," writes Rosemarie Garland-Thomson, "describes an incongruent relationship between two things: a square peg in a round hole. The problem with a misfit, then, inheres not in either of the two things but rather in their juxtaposition, the awkward attempt to fit them together." (2011, pp. 592–593). When Kevin was small, I was still trying to sand down our square pegs to fit into round holes. Until his arrival I didn't question dominant discourses that see the able-bodied child as the norm and the disabled child as the awkward exception to the rule. I still thought it was our job to make our family as much like a family without disabilities as possible. I hadn't concluded yet that it was the ableism of the world at large, and the effort to conform, that made things awkward—not our family itself.

Meanwhile John and I had begun to feel the blunt force of the delays, disappointments, and dysfunctions that often typify services for people with disabilities. As just about anyone who works with such agencies and businesses will tell you, preposterously long wait times and inexplicable incompetencies run wild in the world of disability goods and services. As John said once, "It's like living in communist Hungary circa 1953, but there's no Five Year Plan." Ann Dean, the head physical therapist at our local clinic, urged us to get on the waiting list for a revolutionary new device called a spiral brace. "The brace is coiled like a spring, so it propels the child forward with every step," Ann said admiringly. "We are extraordinarily lucky, because the inventor lives right here in Eugene. When Kevin gets that spiral brace, he will really take off." So, we got on the waiting list for an appointment. And we waited. For months. Strangely enough, we kept falling off the list. Every week we checked in with Ann. Every week she said, "I don't see you on the list." So, every week we put ourselves back on the list. And every week Ann said, "When he gets that spiral brace, he's really going to take off."

When our appointment finally came, the genius inventor started yelling at us in his waiting room. "You should not be here," he shouted. "Ann is supposed to come with you to see me. And this child is nowhere near ready for a spiral brace. What were you thinking?" He led us into his examining room and asked us to take off Kevin's shoes and socks. He grabbed Kevin by the right ankle and yanked his toes up as high as they would go. Kevin started crying. My gut reaction was to whisk my baby away from this botulism toxin of a man, a man capable of going into a tirade over a toddler's foot. We left. On the following Tuesday we had an appointment at the clinic with Ann Dean and one of the clinic doctors. They kept us waiting for an hour and forty-five minutes past our appointment time. Already aggrieved at Ann and the entire world of orthopedics, I now attempted to subdue an increasingly hungry and impatient toddler. When we finally made it into the examining room, I explained how things went wrong at the inventor's office. Ann didn't seem at all fazed by my account. I felt bad about taking Kevin back into a clinical setting just a few days after that visit, so I was extra soothing and gentle with him. I told Ann and the doctor, "Now, Kevin's just had a rough time, so I told him I wouldn't let anyone grab him or yank his foot in here today." When we got the paperwork from this appointment in the mail, the doctor's chart notes said, "Patient is used to being indulged and will only cooperate with providers if bribed and cajoled."

As I wrote earlier, it took me a while to grasp that activities have to work for us. Before I could understand it, I had to glimpse what "works for us" looked like, and that's the vision the OI Preschool gave me. We entered a world where nobody blamed or judged us, where people knew how to change the shape of the hole rather than trying to change the shape of the peg. The preschool put into practice what critical disability theory calls the social model: the idea that people with disabilities don't necessarily need fixing but rather can get along just fine in a world that doesn't exclude them and instead accommodates their differences. As Tobin Siebers writes, the social model "makes it possible to see disability as the effect of an environment hostile to some bodies and not to others, requiring advances in social justice rather than medicine" (2008, p. 54). The team at OI gave us the adaptations and workarounds we needed to bridge the gap between cerebral palsy and the nondisabled world. At preschool Kevin unleashed his enthusiastic and gregarious self, giggling as he launched himself into his new friend Keegan's lap and knocked them both over, wide-eyed with excitement about a visit from Smokey the Bear, whom he called "Funky the Bear."

Dianna, Laurie, Jane, and Meg were more than ready for Kevin when he got there. They didn't blink an eye when I told them Kevin had life-threatening allergies and took over an hour to eat lunch. We were used to entering a new space and rearranging the furniture to make a place for Kevin to sit, but Jane was way ahead of us. She had five or six chairs of increasing size lined up and tried Kevin in each until she found the right one. Then she added foam pads of various sizes until he was safe, comfortable, and upright in his seat. We didn't have to do a thing.

Not having to do a thing is a rare and buoyant feeling for parents of children with disabilities. We often have a bad reputation for excess anxiety and hovering, but we have good reasons for our vigilance (Lalvani & Hale, 2015). Especially when our kids are small, only the wealthier among us ever get to go off duty. I think of myself as a pretty mellow, unhelicopterish mom, but my kids' disabilities have trained me otherwise. Take their potentially fatal peanut allergies, for instance. If a Fun-Size Mr. Goodbar could kill your kid at any moment, what looks to the outside world like hypervigilance looks to us like good parenting. To most people, the words "piñata" or "potluck" may conjure up images of innocuous and festive gatherings. When we hear those words, we think, "Secure the perimeter!" And we are among the lucky parents with steady incomes and respite care. So, to meet a team of caregivers willing and capable of taking over—and for free? Astounding.

The preschool team was also at ease with other kids' gastric tube feeding, cystic fibrosis, choking, gagging, and seizures. Realizing our children were safe in their hands, we moms breathed a sigh of relief and went out for coffee together. When I told stories about our breakthroughs and frustrations, the other moms knew exactly what I was talking about. One day, having coffee at Cyndi's house with Robin, I said, "The people I work with who are parents seem to worry about totally different things than I do." "Like what?" asked Robin. I said, "I work with this woman who has a daughter in first grade, and she's worried about her *penmanship.*" Robin and Cyndi laughed out loud.

"You know what bugs me?" Cyndi asked. "When you take your kid to the mall and everybody stares at you."

"Oh, I know," I said. "And the worst ones? They're the ones who think they're really subtle and wait until you've gone past them, then they turn around and stare at you from behind."

Robin said, "We should all get those T-shirts that say across the back: KEEP STARING. I MIGHT DO A TRICK."

On the mornings I brought Kevin to school, I learned, along with him, how to make friends, play, and communicate with people who can't speak or move much. Alex was a handsome five-year-old with curly honey-colored hair. I didn't know how much emotion he could convey until I sang "Itsy Bitsy Spider" and his face lit up. He radiated delight when his parents, Robin and Carlo, walked into the room. Alex loved to watch other kids running around, swiveling his head as far as humanly possible. Hailey Grace, who passed away at age eleven, had a diva's charisma. She could only see out of the corners of her eyes, so she would look at you sideways and startle you with her deep, hearty guffaw. When she and Alex were lying on the carpet together, they always found each other's hands. Able-bodied playmates like Keegan, Sarah, and Meg's daughter, Lily, would take off their shoes, get down on the carpet, and crawl around playing tag with Kevin. Hopping, bouncing, and pouncing, Kevin always left behind at least one of his socks.

Kevin was lucky to have two years at OI Preschool. It closed right after he graduated. During a freeze in state spending, the school district took money from programs for students with physical impairments to plug budget gaps elsewhere. Saying the OI model was too "resource rich," administrators substituted less qualified teachers. They replaced the OI Preschool with a "highly structured environment" open only to preschoolers with little speech or independent movement, essentially segregating them (Early Childhood CARES, 2018). Ironically, they called the new school Circle of Friends, while cutting many friends out of the circle. I am grateful for Kevin's two years at OI Preschool, and wish many more children and families could experience a community like that.

Although we fit in beautifully at the OI Preschool in most ways, there was one way in which our family misfit, and that way had to do with gender. The story I'm about to tell illustrates why it matters to think about identities like disability, gender, race, and class at the same time. Scholars often call such versatile thinking "intersectionality." Although sometimes criticized as too rigid or schematic, intersectionality yields indispensable truths (Puar, 2005). Kimberlé Crenshaw, who coined the term to describe African American women's lives, explains the need to move beyond single-issue political practices: "And so, when the practices expound identity as woman or person of color as an either/or proposition, they relegate the identity of women of color to a location that resists telling" (1991, p. 1242). When one looks at two or more aspects of identity together, problems and solutions swim into view that were previously out of sight.

Intersectionality, then, refers specifically to combined types of oppression, while Michael Hames-Garcia uses the term "multiplicity" to indicate any blend of identities. (2011, p. xi) My story about masculinity at the orthopedic preschool exemplifies how families, not just individuals, form multiple, complex identities.

Our gender misfitting at the Orthopedic Preschool began with Kevin's clothes. Resisting masculine norms, my husband John dressed Kevin in pink and purple and wanted his hair kept long. Not that I'm a big gender square myself; my favorite school outfit for Kevin was a leopard print turtleneck with black velveteen bellbottoms. The other moms teased me about our fashion choices. Although OI made room for a wide spectrum of abilities and disabilities, it didn't have a wide gender spectrum. The preschool parents and teachers, while not narrow-minded, were straight and cisgender. Many of the moms who became my dear friends were conservative Christians, either Greek Orthodox, Catholic, or fundamentalist. Elia and Miriam's mother, Nanette, said once she would never go to a church that hosted same-sex marriages. Carina, Hailey Grace's mother, told me her pastor preached against homosexuality from the pulpit. All the families were more middle-of-the-road than we were in political opinions, home decor, and adherence to the gender binary.

If the OI preschool was a deeply gendered place, it was not alone in this. Preschool is a key construction site for gender. Sociologist Emily W. Kane writes that the preschool age range "is the period when most children begin to develop a clear understanding of the gender expectations around them" (2006, p. 153). In Kane's interviews, preschool parents expressed fear that their sons would face harsh judgments if they failed to uphold the ideal of traditional masculinity. They saw preschool as "an important, foundational moment, often projecting into the future as they expressed concern about the risk of gender assessment" (2006, p. 167). This fear shows up in the exaggerated gender differences between boys' and girls' clothing. When shopping for Kevin I found it very difficult to find gender-neutral clothing in preschool sizes. The T-shirts all had pictures of either football players or fairies. In her study of 112 children at five preschools, Karin A. Martin found clothing was a key way "the preschool as an institution genders children's bodies" (1998, p. 510).

> The clothes that parents send kids to preschool in shape children's experiences of their bodies in gendered ways. Clothes, particularly their color, signify a child's gender; gender in preschool is in fact color-coded. On average, about 61 percent of the girls wore pink clothing each day. Boys were more likely to wear primary colors, black, florescent green, and orange. Boys never wore pink. (1998, p. 498)

And there was Kevin, dressed in pink and purple among his male playmates in navy blue and camouflage. At the preschool Halloween party, there were lots of boys in Oregon Ducks football uniforms and girls in ballerina tutus. Karin A. Martin concedes that "Parents are not solely responsible for what their children wear to preschool, as they are constrained by what is available and affordable in children's clothing. More important, children, especially at ages three to five, want some say in what they wear to preschool and may insist on some outfits and object to others" (1998, p. 498). Fashion conformity may have been even more exaggerated at the Orthopedic preschool, where many of the children could not declare their clothing preferences or dress themselves. Here was a way in which disability intersected with gender.

Toys also come with gender expectations, and preschoolers get the message loud and clear. Laurie, the occupational therapist, had received a grant to start a Toy Library at the OI preschool. Each child could choose a toy and take it home for a week. She asked me to be the Toy Librarian on Thursdays, helping children make their selections. A boy named Hunter, one of the playmates, was the rowdiest kid in the bunch. He stood in front of the toy cabinet wearing a T-shirt that read, "My Grandpa Rides Motorcycles and Someday I Will, Too." Hunter loved to play dress-up. The toy he was returning that week lent itself to dress-up play: a boy bear with a shirt you could lace up. Hunter looked longingly at the girl bear with a dress you could lace up, but finally chose a toy golf set instead.

This anxiety about gender moved into my heart as well. One day during Kevin's first year in preschool, John said to me, "I'm leaving my identity, Betsy." He wanted to transition to female. It didn't come as a complete shock. I always knew he liked to cross-dress while puttering around his home office or working at the computer. He had been pushing down his desire to become a woman since his early teens in Korea, and now it came knocking more and more insistently at his door. He asked if it would be all right with me if he started taking testosterone-blocking hormones. He made it clear he was content with our life together, still wanted me and our family above all things, and would not transition if it harmed us in any way. The decision would be his and mine together. I started doing some long, slow thinking.

I worried about social ostracism, gossip, and pity. As an interracial couple with one of our kids in an orthopedic walker, we already attracted plenty of stares in lily-white Eugene, Oregon. I could only assume that an interracial, lesbian couple with one of our kids in an orthopedic walker would attract even more stares. I was also still smarting from the loss of our friends with nondisabled children. Would this new kind of difference cause us to lose our new friends from the OI Preschool? Just because people accept some kinds of bodily difference doesn't mean they accept all kinds.

I worried about my own sexuality but found a deep well of queerness and bi-sexuality inside myself, along with my abiding love, passion, and respect for Jordan, the new name John chose. I worried about my ability to handle another change amid the stresses of two young children, cerebral palsy, anaphylactic food allergies, an aging mother, my career, and an almost constant migraine. (One morning at the preschool Robin took me aside and whispered, "Do you know your pants are on inside out?") On the other hand, it was clear to me that something monumental was happening to Jordan that might trump the immediate stressors.

My last worry concerned both our kids, but especially Kevin. He already had a bundle of identities commonly branded unmasculine. He had a physical disability, asthma, and life-threatening food allergies. He is Korean American, and as David L. Eng writes, "the Asian American male is both materially and psychically fem-inized within the context of a larger U.S. cultural imaginary" (2001, p. 2). Was I going to take his Asian American male role model away from him, too? In the midst of these deliberations I found my fears expressed in a parenting book called *Beyond a Physical Disability: The Person Within.*

> There is a difference in a male helping another male compared to a female taking care of a male. One danger is that the development of the male ego can easily be impaired. This is not as likely to happen when there is a male role model in the home. Such a role model can easily point out to the disabled teenager necessary masculine traits. Just because the teenager has a disability is no reason for him to be stripped of his masculinity. (Ayrault, 2001, p. 70)

I wanted no part in stripping Kevin of his masculinity. The risk to his romantic life seemed to bother me the worst. I pictured him fourteen years in the future, home alone on prom night. (As you can tell, I am a world-class worrier.) Then one day at work, I came across a disability studies article by Russell P. Shuttleworth, who had interviewed men with cerebral palsy about their dating lives. Shuttleworth (2002) found three things that helped men with CP move into the world of romantic and sexual relationships. The first was a "supportive context" of people who see you as a whole person. I thought, yes, Jordan and I could facilitate that, especially now we have the affirming community of the preschool. The second was the ability to see negative views of the disabled body as society's problem, not yours. Critical thinkers by temperament and education, Jordan and I could definitely facilitate that. The third was a category called "expanding the masculine repertoire." Shuttleworth wrote,

> Those men who attempted to conduct themselves in rigid accordance with hegemonic masculine ideals and who measured themselves against these ideals were more apt to remain immobilized or socially to withdraw when they fell short; and, indeed, much of the blame for their failure in love was shouldered by their inability to measure up. Those men, however, who perceived hegemonic masculinity as less a total index of their desirability and who could sometimes draw on alternative ideals such as interdependence, prioritizing emotional intimacy, becoming friends first, allowing the other to make the first move sometimes…could better weather rejection and remain open to the possibility of interpersonal connection and sexual intimacy. In this expanded masculinity, ideals often associated with femininity take their place in the masculine repertoire alongside more hegemonic ideals in subjects' psyches and interpersonal practices. (2002, pp. 116–117)

Looking up from the book and out my office window, I had a revelation. Jordan's gender transition could actually be good, not bad, for our son. Clinging to the ideals of traditional masculinity could make Kevin's life harder, not easier, robbing him of resilience and versatility. I started thinking about the problem intersectionally. Kevin benefitted if his family saw negative views of disability as society's problem, not ours. Perhaps, then, Kevin would also benefit if his family saw negative views of gender nonconformity as society's problem, not ours. My mistake lay in thinking of identity as a scoreboard: as if he needed the home run of masculinity to wipe out the two strikes of disability and race.

I needed to envision a spectrum of masculinity as wide and inclusive as the spectrum of ability at the Orthopedic Preschool. Rather than turning Kevin into a social outcast, the relaxing of gender conventions around our house could help him expand his masculine repertoire, just as the inclusive world of the preschool had helped us expand our horizons of what someone with cerebral palsy could do. He was already a patient, loving, acutely aware, and hilarious little boy. Like Jordan, he could become anyone he wanted to be. As Cyndi once said, "Our boys may not be good at walking up to the door and ringing the bell, but they'll be great with the candy and flowers."

NOTE

1. Names have been changed to protect privacy except for people who have chosen to appear by their real names.

REFERENCES

Ayrault, E. W. (2001). *Beyond a physical disability: The person within: A practical guide.* New York, NY: Continuum.

Crenshaw, K. (1991). Mapping the margins: Intersectionality, identity politics, and violence against women of color. *Stanford Law Review, 43*(6), 1241–1299. https://doi.org/10.2307/1229039

Early Childhood CARES (2018). https://earlychildhoodcares.uoregon.edu/

Eng, D. L. (2001). *Racial castration: Managing masculinity in Asian America.* Durham, NC: Duke University Press.

Garland-Thomson, R. (2011). Misfits: A feminist materialist disability concept. *Hypatia: A Journal of Feminist Philosophy, 26*(3), 591–609.

Hames-Garcia, M. (2011). *Identity complex: Making the case for multiplicity.* Minneapolis, MN: University of Minnesota Press.

Kane, E. W. (2006). "No way my boys are going to be like that!" Parents' responses to children's gender nonconformity. *Gender and Society, 20*(2), 149–176. http://doi.org/10.1177/0891243205284276

Lalvani, P., and Hale, C. (2015). Squeaky wheels, mothers from hell, and CEOs of the IEP: Parents, privilege, and the "fight" for inclusive education. *Understanding and Dismantling Privilege, 5*(2), 28–41. http://www.wpcjournal.com/article/view/14433/Lalvani_Hale

Martin, K. A. (1998). Becoming a gendered body: Practices of preschools. *American Sociological Review, 63*(4), 494–511.

Odom, S. L. (2000). Preschool inclusion: What we know and where we go from here. *Topics in Early Childhood Special Education, 20*(1), 20–27.

Puar, J. (2005). Queer times, queer assemblages. *Social Text, 23*(3–4) (84–85), 121–139. http://doi.org/10.1215/01642472-23-3-4_84-85-121

Shuttleworth, R. P. (2002). Defusing the adverse context of disability and desirability as a practice of the self for men with cerebral palsy. In M. Corker & T. Shakespeare (Eds.), *Disability/Postmodernity: Embodying disability theory* (pp. 112–126). London: Continuum.

Siebers, T. (2008). *Disability theory.* Ann Arbor, MI: University of Michigan Press.

Wendell, S. (1996). *The rejected body: Feminist philosophical reflections on disability.* New York, NY: Routledge.

CHAPTER 6

Mothering While Black

Shapeshifting Amid Ableism, Racism, and Autism

LACHAN V. HANNON

"But, I love you…" Avery pouted. His face was still with disappointment as I stopped him from snuggling around my neck.

Mike fussed, "Boy, get off her!"

I'm not sure if it was territorialism I sensed between them, or just a father-son relationship.

Maybe, it was a bit of both. But there was something in my husband's tone that I could not attend to in the moment. I looked at Avery's sad eyes and gently said, "But, I don't want hugs right now, Avery. No, means no. Look at me, please. I need for you to be able to stop when someone tells you to stop. It will save your life." He looked at me with his typical blank wide eyes. "Do you remember when we used to play red light, green light? You would hear me say 'red light' and you'd freeze like a statue in your tracks? That's the same way I need you to listen now. When a girl or boy doesn't want your hugs and says no, they are saying, 'RED LIGHT. STOP.' Do you understand?"

"But, I love you…"

"And, I love you too, but no means no AND stop. You have to always ask permission to touch someone, even your family, even your friends, even when you're playing. You MUST ask permission. Do you understand?"

"… (sigh)…"

In this opening vignette, we meet Avery, who is now my fourteen-year-old son. We've been having this same conversation since he was six. Avery has autism. Unlike many children with autism, he has thrived on hugs, craved human contact, and showed affection through a touch on the nose or a deep pressure hug. Recognizing Avery's growth from a once unpredictable and distant child to an affectionate young boy, everyone in my family has obliged his nonverbal requests for affection. As a mother, I have always wanted my son to grow up knowing how to show affection and express his emotions. But, from the time Avery was diagnosed with autism at 21 months, I knew that nothing in my personal or professional experiences had prepared me for how to mother a Black manchild with a developmental difference that masks itself from anyone who does not take the time to notice his uniqueness.

For me, *mothering while Black* means that there are certain things I have to consider in order to keep my children safe and teach them how to navigate this world. I have to consider where I go, with whom I interact, what I say, how slowly I drive my car, what activities I choose for my children, and a host of other considerations that honestly mean very little to me. Mothering while Black means accepting that, eventually, all roads lead to race. Mothering while Black means that I need my children home every night, alive, having endured only minimal trauma. This is part of Black motherhood.

Mothering a Black boy with autism means that I will have to consider all of these things, and more, while attending to other people's ignorance of an invisible and unpredictable disability that presents differently in each child. For some, my son's blackness will cloud their acknowledgement of a disability. For others, his disability will communicate that he is one of the "safe" ones. For me, it means that I will have to construct different rules for my Black son than those I have for my Black daughter and acknowledge the ways that my own mothering will contradict itself.

Like many parents, my husband and I have rules for our family. However, among these many rules, as the opening vignette shows, I have made one more that Avery will have to learn and follow, and that is, you cannot demonstrate physical affection toward someone without their explicit permission. In my head, I know this rule I'm making will be broken, and not just by him. It will be broken often by me, his sister, his father, his grandparents, his aunties, his cousins, and even his friends. We all hug without permission, hold hands without permission, and express love without permission, under the ableist assumption that we all subscribe to the same social rules. Avery should have been permitted to enjoy this privilege, especially considering that, often, children with autism can experience difficulty with physical touch or expressing emotions. It hurts me to limit Avery's demonstration of love. Yet every day, I require that he hold fast to this rule while he watches the rest of us break it.

At the intersection of ableism, racism and sexism, I know that mothering my daughter and mothering my son will take very different forms. As a mom, I have always made allowances for my son that I would have never made for my neurotypical daughter (often to the disapproval of my husband). I resented what I believed to be double-standards when my own mother made allowances for my brothers. And yet, I find myself doing the same. I recognize the double-standards but ultimately, I am driven, like many Black mothers, by my goal to keep my children safe—safe from bullies, safe from unprepared teachers, and safe from assuming law enforcement and community members.

I constantly negotiate and renegotiate my motherhood as my children and I interact with others and the unforgiving world around us. In this essay, told through a series of vignettes, I hope to illuminate the ways my mothering choices have been challenged, constructed, and reimagined in response to gendered and racialized norms, ableist attitudes, and assumptions about what it means to be a "good mom."

"AIN'T NOTHING WRONG WITH HIM"

I told my grandmother that I was concerned about Avery. "But, he doesn't talk."

She playfully told me, "Well, maybe he doesn't have anything to say."

"He doesn't even babble or make eye contact or act like he can hear anything I'm saying. I think he is deaf. We have an appointment with the audiologist next week."

She reminded me, "Well, he's looking at me. All you have to do is get his attention."

"Grandmom, something is wrong. He stands for hours in the crib, doesn't cry, doesn't play with toys, he stares at his fingers, and lines the Cheerios up on his high chair tray. He is in his own little world. Something is wrong with him."

She stated, "Ain't nothing wrong with that boy."

"…(sigh)…"

My grandmother was the best mother I knew; and somehow, I felt like I was getting motherhood all wrong. It was becoming clear to me that the expectations for me to mother in the ways my grandmother and mother did were insufficient for my new family. Unlike my foremothers, my decisions would be influenced by the presence of a disability no one understood. As a mother, you want to be able to trust your gut and intuition, and, at the time, I thought I trusted mine. But, my gut was often contradictory to the reactions of my family. I second-guessed myself. Were my experiences real or exaggerated? Were my senses deceiving me? Was I overreacting? Were my insecurities getting the best of me? Why wasn't I confident in my mothering? Was something wrong with me? Was guilt fueling my feelings? Was I getting it wrong?

In accounts of refugee and slave literature, there exists the idea of *othermothers* and *othermothering*. More recently, the terms have been used in education literature to describe the relationships between students and women teachers of color (Hill

Collins, 1990; Mawhinney, 2011; Peteet, 1997). Case (1997) explains othermothering as a survival mechanism that served as a "vehicle for educational and cultural transmission" (p. 26). In cultures of othermothering, women in the community would offer maternal assistance to children whose blood mothers were unable to do so, for whatever reason. I was raised in a community of *othermothers* where everyone knew your name, and there were some things that Black people just did. For example, we helped to raise each other's children. We disciplined them and kept them out of trouble as best we could. We celebrated each other's successes as if they were our own. We decided for our children what we believed was best. We expected them to comply with all adult demands. And, we turned to our matriarchs for mothering wisdom and knowledge. These were and continue to be staples in my community. But when families had children with disabilities, those disabilities were rarely discussed, and those children were often eliminated from the collective narrative. As I continue to raise my family, discussions about disability have had to become an important part of our collective narrative.

For me, intersectionality (Crenshaw, 1989; Hill Collins, 2000; hooks, 1989) is the intellectual and emotional space where I can acknowledge how my experiences, assumptions, and choices are informed by my entire existence. This theoretical framework provides an avenue to situate my experiences without having to compartmentalize, prioritize, or justify them. All parts of me are allowed speak to one another and inform my choices and beliefs about motherhood. As such, there are mothering intuitions that I have come to understand, accept, and appreciate. I imagine my Pennsylvania-Dutch great-grandmother would capture this sentiment by saying, "Because I said so, and I know so." Phrases like this would backdrop the reconstructing of what Black motherhood looked like, sounded like, and felt like to me. While my maternal great-grandmother never saw me get married and raise my children, her values of independence and motherhood still shape us today. My difficulty in (re)constructing motherhood is not in how I understand it but rather, in having to explain it to others. While I do my best to make my thinking as clear as possible, my thinking changes as the demands on my family change. Avery is not the only one in my family living with autism. As his immediate family, we are all living with autism—which is like the obstinate uncle that came to visit and never left but helps to keep the family grounded in the things that really matter.

Although my parents were upper middle-class college graduates, many of the beliefs and traditions we lived by reflected those of my grandmothers who grew up in a very different time and place in society. I can remember trying to describe Avery and some of his challenges to my grandmother, and her response was always the same, "Ain't nothing wrong with that boy." In my family, some would say that Black is Black. Others would not acknowledge his autism. The schools would not appreciate his autism until it stretched the limits of their teaching abilities. As a mother, how could I ask for help from the *othermothers* who were supposed to be my support system, if they did not believe that I even needed help? No example of motherhood in my family or community could have demonstrated for me what it would mean to mother a Black boy with autism in our society.

WHO GETS TO BE ANGRY

March 18, 2016

I'd had a long day of teaching high schoolers, and I was greeted by an email with a subject line that read: Avery. I was unaccustomed to emails from Avery's teachers, as it was usually Mike and I who did most of the informing, not Avery's teachers. Apparently, there had been a misunderstanding between Avery and his teacher regarding a missing homework assignment. Avery had completed it but could not locate it. This is often the case with Avery; he has well documented organizational challenges. As a result of not being able to produce his homework, his teacher placed his name on the "No Fun Friday" list. Students on this list must read a book and are separated from the rest of their peers who are playing games and interacting with one another. Avery got angry because he had done his homework and "No Fun Friday" is for people who did not do their homework. The exchange between Avery and the teacher had apparently became antagonistic as Avery openly challenged her authority (presumably because, to him, it did not make sense). The email read, "he began to yell very close to my face, pointing his finger at me, and telling me that it was not fair because he had done his homework...he was yelling at me rather loudly and was in my face saying, 'NO!'"

I was shocked. To my knowledge, Avery had never had a reaction like this toward a teacher. He is usually compliant and cooperative. Years of behavior therapy had taught him only to acquiesce to rules that made no sense. Ironically, his teachers often overlooked him because he does not exhibit "challenging" behaviors. Still, some things just did not add up. A follow-up meeting with the teacher and principal revealed a few key points not mentioned in her email. First, the in-class support staff assigned to help carry out Avery's IEP was not present to help him locate his homework, which is what would typically happen if he could not find it himself. (The teacher herself seemed to have had no intentions to help Avery locate his work!). Second, Avery was publicly humiliated because the teacher made a production of crossing his name off the posted Fun Friday List and adding him to the No Fun Friday list. Third, the teacher is 5'6", and Avery is 4'8". Unless she was sitting, which she reportedly wasn't, there is no way that Avery was in her face. Yet, she perceived him to be, and was threatened by his atypical response. The mother in me knew that Avery's teacher was having her first real encounter with a Black boy with autism and was unprepared.

Anger is a tricky thing. Each of my children is triggered by very different things, but it is their demonstrations of anger and frustration that concern me most. The tantrums of a little Black girl can be interpreted as an unthreatening spoiled brat, but the tantrums of a little Black boy are pathologized as acts of aggression and are further complicated by the unpredictable inflexibility of autism. Avery's expression of anger or frustration has the potential to be a perfect storm.

In this situation, Avery was rightfully angry, but he was not allowed to be. When I asked the teacher how he was supposed to respond, the answer was that he should have complied and not pointed out inconsistencies in rules or their application. He should not challenge a teacher's authority. However, the autism in him would not let him mentally move past the point of inconsistency. Avery was a rule follower, and it helped to keep him grounded. For example, I remember the time I took him to see a production of Imagination Movers. When the show was over, he began to cry and tantrum. I calmly explained to him that the Imagination Movers needed to take a break and go to the bathroom so that they could be on the television by the time we got home. It was a realistic lie, but it was a logical truth for Avery. Avery's teacher was trying to argue against a logical truth—I did my homework and therefore, I should not be punished. My logical truth was that my child was humiliated and expected to remain silent about it. The teacher perceived my Black son to be threatening. How do I raise my Black boy with autism in a way that allows him to express his frustrations without scaring his white teachers?

Despite the landmark Supreme Court case of *Brown vs. Board of Education*, American public schools continue to be racially segregated. Additionally, Black boys are disproportionately classified as needing special education services and educated in classes segregated from the mainstream (Ferri & Conner, 2005; Gillborn, Rollock, Vincent, & Ball, 2016). Black boys who display symptoms of autism are often classified and labeled as having ADHD or emotional and behavior disorders (Morrier, Hess, & Heflin, 2008). In these settings, the primary interventions are designed to teach our boys to be quiet, conform, behave, obey, fit in, act normal, and suppress their feelings and movements for the comfort and convenience of their teachers. Beginning at age three and continuing for five more years, Avery was educated in segregated classrooms that operated in this way. I knew these classrooms all too well, but this is not how we raised our children at home.

At home, we encouraged our children to point out our inconsistencies because we knew how important it was for us to live by rules that made sense and work for all of us. We have had countless conversations justifying our parenting choices to Nile, Avery, and others. Avery required that level of explicitness. But in school, his teachers were not used to supplying that. School more closely resembled my grandmother's philosophy of "because I said so" than the *share the why* approach we had in our home. There were rules that prioritized teachers over students—my word versus your word, and even a simple question could be perceived as challenging authority. Complicating things further were Avery's difficulties with understanding sarcasm and other non-verbal communication patterns that made communication with adults who were not accustomed to explaining themselves difficult. And, if he did not understand, he was not budging from his position. Although I acknowledge it is annoying at times, I have often admired his persistence.

Having to communicate with Avery in this way was so very different than how I was raised and even how I raised my daughter. Nile, in contrast to Avery, is highly verbal and flexible. I offered her explanations and justifications—which my *othermothers* criticized. They would ask me why I felt the need to explain my choices to her or provide so much detail. I'd say that it's because she is a girl, and I want to raise a critical thinker and advocate. I also do not want people taking advantage of her. So, unlike her brother, Nile was allowed to demonstrate her anger. Even though she was berated by her sixth-grade math teacher, we celebrated her persistence when she remained seated for the pledge of allegiance. We encouraged her to stand up for her LGBTQ peers when they were being mistreated. We supported her when she experienced racial microaggressions in her classrooms, hallways, and school community. Nile has a strong voice. Sometimes it is loud and resistant, and sometimes it is quiet and defiant. Even in the times when she has raised her voice in frustration, no one ever described her behavior as aggressive. She is called a leader even though she may have displayed many of the same behaviors as her brother. But she is a girl; and therefore, it is likely she is perceived as less threatening by her teachers and peers. Why is my daughter permitted to be angry, but my son expected to suppress and hide his anger? What am I teaching them, collectively and individually, by requiring that my son control his body but giving my daughter free reign over hers?

DAY OF NO APOLOGIES

We were season pass holders at Sesame Place. We learned from other parents that if you went to the help desk and you told them you had a child with "special needs," you did not have to wait in the long lines. We enjoyed this privilege. We tried so hard to do things that so-called normal families did, like take your kids to Sesame Place. It was always such a production when we would go. I packed our lunches due to Avery's particular dietary needs and made sure we had everything we could possibly need to spend the day out of the house. A stroller was a necessity for any outing, mainly because we could strap Avery in to keep him from eloping. Avery was six and still in diapers. Potty training was challenging, but we were happy with the progress we were making. On this particular Sunday, Sesame Place was closed to the general public and reserved for "special needs families." When a child has a disability, the entire family shares in that experience.

This day at Sesame Place, we did not need a special wristband that allowed us to skip the long lines. Every family represented a special wristband. Every child had to wait in line. Luckily, it was not busy. The lines were short, the characters were not roaming the grounds, the music and strobing lights were kept to a minimum. As season pass holders, we did what we normally do—a few roller coasters, then off to the water park. Everywhere I looked, I could see mothers who were stressed. Children and mothers alike were climbing, running, yelling, screaming, crying, eloping, and while this may sound like a typical day at Sesame Place, the tension was more palpable. Eventually, we made our way to a ride and waited in line. A few patrons behind us stood a mother, probably in her late twenties or early thirties, and her child was having a major meltdown. He was kicking, screaming, and having a terrible time. In the midst of his tantrum, his mother kept apologizing to everyone around her as we all became victims of his flailing arms and legs. The other mothers and fathers smiled politely and nodded, but she was clearly embarrassed and frustrated. It just so happened that as her son was climbing on the railing, he kicked me in my back, so I turned around. Her bags had fallen to the ground, and she was on the brink of a full meltdown herself. When I looked at her, she was trying to gather both her belongings and her son. And, she offered the customary, "I'm so sorry. I'm so sorry." I said to her, "Today is the day of no apologies. We are all here for the same reason and have similar experiences. If ever there was a time or place you didn't have to offer a rationale or justify your mothering choices, today is that day. You do not owe anyone here an apology." Nile and I helped to grab her bags while she calmed her son.

Over the years, I've offered what feels like a million apologies. As a mom, I've apologized when my children misbehave, I've apologized when I've made a mistake, I've apologized for my partner's actions. Raising a child with autism has reminded me of all the ways I did not fit with traditional definitions of normalcy. There is nothing normal about raising a Black boy with autism. Every way of knowing, every act of being, is a result of trials and errors for my husband and me. It has challenged our partnership in unimaginable ways and yet, led us to great experiences that work for all of us.

Where I came from, the mothers were supposed to have it all together. Mothers were supposed to be able to maintain control of their children, support their household, and take care of their partners. After all, isn't that a women's role? Mothers were supposed to have super-powers. In this moment, the mother whose child was having a meltdown was defeated. She needed understanding, not judgement. She needed a helping hand, not a critical eye. She needed to be accepted, not invalidated. We all did. On this day, I chased down children who were not my own, climbed into cubbies for children who were not my own, calmed children who were not my own, and shared experiences with women who were not my friends. Autism bound us together, and autism did not care if you were Black, middle class, married, had other children, or had any other identity thought to either advantage or disadvantage you. On this day, autism was the equalizer. I think somehow, in choosing to be at Sesame Place that day, perhaps my family was not looking for acceptance from the mainstream community but looking for validation within our own community of families-those who have children with autism.

I realized then, that I also did not owe anyone an apology. My child was no more or less contrary than anyone else's, and my choices as a mother did not warrant an explanation. At the same time, I knew that the larger society did not view my child in this way. Although my mothering might not have been instinctual, it was reflexive in that I could adapt and respond with immediacy to Avery and new situations. And I was proud of my adaptability. I participated as the Sesame Place mothers became *othermothers* to one another. In those moments, and in this space, I did not feel "othered."

ALL THE WORLD'S A STAGE

There is something about music that stirs the soul. It has the power to lull and awaken, to depress and uplift, to renew and reveal just who we are. I do not know if there is a connection between autism and music, but if there is one, I am grateful for it.

Avery Performs in "Roar" (Age 7)

Teacher: When the music came on, it seemed as if he couldn't contain himself. It wasn't just his foot tapping. His whole body was moving. He caught my attention, and I nodded my head. Before I could blink, he was up on the stage, and all the students were yelling, "Avery, Avery, Avery."
Avery: Can I have an agent?

Avery Dances to "Te Amo" (Age 8)

Me: Avery, I know you're only in the third grade, but your sister wants to be in the middle school talent show. Will you dance with her?
Avery: Okay.
Me: Do you remember how to samba? It's just like the video we watched.
Avery: Yep.
Me: Are you scared?
Avery: Nope. Can I have an agent?

Avery Teaches Dancing to "Pause" (Age 9)

Me: Avery, I'm going to sit this one out. Do you think you could finish teaching the last dance for my Zumba class?
Avery: Yes.

Me: Are you sure?
Avery: Yep.
Me: Are you nervous?
Avery: I'm okay. Can I have an agent?

Avery Performs in "Cabaret" (Age 11)

Audience member: You did a great job, young man.
Avery (with a flat affect): Ah, yeah, thanks.
Audience member: You seem pretty comfortable up there on stage.
Avery: Yeah, I am.
Avery (to me): Can I have an agent?

Avery Performs in "Gypsy" (Age 12)

Stage Manager: We are so grateful to have Avery in the cast of Gypsy. He is fitting in so well, and the cast members love him. He is so focused and serious about his art. It's hard to believe he has autism.
Me: Thank you. He loves this. He is home here.
Stage Manager: Have you considered getting him an agent?

Avery Performs at "Core" (Age 14)

Company owner: We were looking for a boy to play the main character in this year's recital. Do you think Avery would be interested? He has to sing, dance, and act. Is that okay?
Me: Avery, the faculty would like for you to be in the end of the year production.
Avery: I can do that.
Me: But I haven't even told you what you have to do yet.
Avery: I know, but I'm sure I can do it. Now, can I have an agent!?

Avery feels music in his bones. It exudes from his being. He has always felt at home on the stage, and his amazing memory has always served him well in this way. He reads lines with feeling, emotion, and little coaching. When he finally developed expressive language between the ages of 4 and 5, his teachers would ask him to read aloud. His classmates loved it because Avery's reading was filled with such expression. Often, when presented with the option of choosing between listening to their teacher read aloud or to Avery, students would choose Avery. You could close your eyes and picture what was happening in the story with every word he uttered. At these times, Avery is truly happy.

Through the arts, Avery is able to tap into any emotion he chooses to share and, as his mother, I've come to appreciate and encourage this. Singing, dancing, acting, and instrumentation are his ways of communicating everything he cannot say verbally. In a culture that tells young men they cannot cry or show emotion, and that sends a message to Black boys that their lives do not matter, the arts provide Avery with an outlet to express himself and an opportunity to escape the boundaries of normalcy and ableism. In the world of theater, he's found a community that accepts every part of him—every quirk, every squeal, and every repetitive motion. When Avery is performing, he is engaged and engaging. On stage, Avery has no disabilities.

I learned early in Avery's life that if I was going to connect with him, I had to follow his lead and attend to what made him happy. When he expressed an interest in something, we ran with it. Sometimes this has led to wrestling (even though at one time he could not tolerate being touched), or baseball (even though he did not have the patience for standing around in the outfield). Avery plays whatever instruments he can get his hands on. I recall his formative years when he sat in front of the television, mimicking and echoing the words he heard. I worried, wondering what kind of life he would live if he had trouble communicating. Little did I know that he was keeping inventory of all the emotions, words, and phrases he observed, entering and storing them in his mind's database, ready to extract when his own life handed him similar situations, and to demonstrate in his own style. His ways of being and expressing would unlock a world where imagination and curiosity were prized possessions. On the stage, he would find a safe space; here I would not have to worry about failing him or protecting him.

Recognizing how non-traditional our family is, my husband and I are still evolving in our approach to raising Avery. We encourage him to find ways to explore his passions and foster his curiosity in ways unfamiliar to our parents and grandparents. Trying to make Avery conform to traditional expectations of masculinity, ability, schooling, college, or a typical 9–5 career would completely undermine the very attributes that make him unique and would only impose a false sense of normality. It could also likely alter the very things that make him feel good about himself.

Avery and autism have taught me that my expectations of what mothering looks like will be consistently inconsistent. My experiences have disrupted everything I knew to be true and will probably continue to do so. What I do know is that if mothering a Black boy in America is hard, then mothering a Black boy with autism is unchartered territory. I am learning, gradually, to stop normalizing my son and to stop normalizing my mothering. Instead, as a family, we are choosing to create a new normal. It takes a village to raise a child, and I'm relying on our village to support us in the development of our new norms. And, I've come to understand that it is the village that will need to collectively reimagine motherhood and challenge yesterday's expectations. Avery does not need to tone down his autism to be palatable to all the "normal" people of the world.

I do not pretend to know what tomorrow holds for Avery or my family. As a mother, I am still shape-shifting; I am still becoming. Each day, I am decidedly content with who we are as a family, the choices we have made, and the routines we have established. For now, they work for us, and I will not apologize for them.

REFERENCES

Case, K. I. (1997). African American othermothering in the urban elementary school. *The Urban Review, 29*(1), 25–39. https://doi.org/10.1023/A:1024645710209

Crenshaw, K. (1989). Demarginalizing the intersection of race and sex: A Black feminist critique of antidiscrimination doctrine, feminist theory and antiracist politics. *University of Chicago Legal Forum*, 139–167. Retrieved from https://philpapers.org/archive/CREDTI.pdf?ncid=txtlnkusaolp00000603

Ferri, B. A., & Connor, D. J. (2005). In the shadow of Brown: Special education and overrepresentation of students of color. *Remedial and Special Education, 26*(2), 93–100. https://doi.org/10.1177/07419325050260020401

Gillborn, D., Rollock, N., Vincent, C., & Ball, S. (2016). The Black middle classes, education, racism, and dis/ability. In D. J. Connor, B. A. Ferri, & S. A. Annamma (Eds.), *DisCrit: Disability studies and critical race theory in education* (pp. 35–54). New York, NY: Teachers College Press.

Hill Collins, P. (1990). *Black feminist thought: Knowledge, consciousness, and the politics of empowerment*. Boston, MA: Unwin Hyman.

Hill Collins, P. (2000). Gender, Black feminism, and Black political economy. *The Annals of the American Academy of Political and Social Science, 568*, 41–53. Retrieved from http://www.jstor.org/stable/1049471hooks, b. (1989). *Talking back: Thinking feminist, thinking Black*. Boston, MA: South End Press.

Mawhinney, L. (2011). Othermothering: A personal narrative exploring relationships between Black female faculty and students. *Negro Educational Review, 62–63*(1–4), 213–232.

Morrier, M. J., Hess, K. L., & Heflin, L. J. (2008). Ethnic disproportionality in students with Autism Spectrum Disorders. *Multicultural Education, 16*(1), 31–38. Retrieved from https://files.eric.ed.gov/fulltext/EJ822396.pdf

Peteet, J. (1997). Icons and militants: Mothering in the danger zone. *Signs: Journal of Women in Culture and Society, 23*(1), 103–129. https://doi.org/10.1086/495237

CHAPTER 7

Unbecoming Mother

Selected Notes on Miscarriage and Infertility

ELAINE GERBER

When I first saw the call for chapters for this book, I ignored it. I thought it didn't apply to me. It sought essays about *"the lived experiences of mothers of children who are labelled or culturally defined as disabled."* My "children" were so disabled they didn't survive. All seven of them.

Infertility in general and miscarriage(s) in particular are usually not considered as part of the reproductive story and are definitely not included in mainstream narratives about mothering. At least in standard American culture, these experiences are seen outside the realm of *motherhood*—which is understood as being, exclusively, about positive outcomes of pregnancy. The myth of biomedical progress (with its promise to "fix" infertility and give babies to all childless couples who desire them) in a capitalist culture (with its emphasis on production) leads one to believe that the only successful pregnancies are those in which there is a "product" or a healthy outcome—a baby (Martin, 1987). Further, ableism plays a role in shaping notions of reproduction/ motherhood; in dominant culture, miscarriages and infertility are removed from the realm of the "natural," despite the evidence of their widespread occurrence.

What follows is a reproductive story that does not result in birth. In it, I offer my first-hand experiences of miscarriages and infertility, situating them within broader cultural narratives about reproduction, disability, and ableism. My analysis is shaped by feminist anthropology and by disability studies. I hope to show how assumptions about disability shape expectations around mothering, and to document ways in which assumptions about reproduction are implicated in the creation of disability and the process of disablement.

This is my story of (un)becoming a mother.

***

I grew up believing that pregnancies could be planned. Both my brother and I were born in May, in Houston. My mom was an elementary school teacher, and we had been told repeatedly growing up that "there was no way I was carrying a child to term during the heat of a Texas summer." Plus, she added, "I could maximize my maternity leave," since she would be "off" during the summers. My mom didn't go back to full-time work for the next 5 years after my older brother was born, so I'm not sure whether any of this is true. For all I know, the timing of our arrival could have been fortuitous and convenient, yet accidental. Nonetheless, I know I am not the only one in American culture that has grown up with these myths.

In one of my first jobs after college, I worked at Planned Parenthood with another young woman who had had three kids, all while being on different forms of birth control. She was mocked by other staff and disbelieved—*"sure, condoms fail and aren't used properly, but while using an IUD?!"* She was exactly the kind of woman who "should" have delayed childbearing, according to the norms of society: she was white and middle class and came from a family whose parents had been college-educated. Her story reinforced myths about the ease and fortitude of unintended pregnancies.

In graduate school, I focused on the prevention and elimination of unwanted pregnancy as a way to promote the rights and equality of women. My doctoral work was a study of women's experience using the "abortion pill" in France, back when it was still illegal and unavailable in the U.S. (Gerber, 2002). I was at that time, and remain today, despite the nature of my experiences, committedly "pro-choice." Nonetheless, my own personal experiences with pregnancy have altered how I think about fetuses and "unborn babies," and I agree with Bennett and de Kok (2018) when they write, "Reproductive disappointments can only be truly appreciated in light of reproductive desires" (p. 91). I wanted to have children. Women who have had miscarriages or stillbirths often go on to have live births. I did not.

STIGMA, SHAME, AND THE CULTURAL CONSTRUCTION OF INFERTILITY

"Just do IVF," I was told repeatedly.

Infertility. The word most often used to describe "my condition" doesn't actually do it justice. It provides no definitive description for the varied range of experiences leading to that label and how involved the process is of becoming it, nor does it suggest the profound social repercussions that arise from it. Culturally, the word conjures images of couples trying and trying to conceive, to no avail. Medically, infertility is defined as "a disease of the reproductive system defined by the failure to achieve a clinical pregnancy after 12 months or more of regular unprotected sexual intercourse" (Zegers-Hochschild *et al.*, 2009, p. 1522). Neither begins to explain my story, yet there is no other term for my experience. I have no disease. I was pregnant six times, at least once with twins. How am I infertile?!

Accepting this label—"infertile"—was a struggle for me personally, one that I resisted. I really wanted a family. "Infertility" is still a word that I use only occasionally, and very uncomfortably, to talk about myself. In part because it doesn't even begin to describe my story and thus contributes to the erasure of my experience, and in part because it is still hard to define myself in this harsh way. Accepting the label meant that I was disabled.

Truth is that I was already disabled. I have had a lifelong struggle with chronic, clinical depression. However, at the time of these reproductive experiences, I did not have a disabled identity. I thought of myself, and was perceived by others, as non-disabled.

Cecil's collection, *The Anthropology of Pregnancy Loss* (1996), was one of the first volumes to address involuntary pregnancy loss and how it is experienced, managed, and understood in culturally and historically diverse situations. Collectively, the anthropological literature identifies a number of problematic ways in which infertility is positioned, even today, including: the loss of the "child" as the result of spirituality or fate (god, karma, malfeasance, witchcraft, or sorcery), and punishment for moral failure, wrong-doing, or breaking of taboos, generally by the mother. Blaming women as "defective" or as the cause of infertility is particularly salient in cultural narratives, as are other key assumptions about bodies and disability, not just patriarchy.

Layne (1996) writes that pregnancy loss is an "abrupt, unthinkable deviation from the natural or the normal biological and social progression that pregnancies are expected to entail" (p. 132)—the transformation of "would-be" parents into "parents." Thus, miscarriage poses a significant challenge to deeply held beliefs about the biological and natural order. Further, "unsuccessful pregnancies" also create dissonance with pervasive and powerful cultural myths around medical progress and science—"*Just do IVF.*"

We further learn from the anthropological literature that there is no consensus (cross-culturally or even within U.S. culture) as to the significance of a fetus, let alone what to call "it"—and thus, to its loss (Barley, 1995; Cecil, 1996). There is also no consensus about when life or "personhood" begins around the globe, for example: at 7 years for some Japanese Buddhist traditions (Orenstein, 2002), 6 years of age for boys among the Nuer (Evans-Pritchard, 1956), approximately one year of age among the rural shantytowns of northeast Brazil (Scheper-Hughes, 1992) and in parts of Nigeria (Maclean, 1971), and the moment of conception for some, including in American culture (Morgan, 2009; Taylor, 1998). There is no word in English for a miscarried or aborted fetus (unlike, for example, in Japanese, *mizuko*, or "water baby"), and their deaths are not mourned ritualistically in the same way as they are in some other cultures, e.g., the Japanese *Mizuko-kuyo*—a ceremony in which children lost through abortion, miscarriage, or stillbirth are memorialized and mourned (Brooks, 1981). Additionally, because ethnographic, lived experiences of pregnancy losses are rarely recorded, it is difficult to say with certainty if, and how, they differ qualitatively from other losses. Despite the cultural assumption that women will experience less grief if miscarriage happens early in pregnancy, most researchers have not found an association between the length of gestation and intensity of grief, anxiety, or depression (Brier, 2008; Leis-Newman, 2012).

* * *

People said I looked great. I can't believe people didn't notice. I had dark bags and con-tinually red, sunken eyes. I cried, no, sobbed, for hours and hours a day. I didn't get off the couch. I wanted to die. I couldn't sleep. I couldn't bear leaving the house. I could barely get to work. I declined invitation after invitation to go out with friends. I didn't eat. For approximately five years, there were cycles of extreme bloat and weight gain from hormones and satisfying pregnancy cravings, and then extreme weight loss, as I suffered yet another miscarriage, sunk into horrible depression, and stopped eating. I dropped multiple clothing sizes. And people kept telling me, "You look great!" Either I was exceptionally good at "passing," or maybe people really did not want to know.

Pregnancy loss and infertility remain a private matter. Certainly, norms about when, or whether, a pregnancy is made public impact the experience of loss and how miscarriage is treated. From my own contexts, Judaism teaches us not to name the baby until birth, and traditionally in American culture, it has been customary to wait until after the first trimester to announce the pregnancy. However, technology is changing these conventions. The widespread use of ultrasound imaging affects how, as well as when, pregnancies are announced (Taylor, 2008). Ironically, reproductive technology also contributes to increased loss in early pregnancy and the ambiguity surrounding it: failure rates from IVF are incredibly high and be-cause early pregnancies can now be confirmed, women have gone from being "late" to being "pregnant." Nonetheless, pregnancy loss remains the most private of all "deaths" ritualistically. The impact it has on a woman over the course of her life (and on partners and other family members) is not recognized, despite the fact that it is a very common event. Although accurate statistics are difficult to gather, if one includes both medically-confirmed and unconfirmed pregnancies, estimates are as high as 50% of all pregnancies end in miscarriage (Todd, 2017).

* * *

We were sitting in a quiet space, away from the noise of the convention center. I remember telling a friend and colleague that I had started to miscarry the night before I left for the conference. And, although she felt sorry for me because she could see I was hurting, the conversation quickly moved on. Like I should just get over it, right?!

Culture teaches us that women are supposed to "let go"—to accept the loss with stoicism, forget the unfortunate incident, put it behind them, move on. And, to "replace the dead baby" by getting pregnant again as soon as possible (Cecil, 1996). This is part of a larger cultural narrative among American women to "make something good" come from the tragedy (Layne, 1996). It also reinforces this idea that the only "real" (i.e., natural, legit) pregnancies are those that end in healthy babies. But what about women who do not, or cannot, reach their "rightful destination" as a mom?! I've heard from women who had so-called "replacement children" that they remain traumatized and saddened from their miscarriage(s). One event does not actually negate the other. The pain of miscarriage remains profound and hidden. Author Brkic (2018) described her multiple miscarriages this way:

> The miscarriages were seldom straightforward and often physically painful. Some took weeks to resolve. But far worse was the emptiness that followed each one, and the way I did not know where to park my grief... Our culture insists that women in these situations move on. Worse, we ask them to be complicit in their own forgetting ... We are unsettled when a woman lingers in her grief. We find it creepy. Macabre, even. ... There is an element of shame to miscarriage, in not being able to carry out one's biological imperative. Most women only realize how common it is when they confide in a friend or relative who has also experienced one, or who knows someone who has.

Orenstein (2002) suggests that there are multiple reasons for this "cult of secrecy" around miscarriages. From a general discomfort with death to an uncertainty about the personhood of these early beings to a backlash against "older moms" who are judged for "waiting too long" to have kids. I add that this culture of secrecy—and the shaming of women who can't reproduce—also stems from ableism. We are "womb-shamed" because of the incredible stigma around disability. In ableist narratives, certain bodies are marked as medically problematic, unfit, and unnatural; and the women who have them as "other." The embodiment of infertility, culturally, is partially what makes it a disability.

Ableism refers to discrimination or prejudice towards people considered disabled. On par with racism or sexism, it reflects certain cultural beliefs about people and their bodies, framing some as unfit, unable, and less-than. As such, it is a force which maintains and produces disablement. Further, it is implicated, not only in the creating of negative experiences and discrimination, but also in the maintaining of the social hierarchy about bodies.

The social model of disability (Oliver, 1990), which locates disability within the sociopolitical environment rather than in bodies/minds, could be a useful conceptual tool here. The reality is that infertility might not be located "in" any particular body, but rather between bodies (i.e., the combination of genetic material from two partners) or external to the body (i.e., existing in the environment). My diagnosis was technically "of no known origin," the most common kind of infertility. Nonetheless, infertility is thought of and culturally understood as a "body" problem.

Rather than seeing pregnancy loss as external to ourselves, or as a natural part of the reproductive continuum, we are enfreaked by the experience. I am understood as having a body that goes against nature; that is contrary to what humans are supposed to be able to do. It's *so easy everyone can do it*," yet I couldn't. I felt cursed. Despite intellectually "knowing better"—all the arguments about how women are more than their biological parts and reproductive capacity, and how it might not even be "my body" at all—I still felt "other." Being a woman meant being able to give life; it's supposed to be our power. It's magical. And after 30+ years, I was surprisingly, and severely, disempowered by this. Personally, I needed to grapple with and reconstruct my own identity and femininity. I had internalized ableism.

ABLEISM AND THE POLITICS OF REPRODUCTION

"Has he always been blind?" asks the handyman, a complete stranger. He is in our apartment, fixing the window. I already know exactly where this line of conversation is going. I've heard it so many times. People felt surprisingly comfortable asking personal questions about our sex life, questions that would never have been asked had my partner not been blind. "Yes," I reply, "He was born with it." The worker continued, "Wow, you know, I have such problems with, you know, not thin enough, not attractive enough.... And you…" (here's the clincher), "you, wow, I just really admire you." I got the "I really admire you" all the time. My friend's mom, when I met her for the first time, exclaimed with such surprise and awe to another friend, "She married him blind. She married him blind." Again, the surprise that someone would choose to partner with a blind man to start a family seemed beyond comprehension.

When I was first trying to start a family, it was with my blind partner. While women are usually blamed for infertility, in my case, it was *his* disability status that was significant to the larger cultural narratives shaping my story of reproduction and mothering. To date, there is a huge stigma against blind parents. Blind people in general are not considered to be desirable mates, and blind men in particular are not considered good husband material—*"How could he possibly be a good 'provider,' let alone father?!"* Blind parents report extremely high rates of child removal and loss of parental rights (Powell, 2017), and I personally know several people who have had their children removed from their custody after courts determined that their blindness rendered them unfit to parent.

The positioning of the (presumably) non-disabled wife as a martyr—willing, giving, nurturing, deserving of admiration, saintly—obviously ties to expectations about femininity in general, but also reifies notions about the undesirability of disabled partners. Cultural assumptions about disability as inability, about particular gender roles/characteristics for males and females as biological and "natural," and about sexuality and reproduction as appropriate for certain bodies (but not others) are prolific and intertwined—taken as givens and rarely challenged.

These assumptions were echoed by medical professionals, family members, friends, and the culture at large, with regard to my miscarriages. I got a lot of platitudes. *"God only gives you what you can handle." "Maybe it was meant to be."* And, without knowing any of the details, *"Maybe it was for the best."* How were these multiple losses for the best, I wondered?! It wasn't just people with a Judeo-Christian background or who were adherents of fatalism that said these things. Even people with progressive and non-traditional spiritual views expressed a version of this. *"There's a life lesson here."* Or, *"Karma teaches us the same lesson over and over, until we learn and grow."* I'm pretty sure that whatever "life lessons" I was supposed to learn from all this suffering and pain could have been learned after one miscarriage, not six. Of course, what they were saying reflected deeply-held assumptions about appropriate bodies for parenting: blind people are not meant to be parents, should not parent. *"See, it's God's will."*

Attempts to make sense of these losses through culturally valid explanatory models reflect ableist views about disability. "For the best" implies that the alternative would be worse (i.e., I would have had a severely disabled child if I hadn't miscarried). Not only were these types of comments offensive, they were inaccurate in presuming blindness as the cause. My partner's blindness had nothing to do with "our" infertility. And there are plenty of people with limited eyesight who are loving, devoted, and successful parents.

These assumptions that my infertility was somehow a "blessing" also perpetuate a history of eugenics and of evolutionary concepts of "reproductive fitness" that are inherently ableist (Clare, 2017; Taylor, 2017). Medically, as well as culturally, it was simply understood, without question, as my partner's "fault." Clinicians made my partner test for genetic diseases that could be passed down—even after we provided them with medical records that showed his blindness was not hereditary. They insisted "we" be tested, even after explaining that regardless of the test results, we were not going to abort—we just wanted a child; we didn't care if they were blind. In fact, we would welcome a blind child, we argued; who better to parent them than someone who knows what it's like?! This they could not understand.

I was treated like a martyr for "choosing disability" in my partner, but not in extending those choices to my potential offspring. That choice was deemed unacceptable. I am not sure whether our experiences resulted from the policy of individual clinics, the medical professionals' choices, or were determined by health insurance coverage, but ableism was woven into the structure of medical care we received. In many places, the ableism is formalized through policy. Data from Pakistanis in the UK, for example, show that "fertility providers have the state-sanctioned right to veto access to treatment to patients who do not conform to normative ideas of a 'legitimate' family" (Blell, 2018). In the US, there are multiple states with a "conscience clause" law that allows providers to decline certain health services, including those needed to resolve incomplete miscarriages that result from IVF (Daniels, 2018).

Myths about the availability, ease, and success of IVF simultaneously coexist with narratives about adoption that further shame women for caring so much, for being so deeply impacted by childlessness in the modern era. *"Just complete your family a different way"* was a common retort to my pain—as though this is easy, or even doable, for all women. The truth is there are many barriers to adoption. It is not easy, nor cheap, nor are adoptable children as "widely available" as media and myth make it seem. Even possessing a PhD and a full-time professional job, I doubt that we would have passed a means-test in New York City, even for the fost-adopt program that placed "special needs" children. Add to this the bias against blind parents. We didn't even try adoption.

The history of eugenics and ableism are interwoven. Structural barriers to reproduction for disabled people have been a significant issue historically and remain problematic today. In fact, the right for people to have autonomy over their own bodies, including for reproductive choice (and sexual expression, generally) was a key factor in the independent living movement and the fight for disability rights (Disabilityrightsff, 2011; Hall, 2011; Levine, Nemeth, & Lewin, 2012). I don't know what it's like for women who, by virtue of body or circumstance, grow up not expecting to mother. I cannot imagine what it must have been like for Carrie Buck and the countless other women in the U.S. historically who were sterilized against their will for "feeblemindedness," their opportunity for motherhood stolen from them (Clare, 2017). I always expected to have children. It was never a "choice."

Much of the anthropological scholarship addressing genetic testing and access to "assistive reproductive technologies" (ARTs) highlights the prevalence of medical model perspectives which frame disability in a negative light, a pregnancy outcome to be avoided or eliminated, and thus, could benefit from disability studies' insights. For example, Homans' (1982) work in Britain documents how women would rather abort than give birth to a "deformed baby." These findings are confirmed in other scholarship about prenatal diagnostic testing in the U.S. (Courduriès & Herbrand, 2014; Parens & Asch, 2000). One notable exception is Press and Browner's (1998) work examining the positive value disabled offspring bring to the project of mothering among some Mexican American women. Regarding IVF, both clinical practice and cultural perception emphasize positive outcomes, despite that ~75% of implanted embryos do not result in live births (Centers for Disease Control and Prevention, 2016). This "failure" rate is part and parcel of using IVF, which means that for every successful "miracle baby," there are many more that did not survive. Existing narratives omit the destruction of *disabled lives* in particular.

* * *

When does motherhood begin? When does it end? If life begins at conception, does motherhood begin then too? Why do I not have the right to grieve, or to mark the loss of my babies, my fertility, or my own identity as a mom?

Brkic (2018) compared her experience to those of women depicted in Victorian-era photographs, where they posed with their stillborn babies and dead infants. She wrote, "It occurred to me that I had never been offered an ultrasound picture of a lost pregnancy, or of a doomed one…I left empty-handed, without photographic evidence of those tiny passengers." The ultrasound images she has are all from when her pregnancies were still healthy and developing "normally." She holds onto them, "because they are more than images of doomed pregnancies or babies who would never be. They are photographic evidence of something that is as much a part of me today as my hands and face," and she saves them as a reminder that "I did not have to deny this part of me, even as my culture told me to forget" (para. 18).

I don't have that. I don't have any markers of what was taken from me. I possess no pictures of my babies-not-to-be, ultrasound, or otherwise. What I possess is a haunting aural memory that I cannot forget, no matter how hard I try.

G. was there with his tape recorder, wanting to capture "baby's first picture" in a way that would be meaningful to him. They had the sound on before homing in on the image. The heartbeat was slower than mine, I can hear it still, its beats mixed with the slushy underwater ultrasound noise. They didn't have to say anything, I knew it wasn't good.

"MOVING ON" AND UNSANCTIONED GRIEF

A great feeling of loss has come over me. The world is no longer solid. I feel untethered. Lost.

"Light a candle," I was told. I had reached out to the psychiatrist on staff at the fertility clinic while I was struggling through all this. In our session, I explained that I was an anthropologist, so I appreciated and needed ritual. This is what she told me. Literally, "light a candle." Are you kidding me?!? Thank you, here's your $150… gee, I wish I had thought of that! Then I got up and I left. It was years later before I went back to seek professional help.

I experienced both physical and psychic pain. Grief surrounded my individual pregnancy losses, and the recognition with each subsequent one that I would never have children. I grieved the loss of my fertility overall, and with it, the loss of my identity, my sense of self. The infertility caused a major depression. But the miscarriages—the process of becoming infertile—the repeated cycles of hope and loss, caused anxiety, medical trauma of their own, PTSD; it impacted my executive function and decision-making; I had a stroke. The trauma changed me. I was fundamentally altered. My sense of wholeness, of well-being in the world disappeared. My grief was deeply existential and profound.

Psychologists define unrecognized or "unsanctioned grief" as grief that exists even though society does not acknowledge a need for, or right to it; this is also sometimes referred to as "disenfranchised grief" (Doka, 2002). Examples include grief over unacknowledged LGBTQ partners, ex-spouses, foster children, abortions, and pregnancy loss.[1] With miscarriage, the bereaved may not publicly grieve because the loss is hidden from others, not socially recognized, nor deemed a significant/valuable loss—including by clinicians and medical professionals. Members of one's social network may not even know about the pregnancy, while others, who do know, may not acknowledge the loss as warranting "real" grief. These circumstances prevent people from being able to validate the feelings of the bereaved, and women from feeling socially supported. The psychological literature is clear that stigma is central to the experience, and that the "invisibility" tied to the loss only increases the grief/reactions to the loss (Doka, 2002; Hocker, 2018; Pine, 1990; Worden, 2018).

Death rituals are, by definition, social. But, as discussed, in Western cultures there is no social space or time-honored public acknowledgment for pregnancy loss. Unlike the *Mikuzo-kuyo* ritual (described earlier) there's no burial, no ceremony to commemorate the suffering. No one brought food to my home after I miscarried, to be sure I ate. No one sat *shiva*[2] with me. Neither for the individual souls that evaporated into the ether, nor my identity as a woman. Did my friends and family not share my grief?! No one joined me to mark a year of mourning—a ritual symbolizing that it is time to move on with the project of living, as we do in the Jewish tradition. In my case, there was no singular "date" to mark my loss, there was no line delineating fertile from infertile. My experiences all just bled into each other, this process of unbecoming the mother I thought I was.

Research among infertile women suggests that my experience was not unusual (Sandelowski, 1991). Further, because women can "choose" these days to opt out of motherhood, it further compounds the social isolation and contributes to unsanctioned grief. It can be awkward and contradictory to discuss, making it hard to get support. I was deeply conflicted about my own feelings: as someone who researched, wrote about, and believed that fetuses were *not* "babies," how could I feel such distress at losing one?! And, simultaneously, there are plenty of women who now lead perfectly full lives without children, by choice, and my feminist self supports them and their politics—how could I be so crushed by my lack of children, let alone deserve sympathy from these child-free women? Yet, for most people, the desire to reproduce, to create a family is powerful, and the drive to be intimately/permanently/biologically connected to other beings is a core human need. Recognizing the profound grief that accompanies a miscarriage would help to reframe these losses as significant and worthy of support.

THE SOCIAL AND LIFELONG NATURE OF INFERTILITY

Infertility is a reproductive *event* that exceeds the bounds of what is signified by the word. It is felt throughout one's life-course, not just in the few months after a miscarriage. Its presence is felt in conversations and settings having nothing, seemingly, to do with reproduction itself. If one does not either "get over it" or join the ranks of "natural" women as a mom, it remains a "master status" (Hunt, 2007), present and interwoven into all life events.

What does every reunion begin with? Catching up with friends you haven't seen in a few years! Immediately following, "How are you?" is "How are your kids?" Pictures ensue. Once, at a national conference, I was seated at a table with some colleagues I liked but didn't know well, a few friends, and some people I had not yet met. Immediately upon greeting each other, family photos were whipped out. It was my first time in a social setting like this since experiencing my reproductive traumas, and I didn't see it coming. Today I might have a one-liner ready at my disposal, but back then, I was not at all prepared—I just burst into tears. Publicly. Like, hard sobs, unable to speak, unable to breathe, let alone explain myself. Socially awkward is an understatement. Yeah, rituals of greeting are always hard now.

How do you put a trigger warning around a happy event? The joy that new parents experience over the birth of their baby is assumed to be universally appreciated. There is no acknowledgement that such news about the new arrivals may be difficult for some people to hear. Any deviation from the standard "emotional script" about births and babies is constructed as a character flaw (Scheper-Hughes, 1985). (*What's wrong with you?! Why can't you appreciate the happiness of others?!*) Women, in particular, who deviate from the script are painted as bitter— the kind of woman who "doesn't like kids" (read: unnatural). Simultaneously, as a woman of reproductive age, I received many versions of "*You'll see one day*" or "*Just wait, you'll see…*" without any recognition that childbearing might be difficult or impossible, let alone a source of great pain. I was shown baby pictures countless times, and still am, never once with consideration that this might be difficult for me, and never once was I asked if I wanted to see them. It was given, of course, I would! Doesn't everyone?!

I can't imagine a scenario in a social setting, where it would be appropriate to show pictures of my pregnancies (if I had them)—miscarriage is not a topic of "polite conversation," not appropriate during a family meal or a reunion of long-lost friends, nor at work; there is not a single culturally-coded "happy" or social event where it would it be fitting to talk about it. Traditionally, in some cultures, widows wear special attire, so people know their status and can respond appropriately. How I wish I could wear something that would explain things for me!

I am often informed that because I do not have children I could not possibly know about parenting, raising children, or, even more insulting, what it might be like to lose a child. *"What would you know about it?!"* or *"You don't have kids, how could you possibly know?!"* were comments I heard more times than I care to count, and in all kinds of contexts. Whether the topic is school shootings or the impact of climate change on our future, women like me are silenced. We are not entitled to weigh in or considered to have "standing" or enough at stake; our opinions are not valued. Further, in contexts where children are present and central, conversations tend to hover around age-appropriate topics, comparisons between kids, and other parenting concerns. Narratively, this means my stories rarely get told. It leaves infertile women without a way to participate meaningfully in social activities or conversations and contributes to our silencing.

* * *

"Why would you want to go to a six-year old's birthday party?!" my brother retorted, *when I asked if I was going to be invited to my nephew's party.*

I explained to him how, as a non-parent, there were no kids in my life. As a parent, he goes to 20 children's birthday parties each year, so I can see why he would *not* want to go to another. But without kids, you rarely are invited to any! You do not get to participate in these milestone celebrations, to see kids grow up, or be part of their lives. Not only do you not have children of your own, but you get less access even to the other children in your life. The loss extends outward and includes the loss of social networks and social opportunities.

To be fair, some of my isolation was my own doing. I withdrew, finding it particularly difficult to be around groups of parents and small children. Many women who've experienced pregnancy loss also described feeling "misunderstood"—their rationale for declining invitations not considered valid or legitimate, particularly if it occurred years after the reproductive "event"—leaving them unable to participate in holidays and other celebrations (Layne, 1996). Like me, they felt that no one understood or considered their feelings to be appropriate.

* * *

I had offered to babysit the kids of one of my closest college friends for a few days as they headed to a memorial, so they wouldn't have to bring young children with them. She said, "That's ok. We'll just drop them at my cousin's house. They already have kids, so it's just easier." Ouch.

The social isolation resulting from infertility gets compounded throughout the life-course. A large part of this has to do with how family is structured in American culture (see Courduriès & Herbrand, 2014; Schneider, 1984)—both the emphasis on nuclear family and the tendency for parents to socialize with other parents. Those without "family"—culturally-defined as with children—are further isolated from their peers as they age. Moreover, if you do not have kids of your own in mainstream American culture, it is difficult to have the presence of children in your life. Certainly, teaching is one way that I stay connected to youth. But it is considered "unnatural"—even creepy, to have more than a passing interest in other people's children, particularly if you have none of your own. Losing access to the social world of children is an additional, significant loss.

* * *

Today, I did try to "light a candle." It was Mother's Day. I wanted to light 7 candles, actually, one yahrtzeit[3] for each of the "babies" I had lost. I wanted to plaster this image all over social media, to counter the crayoned cards and short stacks of pancakes made by their kids that my friends were posting. Not that I wanted to rain on anyone's parade, I just wanted people to know what the day meant to me. I wanted people to realize this could be a painful holiday, not just a joyous one. But I didn't. I lit one. And I left it in my bedroom, perpetuating the culture of secrecy. I convinced myself that it wasn't due to stigma/shame, but because my mother was coming over, and I didn't want her to see them, to have to feel bad—either for me, or for what she'd lost too. But truthfully, I continue to feel ambiguous about my suffering and what to do with it.

Infertility isn't an individual issue; it's social. No one brought my mother food either, to acknowledge her loss of grandchildren and provide support. She, too, has to sit smiling while her peers boast and brag. My mom has nowhere to park her grief. Nor does my dad. My nieces and nephews don't get to go through life with cousins. Further, the inability to cement a relationship through children fractures partnerships. It did mine. Statistics show that couples often separate due to fertility problems (Firth, 2014). Because American culture emphasizes a very narrow idea of family, one that privileges nuclear family, of course people didn't see the loss as extending to my mom, my cousins, nor the ways that it impacted my partner or relationship. But miscarriages and infertility impact everyone. And, not only is it social, it is lifelong. Life cycle events, such as weddings and the arrival of grandchildren, further situate the experience of infertility as lifelong and mark the miscarriage(s) with ongoing significance.

The social isolation that results is, in large part, what makes infertility so painful. That this pain is understood as the result of embodiment is what makes it disabling. A disability studies framework can shed light on how my body (with or without impairment) is implicated for what are essentially social phenomena. Culturally-pervasive ableist narratives position only those with particular bodies (those which are able to reproduce) as capable of full adulthood status. Others are socially and linguistically positioned as not full adults, and sometimes, as not fully human (e.g., as incapable of "real" empathy). Invalidated adulthood status is part of the disabling experience of infertility, and it is characteristic of the disability experience more generally (Longmore, 1995).

CONCLUSION

Previous feminist scholarship around reproduction and infertility has shown that it is women and their bodies that are the targets of stigma (Courduriès & Herbrand, 2014; Ginsburg & Rapp, 1995; Inhorn & van Balen, 2002), but these critiques have yet to explore the role of ableism in that process, as I hoped to here. Stories of miscarriage can inform a more complete understanding of mothering and reproduction. Specifically, what would it mean to consider infertility as a disability, through disability studies perspectives, rather than a disease? What would it look like if we were to discuss infertility and pregnancy loss as part of "reproductive diversity" and as an acceptable way of being in the world? Given that potentially 50% of pregnancies end in miscarriage (Todd, 2017), it is indeed a part and parcel of "healthy" and "normal" reproduction, even if undesirable. Perhaps we might start to see how the "othering" of those who cannot reproduce is located in the sociocultural environment, not in the body. Reframing pregnancy loss as a "natural" experience of reproduction could do a lot to create solidarity and reduce stigma.

It's been over 5 years since my last miscarriage. I am no longer trying to re-produce, but this hardly means I am "over it." Miscarriage losses and infertility shape one's reality and remain for life. The significance and role it plays in one's life course may change, but it is never over, complete, finished, irrelevant. There's no "magic eraser" that removes the scars of trauma from our memories and our bodies. I have rebuilt a life for myself. I got myself a dog and a new partner. Parts of my life are absolutely amazing, in ways I never could have imagined possible, even before all this. And I am incredibly grateful for my success, my privilege, and my luck. I can feel happiness again. I certainly am no longer suicidal. Thoughts about babies, motherhood, disability, and loss are no longer constant. However, not a day goes by when the implications, the consequences, are not present.

Truth is, I love kids. But my narrative is omitted from the cultural story of motherhood. I am still struggling to build a new narrative, a reconstructed life-story that encompasses the history of my lived experience and which allows me to feel whole. Feeling isolated is common for infertile women. So, these days, I often stay home, and now that I no longer live in the city, I garden.

NOTES

1. I would add to this list: kids lost to adoption, migration & deportation policies, warfare, do-mestic violence, abuse, and myriad other large-scale structural conditions that force unimagi-nable "choices" onto the lives and reproductive decisions of women (Petchesky, 1984; Roberts, 1997). Solidarity.

2. *Shiva* is the week-long period of mourning in Jewish culture that follows a loved one's death. Traditionally, during this time family members gather in one home to receive visitors who have come to pay their respects.
3. *Yahrtzeit* is a Yiddish word that means "anniversary" and is used specifically to refer to the day on which a person has died. There are various customs associated with the passing, including the lighting of a 24-hour candle each year, to honor the memory of the departed.

REFERENCES

Barley, N. (1995). *Grave matters*. New York, NY: Henry Holt & Co.

Bennett, L. R., & de Kok, B. (2018). Reproductive desires and disappointments. *Medical Anthropology, 37*(2), 91–100.

Blell, M. (2018). British Pakistani Muslim masculinity, (in)fertility, and the clinical encounter. *Medical Anthropology, 37*(2), 117–130.

Brier, N. (2008). Grief following miscarriage: A comprehensive review of the literature. *Journal of Women's Health, 17*(3), 451–64.

Brkic, C. A. (2018, May 17). Framing a loss: How Victorian death photography helped me process my own miscarriages. *Slate*. Retrieved from https://slate.com/human-interest/2018/05/how-victorian-death-photography-helped-me-process-miscarriage.html

Brooks, A. P. (1981). Mizuko kuyō and Japanese Buddhism. *Japanese Journal of Religious Studies, 8*(3–4), 119–147.

Cecil, R. (1996). *The anthropology of pregnancy loss: Comparative studies in miscarriage, stillbirth, and neonatal death*. Oxford, UK: Berg Publishers.

Centers for Disease Control and Prevention, National Center for Chronic Disease Prevention and Health Promotion, Division of Reproductive Health. (2016). *Assisted Reproductive Technology (ART) data* [Data file]. Retrieved from https://nccd.cdc.gov/drh_art/rdPage.aspx?rdReport=DRH_ART.ClinicInfo&rdRequestForward=True&ClinicId=49&ShowNational=1

Clare, E. (2017). *Brilliant imperfection: Grappling with cure*. Durham, NC: Duke University Press.

Courduriès, J., & Herbrand, C. (2014). Gender, kinship and assisted reproductive technologies: Future directions after 30 years of research. *Enfances Familles Générations [En ligne], 21*.

Daniels, M. (2018, June 25). Woman denied miscarriage drug on moral grounds. *The Detroit News*. Retrieved from https://www.detroitnews.com/story/news/nation/2018/06/25/miscarriage-medication-pharmacist/36368633/

Disabilityrightsff [Screen name]. (2011, November 24). *Weird and wonderful documentary teaser* [Video file]. Retrieved from https://www.youtube.com/watch?v=e5Ccrkp5Y6w

Doka, K. J. (2002). Disenfranchised grief. In K. J. Doka (Ed.), *Living with grief: Loss in later life* (pp. 159–168). Washington, DC: The Hospice Foundation of America.

Evans-Pritchard, E. E. (1956). *Nuer Religion*. Oxford, UK: Oxford University Press.

Firth, S. (2014). Study: Infertile couples 3 times more likely to divorce. *U.S. News Civic*. Retrieved from https://www.usnews.com/news/articles/2014/01/31/study-infertile-couples-3-times-more-likely-to-divorce

Gerber, E. G. (2002). Deconstructing pregnancy: RU486, seeing "eggs," and the ambiguity of very early conceptions. *Medical Anthropology Quarterly, 16*(1), 92–108.

Ginsburg, F. D., & Rapp, R. (1995). *Conceiving the new world order: The global politics of reproduction*. Berkeley, CA: University of California Press.

Hall, K. Q. (2011). *Feminist disability studies*. Bloomington, IN: Indiana University Press.

Hocker, J. L. (2018). *The trail to tincup: Love stories at life's end*. Berkeley, CA: She Writes Press.

Homans, H. (1982). Pregnancy and birth as rites of passage for two groups of women in Britain. In C. P. MacCormack (Ed.), *Ethnography of fertility and birth* (pp. 231–268). New York, NY: Academic Press.

Hunt, S. (2007). Master status. In G. Ritzer (Ed.), *The Blackwell encyclopedia of sociology* (Vol. 11). Hoboken, NJ: Wiley.

Inhorn, M. C., & van Balen, F. (Eds.). (2002). *Infertility around the globe: New thinking on childlessness, gender, and reproductive technologies*. Berkeley, CA: The University of California Press.

Layne, L. L. (1996). "Never such innocence again": Irony, nature, and technoscience in narratives of pregnancy loss. In R. Cecil (Ed.), *The anthropology of pregnancy loss: Comparative studies in miscarriage, stillbirth, and neonatal death* (pp. 131–152). Oxford, UK: Berg Publishers.

Leis-Newman, E. (2012). Miscarriage and loss. *American Psychological Association*. Retrieved from https://www.apa.org/monitor/2012/06/miscarriage.aspx

Levine, J. (Producer), Nemeth, S. (Producer), & Lewin, B. (Director). (2012). *The sessions* [Motion picture]. United States: Fox.

Longmore, P. K. (1995). Medical decision making and people with disabilities: A clash of cultures. *Journal of Law, Medicine, & Ethics, 23*(1), 82–87.

Maclean, U. (1971). *Magical medicine: A Nigerian case-study*. London: The Penguin Press.

Martin, E. (1987). *The woman in the body*. Boston, MA: Beacon Press.

Morgan, L. (2009). *Icons of life: A cultural history of human embryos*. Berkeley, CA: University of California Press.

Oliver, M. (1990). *The politics of disablement*. Basingstoke, UK: Macmillan.

Orenstein, P. (2002, April 21). Mourning my miscarriage. *The New York Times Magazine*. Retrieved from https://www.nytimes.com/2002/04/21/magazine/mourning-my-miscarriage.html

Parens, E., & Asch, A. (Eds.). (2000). *Prenatal testing and disability rights*. Washington, DC: Georgetown University Press.

Petchesky, R. P. (1984). *Abortion and women's choice: The state, sexuality, and reproductive freedom*. London: Longman Publishing Group.

Pine, V. R. (1990). *Unrecognized and unsanctioned grief: The nature and counseling of unacknowledged loss*. Springfield, IL: Charles C. Thomas Publisher.

Plath, S. (1962). *Three women*. Warwick, UK: Stratford Playscripts.

Powell, R. (2014, June 29). Can parents lose custody simply because they are disabled? *American Bar Association*. Retrieved from https://www.americanbar.org/groups/gpsolo/publications/gp_solo/2014/march_april/can_parents_lose_custody_simply_because_they_are_disabled/

Press, N., & Browner, C. H. (1998). Characteristics of women who refuse an offer of prenatal diagnosis: Data from the California MSAFP experience. *American Journal of Medical Genetics, 78*, 433–445.

Roberts, D. E. (1997). *Killing the black body: Race, reproduction, and the meaning of liberty*. New York, NY: Pantheon Books.

Sandelowski, M. (1991). Compelled to try: The never-enough quality of conceptive technology. *Medical Anthropology Quarterly, 5*(1), 29–47.

Scheper-Hughes, N. (1985). Culture, scarcity, and maternal thinking: Maternal detachment and infant survival in a Brazilian shantytown. *Ethos, 13*(4), 291–317.

Scheper-Hughes, N. (1992). *Death without weeping: The violence of everyday life in Brazil*. Berkeley, CA: University of California Press.

Schneider, D. M. (1984). *A critique of the study of kinship*. Ann Arbor, MI: University of Michigan Press.

Taylor, J. (1998). Image of contradiction: Obstetrical ultrasound in American culture. In S. Franklin & H. Ragoné (Eds.), *Reproducing reproduction: Kinship, power, and technological innovation* (pp. 15–45). Philadelphia, PA: University of Pennsylvania Press.

Taylor, J. (2008). *The public life of the fetal sonogram: Technology, consumption, and the politics of reproduction*. New Brunswick, NJ: Rutgers University Press.

Taylor, S. (2017). *Beasts of burden: Animal and disability liberation*. New York, NY: The New Press.

Todd, N. (2017, July 13). Pregnancy and miscarriage. *WebMD, LLC*. Retrieved from https://www.webmd.com/baby/guide/pregnancy-miscarriage#1

Worden, J. W. (2018). *Grief counseling and grief therapy: A handbook for the mental health practitioner* (5th ed.). New York, NY: Springer Publishing, LLC.

Zegers-Hochschild, F., Adamson, G. D., de Mouzon, J., Ishihara, O., Mansour, R., Nygren, K., … Vanderpoel, S. (2009). International Committee for Monitoring Assisted Reproductive Technology (ICMART) and the World Health Organization (WHO) revised glossary of ART terminology, 2009. *Fertility and Sterility, 92*(5), 1520–1524.

CHAPTER 8

Bad Mother

MARÍA CIOÈ-PEÑA AND LAURA CASTRO SANTAMARÍA

At any given time, a person can access the news and come across a report about a mother and her child. Often, the audience will take in some bits of information, and then proceed to categorize that mother as "good" or "bad." Stories about *bad* mothers are, in some ways, the most appealing. Perhaps it's because we believe ourselves to be a society that cares for its young or, more likely, because it helps others measure their own parenting or humanity. This is a story about a moment in time that constructed one mother as a "bad mother" and turned another into a godmother. In order to understand how these lives became intertwined, we must start at the beginning. In 2010, I, María, had been Justine's teacher for three years. This was also my third year as a bilingual special education teacher—the lead teacher in a self-contained class, managing between nine to twelve students and up to five paraprofessionals at any given time. During these three years, Laura, Justine's mother, was an active parent in the class and we developed a very friendly, yet professional relationship. She was a stay-at-home mom who was raising three children, all of whom had, at some point, received some type of special education service. Justine was her first child and the one whose path in the world was the hardest to carve out. We have decided to tell of our experiences across three time periods. First, we will share our memories of an event that occurred in April 2010, and of the days and weeks that followed. Then we share our present reflections of the way these events continue to linger in our lives years later, the underlying ideas that have shaped us, and the ways in which we have since changed. Lastly, we each speak to Justine directly, in hopes of sharing with her some of what we've learned as mothers.

APRIL 2010

María

The first thing I remember about that day was that the principal called me into her office. She told me, and I do not remember why it was, that Justine had gone to the nurse from another class. She had not been with me; I had not sent her. Someone sent her to the nurse. Regardless, when Justine had been in the nurse's office, they noticed a bruise, and she had mentioned that her mother had hit her, and now, I had to call Administration for Children Services (ACS)—New York State's Child Protection Services (CPS) agency and report it.

The one thing I always ask myself when I think back on this is, "Why me?" I think I asked then, but I do not know, I'm not sure. Why did *I* have to call? I did not see the bruise; Justine did not mention anything to me, so why was I the one who had to make the call to CPS? I remember being put in the guidance counselor's office with a telephone and they told me what number to dial and exactly what to say. That's it. I asked, "What now?" And they said, "Nothing, the city takes care of it." I asked, "Are we going to tell mom?" And I was told, "Do not say anything; you cannot mention anything to her." Maybe they thought that Laura was going to leave, or that she was going to take the children somewhere. I do not know, but I was told I could not mention anything to her. At this point, I had already been Justine's teacher for three years, and Laura and I had a close relationship. I knew I had to let her know.

Soon after, I called Eric—a new boyfriend at the time; we had just started dating. I called him, crying, told him what had happened, and said, "I want to call Laura and tell her what happened, but the school told me not to." He said, "Call her, just wait until you leave work; what you do as an independent person outside of school has nothing to do with your role as a teacher."[1] The moment I got home, I called Laura and told her that I had called the CPS. I quickly explained why and told her that I did not know exactly how it worked, but what she could anticipate was a home visit. That they were going to look through the house and check on the children, but also that I did not know more than that. My primary concern was that the children were going to be taken away.

This was the first time I had ever been in a situation that required calling CPS. What I knew about CPS stemmed from my memories as a child growing up in New York City. I remember that when I was younger, I once threatened my mother, "We live in America now and you cannot hit me, and if you hit me the city comes, and it will take me." I recall my mom saying, "Okay, I will help you prepare your suitcases, but you should know, those kids don't fare well." That was the last time I ever mentioned it. As a teacher, I had learned about CPS and my responsibilities, but I understood it only with regard to cases of extreme abuse. Culturally, I also knew that parenting styles and perceptions of abuse could be different within immigrant communities. As a child, my mom hit me, she hit my sister, and yet I never perceived this as abuse or my mother as an abuser. Perhaps because of my upbringing I did not view hitting as abuse, at least not in this situation. I did not feel that this was one of those grave situations where CPS needed to be called.

Justine always came to school well dressed, with her lunch, and well prepared. I never thought she was being abused. After the call, I worried about what was going to happen. I was afraid that Laura would hate me and distance herself from me. In the end, the two of us grew closer, but Laura did distance herself from the school; she stopped coming to the school or participating in events or meetings. I think the only time she came back was for graduation; she wouldn't come for anything else.

At the time that this happened, I wasn't a mother; I wouldn't become a mother for another five years. Now that I am a mom, I have experienced times when I feel overwhelmed, and I only have two children, both of whom are considered *normal*. I also have so much help: I have access to multiple types of childcare; I have people who clean my house, deliver my groceries; I have a partner who is an active parent; I have my parents, my in-laws and friends to call on when things get tough. I do not shoulder the burden alone, and some may even criticize me for outsourcing some of the mothering. Yet, I often feel as if there is no room to make mistakes as a mother.

As a mother, you are supposed to be perfect; you always feel this looming threat that anyone can call CPS if you step out of line. Outsiders are allowed to be so critical with very little information. I have thought about the moments in which I've given my son three spanks; moments in which I was unable to control my emotions, feeling instant regret, and quickly saying, "I'm sorry, I should not have done that." But sometimes that's not enough. And I recognize that for some moms, that instant feeling of regret and that subsequent apology is not enough to redeem them in the eyes of society and from this idea of being a bad mother. Often, the measure of a good mom and a bad mom has more to do with class, race, and education, than mothering styles and love.

For a mom like Laura who is, on the surface, a more obvious immigrant than I appear, the stakes are higher, the expectations are greater, and the space for forgiveness is much smaller. Even though, like her, I am an immigrant, I am also steeped in privilege: I am married to a doctor, I've always had legal status, and I am a college professor. Meanwhile, I feel the same frustrations as her. The difference is only in the way we are judged. It is no wonder that at one point, Laura shared with me her desire to commit suicide. I too have had very dark thoughts in those early stages of motherhood.

On that day in April, I knew the stakes and I knew what I had done. I had to take responsibility. I couldn't just make the call, hang up the phone, and walk away.

APRIL 2010

Laura[2]

All of this started because she had homework, this was all because of homework. She was a special needs girl. She had homework. She had not done it, and spring break was almost over, and she was getting ready to go back to school. So, I sat with her, and she was doing the work, but she did not understand. To me, it was very easy, but I, in my ignorance, I would say, of not knowing that she was a special needs child and the extent of her needs, I wanted her to do it. I was looking at the work; the task was very easy, it was easy to do. Of course, if she is a special needs girl, it is obviously not the same as a normal child. She did not know how to do it, and I wanted her to do it, and she did not know. No matter how many different ways I explained it, she did not get it. Until I got worn out, and it was then that I hit her, twice, with a stick that was here at home. That's why I hit her.

When the school called CPS, I did not know about it. Instead the teacher herself called me saying, "I called CPS and you are going to get a visit." In just a few words, the teacher prepared me, in case I did not know how this happened and what to expect. They came from CPS, they went through everything in the house. I was upset, not with the teacher, rather, I was upset with the school. Because I believe that first, they should have called me and asked me why the girl had a bruise and how it occurred. They knew I made this mark, obviously, because nobody else could have done it other than me. But I believed, and I still believe, that first they have to call the parents and ask, "Why did this injury happen?" before calling CPS.

I was not upset with the teacher, on the contrary, we built a very good relationship, but I stepped away from the school. I stopped attending activities and most events because I was upset with the school, with the principal, and with the teacher's aide. It's my understanding that she had a lot to do with this. It seems that my daughter complained about the pain, she told Tina[3], and Tina took her to the nurse. Tina was the one who saw the mark. This is how I remember it. It was then that the decision was made to call CPS.

The truth is that it did scare me when the teacher told me that CPS was coming. I was very scared, I thought that the children were going to be taken from me. At that time, I already had two other children. I thought the children were going to be taken out of the house. There was a time when I also thought that maybe I was going to go to jail. But, yes, I got scared and panicked, because if the children were removed from the house, I started to think about where they would go, if they would have the right amenities. In other words, would the children be well-groomed, clean, well-fed, would they sleep well? Things like that. That's what I thought about in that situation. I really do not regret having hit my daughter, but I also don't think children should be beaten.

In this situation, I hit her because, while she is a special needs girl, I was frustrated. I wanted her to work according to normal children. It wasn't until later that I understood. When we took her to the doctor, I understood that the child had a learning delay, which I did not know. I knew that the girl was not well, but I did not know that she had a delay until the neurologist told me. Then I got control and I stopped getting frustrated.

I knew there were going to be consequences for hitting her. Yes, that the children had to be removed, that they were going to take them. I already had two more, and I even thought that maybe I would have to go to prison or, because of my immigration status at the time, I thought maybe I was going to be deported and separated from the children because they are citizens. After all this, I was having visitors coming to observe the children; they even had to go to the other girl's school—she was in kindergarten. They went there to observe her in the school; they had to talk to the staff. I realized this because later the kindergarten teacher would look at me like a strange creature.

The girls went to different schools, so they also went to check at the other girl's school. This was really terrible because Melody had just started; it was her first year of kindergarten. This was my introduction to that community. I also had a baby, Kevin. Having another girl around four or five years, and a special girl was frustrating. I wanted to tear my hair out. I did not have a babysitter; I did everything. I cleaned, cooked, and took care of the children. I had to wake them, I had to take them to school. Everything was me. Their dad helped, but not much. My parents lived with me, but they could not help much either; they worked all the time. It was one frustration after another, that's why I got to the point of hitting the girl.

I thought that what had happened in that episode was not me. I felt very bad—very stressed, because I was afraid that the children would be removed from my house. I wanted to kill myself because I felt very frustrated, stressed, and depressed—I felt cornered. I felt that everyone saw me as a bad mother, like the abusive mother. I felt that everyone pointed their finger at me, "That mother is an abuser." "That mother is a beater." I was this mother, that mother. There was a lot of social pressure, and pressure with the children, and pressure with the CPS. It was very overwhelming.

I expected to be told, "Look, why don't you work with the kids like this? Or help them in this way." Or that they would offer me help by naming a place where I would take her, so they could help her with certain things, like homework and school work. But no, there was none of that kind of help. The only help they gave me was that I had to go to family therapy. I went to family therapy at the family center with the children. That was the only help, but it really was not helpful because I had to go with all three kids. It was another task because I had to go alone with the three of them. We would go, and the children would fight and argue, and one could not even talk because there they were crying. It was another task and another frustration. So, for me, that was not help. I wanted help where, like I just mentioned, I could take Justine, where people who knew about her disability could help her and help me to help her. But no, there was no help like that.

I think they should have called me and asked what had happened. They could have told me, "Look, lady, the girl was beaten, we are informing you that it should not be like that, and for reasons of rules we have to call CPS and they will visit." I should've been informed. Another thing, that school was mostly being run by Latinos, Hispanics. Everyone knows that Latinos give spankings with this or that. La chancla voladora [*The flying flip flop*], they call it. They all knew that kind of upbringing. Why not tell me before? I can understand that if it were in another area where there are more Whites, whiter people, where they don't really use any of that, but it was a school run by Latinos, where they could have told me, "In our culture kids grow up like this, but know that in the United States things are different." But the children were told. They were told that if they were beaten, if they went to school bruised, they had to call the police. Now my son says, "You cannot hit me, you cannot touch me, because I'm going to call the police." Well, perfect.

AUGUST 2018

María

Since this happened, I have come to understand these events as a more systemic issue rather than just an incident experienced by Laura and me. This event had an impact on my entire life; the ripples extended farther than I could ever imagine. In many ways, it made me more critical in my work as a teacher and researcher, but also more understanding and forgiving as a friend, mother, and human being. For Laura, this was also a life changing event, but in very different ways, much of which I wouldn't know until I heard her version of the story later. In the years since this happened, I have come to realize that, for Laura, the fact that the school called child protective services without ever reaching out to her felt like a betrayal. In some ways, I shared that sentiment. Perhaps this is why I called her even though it was a professional risk.

According to the state of New York, all teachers are mandated reporters, and as mandated reporters they are:

> not required to notify the parents or other persons legally responsible either before or after your call to [Child Protective Services]. In fact, in some cases, alerting the parent may hinder the local CPS investigation and adversely affect its ability to assess the safety of the children. (Office of Children and Family Services, 2018)

However, this lack of a requirement for contact is often misunderstood, easily giving educators the impression that to contact the family is prohibited when it is, at most, discouraged. Like calls to CPS, the decision to contact a family should be made on a case by case basis (Monroe County Department of Human Services, 2018). In this case, notifying the parent did not change the outcome; CPS still conducted a home visit, still opened a case. What did change was Laura's ability to understand what was taking place and, in some ways, emotionally prepare for what would be coming. The lack of communication also led to a breakdown in her relationship with the school, which, arguably, resulted in more harm than good.

My conversations with Laura have revealed to me the ways in which ideas of normalcy and disability impact a mother's ability to parent their child. Even though Justine had been in special education since kindergarten, it was not until Laura met with a neurologist when Justine was in 5th grade that she felt she had confirmation that Justine was cognitively different. At no point in her journey through special education had anyone taken the time to explain to Laura how Justine learned, what this would look like at home, or how this would shape her role as a mother. We had failed to offer her support or even information, yet we were quick to call her out in a manner that felt menacing and retaliatory.

As a teacher in NYC, I understood that I was a mandated reporter. In graduate school, I had been trained to look for signs of abuse and learned the procedures to follow if I suspected a child was being abused. Teachers all over the country are tasked with this momentous responsibility (Monroe County Department of Human Services, 2018; Office of Children and Family Services, 2018; Pervall, 2012). Failing to report can have grave consequences for both the child and the mandated reporter (Palusci, Datner, & Wilkins, 2015; Schottelkotte, 2018). Perhaps it is because of these potential consequences that most of the existing research around the involvement of child protective services relates much more to teacher training and underrepresentation than the effects that calling CPS have on a family (Fuller & Nieto, 2014; Perrigo, Berkovits, Cederbaum, Williams, & Hurlburt, 2018). But, as I now know, the call is not as detached of an event as it may seem to the caller.

In reality, the school did not serve as Laura's community; instead, it represented the dominant culture which makes and enforces rules about which parenting practices are acceptable and which are "barbaric." Automatically calling CPS does not take into account cultural and social nuances that may exist. Perhaps it is these nuances that made me hesitant to call, like it does so many others (McTavish *et al.*, 2017). Or, perhaps, it was because I understood that this space was serving as yet another school to prison pipeline, one that extended beyond students and sought to punish, rather than rehabilitate, parents (Clifford & Silver-Greenberg, 2018; Meiners & Tolliver, 2016; Sherer, 2011).

CPS exists for a multitude of reasons, but its primary mission is to protect children. While this mission is meaningful and necessary, we must remember that children are parts of family units and that abuses, as well as those acts deemed abusive, are often a call for help. Society, and schools in particular, should offer that help, not just to the child, but also to the families—especially the mothers. Individuals who are labeled as abusers are often mothers who may need help in learning new ways to cope with stressors and to seek support before an episode occurs. Without judgment and without labels. Mothers of children with disabilities already manage so many labels, they don't need another. What they need, and are likely to welcome, is support and guidance from their communities.

I still recall the episode as one of those moments in my life that defined my career and brought me to where I have arrived. Perhaps, more importantly, this has allowed me to be more generous, not only with how I view other mothers, but also how I view myself.

In the end, I found a deep and lasting connection with the family. That has been good for me, and I also think it was a good thing for my relationship with Justine. In those first years after this happened, we spent a lot of time together until I felt that things were more stable, that the whole family was well. And it was not only for Justine, I knew that it also helped Laura. Over the years, Laura and I have shared holidays and big family events, we've cared for each other when we got sick, and supported each other when we encountered major life changes. And sometimes, on lazy afternoons, we call each other when we just need to talk to a friend.

AUGUST 2018

Laura

There is no good mother. No—yes, there are good mothers, but there are no bad mothers. If a mother hits, spanks, scolds, or whatever, for me, that mother does it because she cares about us and because she loves us. But a bad mother, for me, does not exist. I do not see it that way because moms are always scolding and nagging, but they always do it to help us be better.

If I had hit my kids in the ways that my parents beat me, well, not my parents, my mom, because the one who hit was my mom, not my dad. My dad was more, "They are girls, leave them, they are tiny, leave them," and my mother said, "No, what girls?" She hit me a lot. That was her way to correct, to educate—to beat me. I have experienced everything. I tasted the belt, stick, flip flop, spoon, the ladle; my mom hit with whatever she found—extension cords, branch, a stick. If she was in the kitchen and I did something wrong, boom, I'd get hit with the spoon. When she would throw something, I would run away. I do not know how that lady did it, but she was a good marksman. It was actually pretty funny, in a way.

I am not raising my children in the way I was raised. Not with blows. I was beaten often and harshly. After going through that with my mom, when I became a mother, when my first daughter was born, I said, I was not going to beat them.

I do not want the same story to be repeated. However, it does bother me that the city gets involved in the way I raise my children. On several occasions, I wanted to shake the woman from CPS, lash out at her, release my rage, my frustration. Ask why they come to check me out, come and see me. I made a mistake, but I am still trying to do what is best for my children. The CPS visits were a headache. It felt super unfair. From then on, every time my youngest misbehaves, he says, "You cannot touch me." But that's not true. The social worker said, "It's not that you cannot hit them, you can hit them. But you can only hit them with an open hand, with the palm of your hand, it has to be open. It cannot be with any object other than with the hand, you cannot use a shoe, you cannot use a stick, nothing, but with your hand you can hit them." So, I tell them, "The woman says I can spank you, and that I can spank you this way, with an open hand. The worker told me that I could." They don't believe me. So, I told her, "Before you leave, explain that to them. Tell them." Do you think she told them? She only said what was good for her. She never supported me in front of my children. She only criticized me.

Ultimately, I feel frustrated, and it bothers me because I am trying to get my children to walk on a straight line. And it's not that I want to go around hitting them, but there are episodes in which, at one point, they should be punished. You know, before this, I had never hit them. The episode that happened with Justine, it was a totally different situation than my upbringing. Imagine this: when you are pregnant, and a baby is coming, you do not know what you are going to have, if it's going to be a boy or a girl. I wanted a boy; the father wanted a girl. Obviously, a girl was born. As a mother, you dream and hope a lot for them. When my daughter was born, I wanted her to go to school, go to college, be a professional. I didn't exactly want her to be everything I wasn't, but I did want her to be afforded every opportunity that I was denied. I didn't care if she wanted to be a dancer, if she wanted to be a teacher or whatever, but at the very least, I wanted my daughter to graduate high school and go to college. Unfortunately, it's not like that. I do not regret having my daughter, nor do I think longingly about what could've been. I have always loved her, regardless of her condition. Everyone knows it, and everyone sees it.

Yes, there was a time when I felt sorry for myself because I saw that the other children would try to play with her—I would see them try to talk to her and she couldn't keep up, she couldn't respond. Slowly, the children would move away from her, they would go play with the other children, the ones who did not have a disability, kids who weren't like her. Of course, I felt bad, sometimes I would call her over, "Come here, don't play there anymore."

So, yes, years ago, up until like five years ago, so not long ago at all, I did feel very upset with society, with the way society treated her and me because I have a disabled daughter. I felt shame, I was embarrassed to say, "My daughter has a disability." I was ashamed to say, "My daughter is retarded." It sounds awful, but it is a word that cost me a lot to say and speak it: retarded. But now, if I go somewhere, I say, "my girl is disabled." If I'm asked, "what kind of disability?" I say, "My daughter has mental retardation[4], she listens poorly, she is mentally delayed." Before it was like a taboo to say, "mental retardation." It was very heavy for me to say that word, it taxed me, I did not want to say it. Not anymore though, because now if I go out, and someone asks or anything, or if the girl is this or that, I simply say my girl has the mind of an eight or nine-year-old child, and she has a diagnosis of mental retardation. My child did not change, but I did. A few years ago, I started going to therapy on my own. Going to individual therapy, telling my therapist the situation, the problems, my feelings about everything. The therapist taught me how to manage, how to cope, and how to deal with the community out there, on the street, how to manage it. It was how everything changed—with therapy.

Before therapy, I worried that if I acknowledged that my girl has mental retardation everyone was going to point at me, they are going to reject me, they were going to reject her. Some people still reject us, some still look and point. I can understand being stared at by children—they are children, they do not know, but I cannot understand the staring that comes from adults. It's the adults who still look at her like a thing—a thing they reject. Still, with children, they do not understand, but they would if the parents explained things to them. When that happens, I think "how ignorant." For me, these people are ignorant, and maybe I'm seeing it like that because of my daughter. I also try to put myself in the role of those people, what would happen if I did not have a daughter like this? Would I be the same? Would it be like I am now? I ask myself those questions. See, there are so many pressures, so many things to worry about.

Yet, even with all this pressure, I try to be different than my mother. Even after this episode, I tried to ensure that my relationship with Justine grew stronger. After I hit her, I asked her forgiveness. That same day after I hit her, all afternoon I apologized because it was the first time I hit her. That same day, I apologized. From then on, to this date, I have apologized whenever I can. For this reason, the relationship between Justine and I have not changed. It has strengthened. I see that it grows stronger. I apologized.

No, for me there's no such thing as a bad mother. I had a bad moment, but I am not a bad mother.

OCTOBER 2018

We close this chapter with two letters for Justine, one from Laura and one from me—María. We wrote these letters with the intention of giving them to her in the future. We wrote these letters because we know that one day Justine may become a mother. We wrote them because one day she may come face to face with her own stressors, difficult decisions, and conversations, and even errors in judgment. In those moments, we want her to know she's not alone.

Figure 8.1. A letter from Mami.

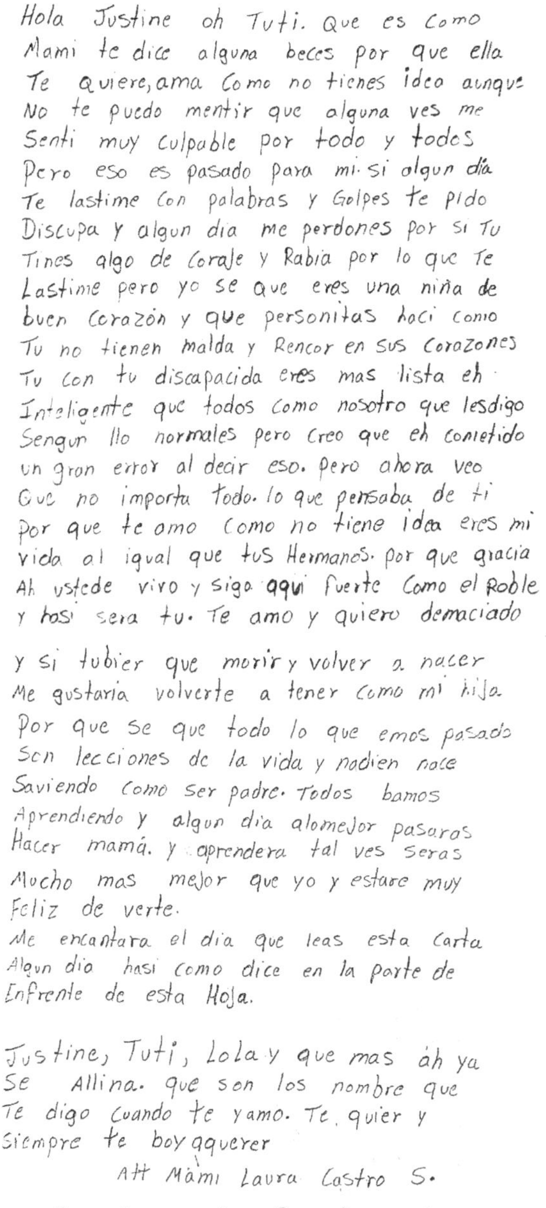

Hola Justine oh Tuti. Que es como
Mami te dice alguna beces por que ella
Te Quiere, ama Como no tienes ideo aunque
No te puedo mentir que alguna ves me
Senti muy Culpable por todo y todos
Pero eso es pasado para mi·si algun día
Te lastime Con palabras y Golpes te pido
Discupa y algun dia me perdones por si Tu
Tines algo de Coraje y Rabia por lo que Te
Lastime pero yo se que eres una niña de
buen Corazón y que personitas hoci Como
Tu no tienen malda y Rencor en sus Corazones
Tu Con tu discapacida eres mas lista eh
Inteligente que todos Como nosotro que lesdigo
Sengun llo normales pero Creo que eh cometido
un gran error al decir eso. pero ahora veo
Que no importa todo. lo que pensaba de ti
Por que te amo Como no tiene idea eres mi
vida al igual que tus Hermanos. por que giacia
Ah ustede vivo y sigo aqui fuerte Como el Roble
y hasi sera tu. Te amo y quiero demaciado

y si tubier que morir y volver a nacer
Me gustaria volverte a tener Como mi hija.
Por que se que todo lo que emos pasado
Son lecciones de la vida y nadien nace
Saviendo Como ser padre. Todos bamos
Aprendiendo y algun dia alomejor pasaras
Hacer mamá. y aprendera tal ves seras
Mucho mas mejor que yo y estare muy
Feliz de verte.
Me encantara el dia que leas esta Carta
Algun dia hasi Como dice en la parte de
Enfrente de esta Hoja.

Justine, Tuti, Lola y que mas ah ya
Se Allina. que son los nombre que
Te digo Cuando te yamo. Te quier y
Siempre te boy aquerer
            Att Mami Laura Castro S.

Source: Personal property, Laura Castro Santamaría.

Hello Justine,
Or Tuti, which is how Mommy calls you sometimes because she loves you. You have no idea how much I love you.
I cannot deny this to you, I feel very guilty for everything that happened. But, that is in the past for me. If I ever hurt you with words and blows, I apologize. If you still carry some anger and rage from when I hurt you, I hope one day you can forgive me.
Still, I know that you are a good-hearted girl and that young people like you do not have malice and resentment in their hearts. You, with your disability, are smart, and smarter than us "normals." I think I've even made a big mistake in saying it in that way. I hope you can see that it does not matter what I thought of you and your disability, because I love you more than you can ever know.
You are my life, just like your siblings. Thanks to you all I live, and remain, as strong as the oak, and one day you will be too. I love you so much and if I had to die and be born again, I would like to have you as my daughter again, because I know that everything we have gone through are lessons in life and nobody is born knowing how to be a mother. We are all learning. Someday, maybe you will become a mom and you will learn. Maybe you'll be much better than me. I'll be very happy to see that.
I look forward to that day and the day you read this letter.
Justine, tuti, Lola, and every other nickname I've given you, I love you, and I will always love you.

Attention, your Mama,
Laura Castro S.[5]

* * *

Querida Agustinita,
What a wonder it has been to see you grow from a rambunctious little girl to a caring, generous and independent adult.
I know that over the years you have had to witness and endure many difficult situations. I know that over the years, you have struggled to understand your mother while navigating your own introduction to womanhood. I also know that you've probably had a hard time understanding your mom throughout this time.
I was once a young girl who questioned her mother's choices, and at times felt like everything was a haze. Then one day I became a mom and I understood life so much better than when I was younger. Justine, being a mother is so, so hard. It is a beautiful experience, but it doesn't always feel like that. Sometimes it feels overwhelming, lonely and like a burden. For some moms those days are few and far between, but for others they are more regular and that can be hard—on everyone.
As a first-time mom, you have no idea what you are doing, and, in some ways, the oldest child often pays the price for that naiveté. But, have no doubt that you and me and Emiliano, the first-born children, are, and have always been, deeply loved. That love

may not always come through in the manner we would prefer but it is no less potent. We first-time mothers are just trying to do the best we can.

One of the greatest joys of motherhood for me has been my ability to connect with my own mother in ways that I never could have otherwise. I hope that one day you are blessed with the opportunity to mother another being (whether that be a child is entirely up to you). I hope that in your own mothering you will be granted a bit of clarity into your mother's choices and are able to recognize that she was doing the best she could with what she had at the time. Any failings were not a reflection of her love for you, but rather, the life-altering power of motherhood. I hope that in this awareness you will also find space to forgive yourself and atone at those moments when you inevitably let yourself or that being down. Lastly, I'm sorry that I haven't been able to be as active in your life as when you were younger. Part of the reason is because my children are very young and mothering them is all-encompassing, part of it is the physical distance between us. But mostly, it's because you don't need me like you used to, and that is a wonderful thing. Just remember that if you ever you do, I am always just one call away :)

Se te quiere de sobras,
  Ms. Peña

NOTES

1. In hindsight, what I do as a teacher has everything to do with me as person and vice versa, but this made sense at the time and more importantly, it's what I needed to hear in that moment.
2. The recollections were originally orally recorded in Spanish, then translated to English and edited for clarity by María and confirmed with Laura. The content is unchanged, as is the sequence of presentation.
3. Name changed to maintain privacy.
4. While the term Intellectual Disability has officially replaced the use of "mental retardation (MR)" within the United States and other western countries, MR remains the common term of use within Spanish-speaking communities both inside and outside of the United States.
5. Translated and edited for clarity by María Cioè-Peña.

REFERENCES

Clifford, S., & Silver-Greenberg, J. (2018). Foster care as punishment: The new reality of "Jane Crow." *The New York Times.* Retrieved from https://www.nytimes.com/2017/07/21/nyregion/foster-care-nyc-jane-crow.html

Fuller, T., & Nieto, M. (2014). Child welfare services and risk of child maltreatment rereports: Do services ameliorate initial risk? *Children and Youth Services Review, 47,* 46–54. doi:10.1016/j.childyouth.2013.11.015

McTavish, J. R., Kimber, M., Devries, K., Colombini, M., MacGregor, J. C. D., Wathen, C. N., … MacMillan, H. L. (2017). Mandated reporters' experiences with reporting child maltreatment: A meta-synthesis of qualitative studies. *BMJ Open,* 7(10). http://dx.doi.org/10.1136/bmjopen-2016-013942

Meiners, E., & Tolliver, C. (2016). Refusing to be complicit in our prison nation: Teachers rethinking mandated reporting. *Radical Teacher,* 106, 106–114. http://dx.doi.org/10.5195/rt.2016.286

Monroe County Department of Human Services. (2018). *Should I tell the family?* Do Right by Kids. Retrieved from https://www.dorightbykids.org/how-do-i-call-in-a-report/should-i-tell-the-family/

Office of Children and Family Services. (2018). *Summary guide for mandated reporters in New York State.* Retrieved from https://ocfs.ny.gov/main/publications/Pub1159.pdf

Palusci, V. J., Datner, E., & Wilkins, C. (2015). Developmental disabilities: Abuse and neglect in children and adults. *International Journal of Child Health and Human Development, 8*(4), 407–428.

Perrigo, J. L., Berkovits, L. D., Cederbaum, J. A., Williams, M. E., & Hurlburt, M. S. (2018). Child abuse and neglect re-report rates for young children with developmental delays. *Child Abuse & Neglect, 83,* 1–9. doi:10.1016/j.chiabu.2018.05.029

Pervall, H. J. (2012). *Reporting child abuse and neglect: Aspects and summaries of state laws.* New York, NY: Nova Science Publishers.

Schottelkotte, S. (2018). Former school administrator pleads, gets probation for not reporting abuse. *The Ledger.* Retrieved from https://www.theledger.com/news/20180914/former-school-administrator-pleads-gets-probation-for-not-reporting-abuse

Sherer, I. (2011). Oh, my father hit me. *Health Affairs, 30*(7), 1382–1385.

CHAPTER 9

The Strange Case OF THE Two Journals

Ableism, Academia, and the Birth of a Child

PRIYA LALVANI

May 18th, 1995
It's a sunny Thursday morning. After twenty-eight hours in labor, I look down at the tiny little girl in my arms. So small and so beautiful. She has dark hair and perfect little fingers and toes. She has brown eyes. She also has Down syndrome.

January 24th, 2002
Minal is one week old today… After it was confirmed that she has Down syndrome, I didn't react very much. Why did I not? I still have a beautiful little girl. But life is never going to be the same.

These are entries from my two journals, written seven years apart, each providing a snapshot of a mother's reflections after the birth of a child—more specifically, a daughter diagnosed with Trisomy 21, or Down syndrome. The journals go on to document events and interactions following the birthing of these two daughters. However, as those who know me might point out, I have *one* daughter (and also, one son). And yet, there are two journals about becoming a mother to two daughters with Down syndrome.

I should explain. When I wrote the first journal in 1995, I had *not* actually given birth to a child with Down syndrome (or any child at all). Rather, the first excerpt above is taken from an entry in a "mock journal"—an assignment I completed for a graduate course in special education in which I was enrolled at the time. I had entered the program with several years of experience as a therapist working with adolescents and young adults with intellectual and developmental disabilities and their families. However, I had never met a baby with Down syndrome or a mother of a newborn child with a disability. Perhaps the course assignment originated from this (correct) assumption and, I can surmise, my professor's aim was to raise awareness among future professionals through this "simulation" activity. Imagining ourselves to be new mothers of babies born with disabilities (*"any* disability," we were instructed), we were to engage in journaling for the duration of the semester and through it, narrate our stories. Specifically, we were to document what we might experience, how we might react, and what actions we might take after the birthing of our imaginary children. Choosing Down syndrome as the diagnosis, I recall I embarked on the task enthusiastically; I was eager to demonstrate all that I had learned through my prior professional background and training.

On January 17th, 2002, almost seven years later, I did indeed birth a daughter on a sunny Thursday morning. This daughter, too, like the imaginary one, was diagnosed shortly after her birth with Trisomy 21. My husband, then four-year-old son, and I welcomed the new member of our family. A week after her birth, I put pen to paper and began documenting my emotions and the events that transpired, attempting to make sense of them. And so, for the second time in my life, I found myself narrating a story about the birth of a child with Down syndrome—albeit this time, a rather different story.

In referring to the two journals, it is tempting to designate the course assignment as the "fake" journal, and second one as the "real" journal. However, I will resist this urge, not only because it would be reductive but also because it would not be an accurate delineation. Although, clearly, only one of these journals reflects my lived experiences, I will steer away from calling that one "real" because, like all personal narratives, it represents subjective interpretations of events and interactions that occurred. To be fair, the experiences described in both journals are, in varying degrees, embedded in constructed notions of disability and shaped by dominant culture. Therefore, making no claims to any truths about the ways in which mothers experience the birth of a child with a disability, and rejecting notions about the universality of this experience, I will henceforth simply refer to the two documents as journal #1 (the course assignment) and journal #2 (my personal reflections after the birth of my daughter).

WHY REVISIT OLD JOURNALS? WHY NOW?

One might wonder why I felt the need, so many years later, to revisit the two stories of motherhood I had once told in order to tell this third one. By way of explanation and to be transparent about my stake in this project, I'd like to offer some further personal contexts. I am, among many other things, a mother, a disability studies scholar, and a teacher educator. These identities are interconnected, and, for me, these roles are inextricably linked. Much of my scholarly work has been focused on exploring the experiences of parents of children with disabilities and the ways in which these are represented and studied (see for example: Lalvani, 2011, 2014; Lalvani & Polvere, 2013). In my own teaching, I place strong emphasis on questioning assumptions about various groups of families and I aim to draw critical attention to ableist cultural narratives about parents and siblings of children with disabilities. However, since coursework related to families of children with disabilities is commonly offered (and often a requirement) within many special education and other professional certification programs in the US, I have frequently found myself curious about how this group becomes positioned in the discourses of higher education. How, for example, through the stated objectives of specific courses, their assignments and their activities, do assumptions about disability and parents of children with disabilities become reified? Would the "knowledge" that is reproduced within these spaces resonate with the narratives of family members themselves? These are some questions which drove me to unearth the two forgotten journals; I hoped that I might find within their texts some answers.

The story I tell here is informed by disability studies (DS) perspectives that frame disability as a socio-politically constructed phenomenon. DS is concerned with the removal of attitudinal and environmental barriers faced by people with disabilities (Hahn, 1997; Linton, 1998). In other words, rather than focusing on the impact of impairments per se, DS focuses its gaze on the impact of *ableism*—the persistent devaluing of people with disabilities in society or viewpoints in which disability is cast as an inherently undesirable state of being (Campbell, 2009). Additionally, I utilize the theoretical lenses of social constructionism (Gergen, 1985) and discourse analysis (Bruner, 1990), both of which reject the notion that stories merely recount events or transmit a set of existing realities, viewing them instead as social devices through which meaning unfolds (Bamberg, 2004). With these conceptual tools, I set out to explore the constructed meaning of disability in society through a juxtaposition of two stories of motherhood: the first, a story entrenched in the public imagination and in the institutional discourses of special education, and the second, a story of my lived experience.

THE LIFE OF MY STORY

Through the stories we tell, we make meaning of our lives and of the world around us (McAdams, 2008). However, life stories do not exist in a vacuum; they reflect cultural values and power differentials in societies. A story about the birth of a child with a disability cannot be understood without first gaining an understanding of the attitudes towards disability and the expectations of motherhood that exist in a given society. To this end, I offer my own story about becoming a mother to a child with a disability as a means to explore the ways in which this experience is situated in cultural and institutional discourses and practices.

Ellis (2004) aptly stated that the difficult part of doing an autoethnography is the feeling of vulnerability; the process often displays hidden aspects of intimate and personal life, highlights emotions laid bare, opens one up to judgments, and threatens to change the present narrative. Thus, I was forewarned that revisiting my journals for the purpose of this project would not be without emotional perils. Still, I was curious about the extent to which the narrative I had generated for the benefit of my professor's approval bore resemblance to my actual experiences. Throughout the process, it was necessary to remain grounded in an understanding that, ultimately, narrative research and autoethnography is interpretive work. Hence, I explicitly acknowledge that my analysis of my past experiences is done through the subjective lens of my present identity. This is *my story of* my story.

UNQUESTIONED ASSUMPTIONS OF "GRIEF"

In my own body of scholarly work, I have made the claim that cultural master narratives on the birth of a child with a disability center on themes of grief, loss, burden, and "tragedy" (Lalvani, 2014; Lalvani & Polvere, 2013). Clearly, I had a stake in what my two journals would reveal about this. It came as no surprise that accounts of sadness, depression, and anger are interjected throughout journal #1. In this document, references to "grief" are hardly subtle. In fact, the paper is conceptually framed, in its entirety, within Kubler-Ross' (1969) stage theory of grief. In her extensive work on death and dying, Kubler-Ross explicated that individuals generally move through five stages (denial, anger, bargaining, depression, and acceptance) in their process of grieving. Although her theory focused more specifically on the psychological processing of death or a terminal illness, over time, mental health professionals have applied this theory erroneously to individuals' reactions to other forms of loss, which is to say, situations that are socio-culturally interpreted as a loss.

The story that unfolds in journal #1 follows a linear trajectory wherein I, the hypothetical mother, find myself going through each of the five stages in Kubler-Ross' model. These excerpts taken from various entries in it illustrate:

May 25th, 1995
The fact that my child has a disability seems unreal. This could not be happening to me. Maybe it's a mistake. I keep waiting for someone to say they made an error.... Once she starts growing, the doctors will see that they were wrong.

June 18th, 1995
I'm angry at the doctors and I get a different story from each of them.... I'm angry at my mother.... I'm angry at the world.... Most of all I'm angry at myself.

July 9th, 1995
As the days go by, I feel less angry. Now it's an overwhelming depression that has taken over. It's hard to get anything done. Even the task of taking care of my daughter seems like an ordeal.

August 4th, 1995
I am not a religious person, but lately I find myself praying often, bargaining with god.

Sept. 15th, 1995
I look down at the little girl in my arms. The anger and sadness of past months has subsided. In its place, there is hope. Once again, I notice how beautiful she is.

I cringe (more than a little) when reading this document I produced to fulfill the requirements of a graduate course 23 years ago. The unidimensional, cliché-filled narrative in which the mother trudges from one stage of grief to the next, arriving finally at "hope," is reductive. The mother in this tale is rendered a caricature. The only defense I can hope to claim is that, as I recall, my aim was to do well on the assignment and I had intuited that framing the paper in grief theory would constitute the *correct* approach—one that would satisfy the criteria for this academic exercise and demonstrate my understanding of the course content. To that end, it seems I was successful; I note, with irony, that I received an excellent grade for this assignment. Yet it is alarming that, as a professional who worked with families of children with disabilities at the time, I had approached this assignment through medical model perspectives in which disability is viewed as an unequivocal tragedy—the kind of thinking I have since critiqued as being deeply problematic.

None of this, however, is surprising. Grounded in grief theory, the framing of the birth of a child with a disability as a profound loss has been a mainstay in the professional discourses of mental health, rehabilitation, social work, and special education for decades (Ferguson & Ferguson, 2006). Although journal #1 was written 23 years ago and therefore one might (rightfully) question its relevance for more current times, it is worth noting that professionals continue to be indoctrinated to expect that parents of children with disabilities may mourn the loss of the "perfect child" after their initial "denial" of their child's disability; these ideas are explicitly communicated through literature targeted to pre-service professionals (e.g., Gorman, 2004; Kroth & Edge, 2007; Seligman & Darling, 2009). In a recent study in which I examined teachers' beliefs about families of children with disabilities, I found the language of tragedy, burden, denial, and loss to be pervasive (Lalvani, 2015).

Okay, I'll admit, journal #1 is an easy target. Perhaps it might be more relevant to ask whether grief had characterized my lived experiences. I had known from the beginning of this project that an interrogation of my personal narrative would be the far harder task, and hence, it was with trepidation that I dusted off journal #2, hoping fervently that it did not contain accounts of sadness. It did.

January 24th, 2002
Feeling overwhelmed. And have had a sense of depression hanging over my head all day. Today the sun did not shine. And no visitors today. I have been depressed and weepy.

Similar to the entry above, journal #2 has several others in which I express my initial feelings of melancholy, my confusion, and my fears about the future. However, the negative feelings described, even in the earliest entries of this journal, are more nuanced and simultaneously accompanied by a conflicting internal dialogue. For instance, within the same entry as the one above, I write this about my reaction to hearing the diagnosis from the geneticist:

January 24th, 2002
Were we devastated? I'm not sure I was. I don't feel devastated. I feel as if I should, though.

And, on another day:

February 22nd, 2002
Why do I not feel more upset than I do? Why do I not feel angrier, more devastated, and more distraught? Why does it not matter as much as it should? Am I denying? Am I pretending?

It seems my reactions were inconsistent with my expectations about how I "should" have been reacting; in these entries, I express surprise that I don't feel *enough* negative emotions. Indoctrinated as I was in medical model perspectives through my professional training, in this entry, I question whether my lack of sufficient distress might signal that I am in denial. I second-guess my own feelings in the absence of any sense of the "devastation" which I believed "should" characterize my experience.

In journal #2, the stages of grief do not play out; they are largely absent from the narrative. Although there are certainly accounts of negative emotions, confusion, and frustration in this narrative, they are not the overriding emotions and they do not define the story as they do in journal #1. Other parts of this story include many accounts of joy and the more mundane aspects of parenting, both of which were entirely unaccounted for in journal #1.

CONTEXTUALIZING "GRIEF"

November 11th, 2004
All the moms in the moms-group said they cried when they heard the news. Everyone in that group thinks you're supposed to! When Minal was born, I just didn't feel like that would be right. I mean, ethically. Because it would be an injustice or an insult to my daughter. I would need to know what I was crying about. And I didn't.

In a vast body of research on parents' experiences of the birth or diagnosis of a child with a disability, there is one common finding: parents report an initial reaction of shock or profound sadness (e.g., Douglas, 2014; Goff *et al.*, 2013; Lalvani, 2011). As Piepmeier (2012) points out, even in published memoirs of the parents themselves, narratives of initial grief and despair are pervasive and often a defining aspect. Although the experience of "grief" in response to a child's diagnosis of disability is well researched, less explored are the sociocultural contexts in which the grief is situated; less examined are the institutional discourses and practices which implicitly (or explicitly) communicate that grief is indeed an expected and appropriate response. Perhaps, then, instead of focusing on the question of *whether* parents grieve, we might turn our gaze to the sociocultural environment and ask a different question: If a parent experiences negative emotions in response to a diagnosis of disability, to *what* is the grief attributed? *Where* is the source of that grief?

Journal #1 seems to be clear on this issue: the mother's grief is the result of the diagnosis of Down syndrome per se and the negative outcomes that are expected to ensue from it. Here, the "problem" is attributed solely to the impairments of the child. In various entries in this journal, I make assumptions that my life will be extremely hard. I imagine that I will no longer be able to have a career and that my child will be constantly sick. The mother at the center of this tale seems to have an ongoing preoccupation with the ways in which caring for a child with a disability is an unrelentingly worrisome, anxiety-filled, and difficult endeavor.

July 29th, 1995
She is so fragile, and I worry constantly that she will get hurt or sick.

In traditional research, which seeks to examine stress among families of children with disabilities, the source of parents' stress is assumed to result solely from their children's impairments, leaving ableism in the environment largely unquestioned; issues related to access, inclusivity, and stigma are generally not acknowledged as stressors (for a full discussion, see: Lalvani & Polvere, 2013). Mirroring these dominant views, in journal #1, the difficulties anticipated by my alter ego are assumed to reside in the child. There is little indication in this document that, as a graduate student enrolled in a course that aimed to explore parents' perspectives, I had developed any understanding of the ways in which the stressors associated with mothering a child with Down syndrome might also be located in oppressive discourses about normative motherhood or in the stigmatized position that disability occupies in society (Fine and Asch, 1998). Nor is there indication of awareness that the way in which a diagnosis of disability is communicated by medical professionals might also shape a mother's experience. Instead, the unquestioned belief that a child with a disability represents profound loss is reified and institutionally sanctioned through my engagement in this academic activity and through the highly positive feedback I received for it.

The entries in journal #2 tell a different story. Here, from the very first hours after the birth of my daughter, I seem less concerned with the diagnosis per se, and more concerned with the meaning ascribed to it. I am hyper-focused on the ways in which those around me are reacting to my daughter's birth. In entry after entry, I've documented every glance averted from me, every furrowing of the brow, and every message of condolence I received.

January 24th, 2002
People's reactions have been interesting! I've made mental notes of how each person re-
sponded. Norman and I don't like it when people say, "I'm sorry." Or, "I'm SO sorry!" I
know they're taken by surprise. They don't know what to say. They mean well. But I'm
getting tired of "I'm so sorry." I'm getting tired of saying to them (or thinking): Don't be
sorry!!

It is worth noting that in journal #2, there are multiple entries about my interactions with my obstetrician following the birth. In these, I reflect on her affect, which I interpret to be one of sadness or discomfort, and her body language, which I interpret as conveying regret. I write that I am perplexed, irritated, and, at some level, wounded by what I perceive to be her appraisal of the birth of my daughter as a negative event—an event that could have been prevented. I make note of her genuine efforts to be kind to me, which I understand to be well-intentioned but resulting from her feelings of sympathy.

March 1st, 2002
Had appointment with Dr. M. today… The last time I saw her was in the delivery room.
Today, again, she looked as if she felt really badly for what happened. She spent extra time
with me, to be kind. I wanted to say: "It's okay! Really."

April 5th, 2002
At hospital, I ran into Dr. M. When she saw me, she looked so saddened. Why?! Again, I
felt like I wanted to assure her: "It's really okay! I'm quite happy at this moment. And I'm
happy to see you!"

The doctor is not the only one with whose reactions I was concerned. In journal #2, there are multiple entries that describe interactions with family members, friends, neighbors, and co-workers. In attempting to make sense of my experiences, I sought to understand how others interpreted Minal's birth. If there is one thing that journal #2 confirms unequivocally, it is this: acts of meaning-making do not take place in a social vacuum.

February 2nd, 2002
Today went out for errands and was at Sobsey's Market. Was really annoyed when Jake,
and also the Millers, did not congratulate me about the baby! Maybe they forgot?? But
now a thought has occurred to me. Did they deliberately not mention it? Because they did

not know what to say? It makes me annoyed when people are awkward when I'm there, and they don't know what to say.

Journal #2 tells a story of motherhood in the context of a culture steeped in ableism. In this story, I am routinely informed by people that they can "hardly tell" or that "it's really not noticeable" that my baby has Down syndrome. Or that I must have been "chosen by god" to have this baby because most people could not "handle it." I am sometimes elevated to the status of a "saint" for being so "accepting" of "my new challenge." I soon come to understand that my membership to the constructed category of normative motherhood has been revoked. I'm no longer viewed as *just* a mother; I'm informed that I am a "special mother." Apparently, this special status entails being asked, relentlessly, if I knew about my daughter's diagnosis prenatally. And when I answer: "No, I did not," it often entails being confronted outright. "Why?!" they ask. "Why would you choose *not* to find out," they remark in puzzlement. Surely, other *choices* could have been made, they suggest. The implications of these remarks were not missed by me. The value of the existence of my daughter was in question.

July 12th, 2002
Okay, so there are those who think it's not worth bringing her into the world, those who do, and those who fall somewhere in the middle. I know it's not that simple. And maybe I'm being too harsh. But I just need to know. I'm confused. When they tell me they would not choose to give birth to a child with a disability if they knew beforehand, then are they saying Minal doesn't need to exist? Or that they don't understand why she exists?

As time goes by, the constant interrogations of my reproductive decisions turn into more explicit statements in which friends and acquaintances inform me outright that they would make very different decisions if they were in a similar situation. In these interpersonal exchanges, I am positioned as having made an irrational choice and my daughter is positioned as an undesirable kind of child.

June 11th, 2004
Alina called to say she found out she might be carrying a fetus with a possible birth defect, and basically straightforward said that she's going to end her pregnancy if that is the case. It's been 3 weeks since she told me this and it's still hard for me to think about it… I'm trying to be a good friend to her at this time. Not sure why it was so hard for me to hear it. It's not really news to me. Most of my friends have already made this clear- that this is the choice they'd make.

Many scholars who explored the psychological and cultural impact of prenatal genetic testing have asserted that the pervasive routinization of this technology alters expectations of motherhood and constructs negative meanings of disability (Parens & Asch, 2000; Rapp, 2000; Rothman, 1993). In cultural discourses, mothers who could have "chosen" to avoid the birth of a child with a disability are either cast as having made an irresponsible decision or, alternatively, they are elevated to the status of "special" mothers who are "chosen by God to have special children" (Landsman, 1999, p. 136). Additionally, as Parens and Asch (2000) pointed out, mothers of children with disabilities (that can be detected prenatally) are among a unique group who often find themselves in the position of having to justify their choice to have their *particular* babies.

Many entries in journal #2 point to my increasing awareness of my motherhood as a stigmatized status. Goffman (1963) explained the concept of stigma as the marking of certain people, either physically or through psychological means, such that they can be identified as fundamentally different. By the time my daughter was a few months old, I start to sense that I am viewed as *other*. Although I am among people, I am no longer considered to be one of them.

July 12th, 2002
I feel as if I have suddenly moved to another planet and I need to understand where my new planet is, in relation to the universe.

Undeniably, culturally-constructed understandings about normative families shape the experience of the birth of a child with a disability. However, individuals are not passively influenced by their environments. Rather, when positioned negatively in social discourses, they can develop counter-narratives through which they reject dominant narratives and make sense of their experiences in alternative ways (Bamberg, 2004). In journal #2, I resist the assumptions which surround me. In my emerging counter-narrative, I rail against the discourses in which my motherhood is positioned as non-normative, and in which my daughter's personhood and value are questioned.

November 11th, 2003
I want to change everything about this picture. I want to rewrite the story! If I could just have a chance, I would rewrite the whole story. And in the new story, mothers would never be expected to feel "devastated," and they would never have to justify to anyone why they did not have an amnio.

Although both journals suggest an evolution in thinking over time—or a shift toward new interpretations of being a mother of a child with a disability, it is worth noting that the shifts described in each are vastly different in their nature. In journal #1, adhering strictly to the grief model in which the entire journal is theoretically framed, the mother advances through the various stages of grieving until she arrives at "acceptance." As such, this document conforms to, and reifies, clinical perspectives in which parents' coming to terms with the "reality" of their children's disabilities is indicative of a healthy outcome in a sequence of adjustment. Rooted in the medical model, here, disability is understood as an absolute category and the "acceptance" of it by parents, as the desired transformation.

In journal #2, the shift is not toward "acceptance of the disability," but rather, toward an increasing awareness and emerging critique of the pervasiveness of ableist beliefs and practices in society.

June 5th, 2003
Why is a prenatal diagnosis always followed immediately by presenting the options for ter-minating? Even worse, diagnosis after birth seems to throw the doctors for a loop! Dr. M. clearly viewed Minal's birth as some sort of failure to detect.

Additionally, in journal #2, there is also an increasing focus on what it means to live with a disability in an ableist world. In numerous entries, I express concerns re-lated to inclusivity and acceptance for my daughter in schools and in the community.

Feb. 25th, 2003
So much anxiety…Will Minal be accepted? Will kids and parents accept her? Will they play with her? Will they tease her? Will they include her?

This entry echoes the narratives of many other parents for whom the social implications of disability, specifically the possibility of social rejection of their chil-dren, is a significant concern (Lalvani, 2011). Often, for mothers, the "problems" related to a disability are not located within the bodies or minds of their children, but rather, within environments that are less than welcoming of individuals with disabilities. Indeed, mothering a child with a disability has much to do with navi-gating access, resisting stigma, and seeking (or creating) communities of belonging.

PROFESSIONAL AS *EXPERT* AND PARENT AS *PATHOLOGICAL*

Both journals contain many entries about interactions with professionals (spe-cifically physicians, social workers, or psychotherapists); however, there are vast differences with regard to the ways in which professionals are discussed in each. In journal #1, they are positioned as the *experts* who know all about disabilities, or as people who can ameliorate the many problems associated with having a child with a disability. In it, I express a belief that my own professional training will be an asset, making it easier for me to navigate the difficult tasks ahead.

August 28th, 1995
Working in the field of developmental disabilities has made me aware that caring for a child with a disability is not easy… I feel thankful for my training and knowledge in this area.

In the ableist tale that is journal #1, while representing professionals as capable and competent in their responses to children with disabilities, I simultaneously cast the mother as anxious, over-protective, irrationally fearful, and mistrustful of people handling her child.

July 29th, 1995
She seems so fragile and vulnerable and I worry constantly that she will get sick or hurt. I try to spend all my time with her and get anxious when she's with other people. She needs to be protected. I don't trust others around her and I don't like it when they hold her. They cannot understand how fragile she is.

Professionals have long operated from assumptions that the lives of families of children with disabilities are defined by immense stress and never-ending struggles, the source of which are located in children's impairments rather than in hostile environments or inaccessible, non-inclusive spaces. Additionally, as Valle (2009) noted, in professional discourses, mothers often become constructed as being too subjective or emotional, and, therefore, needing guidance by experts. These notions have their roots in early psychoanalytic training in which professionals were explicitly cautioned against engaging with parents of "troubled" children because it was believed that their irrationality, guilt, indulgence, or excessive demands would either interfere with children's treatment or cause children to retreat and become neurotic (Donner, 1986; Friesen & Koroloff, 1990). The legacy of these theories has endured; the belief that the judgement of parents of children with disabilities might be compromised by their feelings of grief or their "denial" of their children's disabilities continues to be a pervasive theme in professional discourses (Lalvani, 2015, 2017).

Journal #2 reveals a different story about family-professional interactions. Here, professionals are not positioned as experts. On the contrary, I express frustration over their lack of understanding about how to discuss disability and how to engage with families of children with disabilities. Their body language, affect, and language are identified in multiple entries as sources of my distress.

June 5th, 2003
I feel angry that medical professionals, doctors, hospital staff, are all ignorant about this. Why do they not receive training on how to deliver the news (about disability), how to follow up, how to talk to parents? …Hey, maybe there's a dissertation topic here!?

Mothers' early experiences of the birth of a child with a disability can be profoundly impacted by the language and actions of physicians and other professionals. In some studies, mothers reported that their physicians emphasized only the negative aspects of the child's disability, provided inaccurate and outdated information, or communicated notions of damage, stigma, and loss (Goff *et al.*, 2013; Lalvani, 2011; Skotko, 2005; Sooben, 2010). Yet, in cultural discourses and in traditional research literature, any stress that this group of parents may experience is believed to result from their children's impairment rather than from institutional practices that construct or reify their otherness. The "damage" is unquestioningly assumed to reside in the child; the damaging actions and inactions of professionals are left largely unexamined.

RIGHTING NARRATIVES

Through this autoethnography, I've interrogated the problematic assumptions I made as a young professional and graduate student, in an effort to answer a question I have often posed to students in my classes: What do professionals need to understand about families of children with disabilities? My experiences are not intended to represent those of all mothers of children with disabilities, nor do I speak for individuals with disabilities themselves. What then, if anything, can be gained from my story?

For one, perhaps it is time for professionals to retire the grief model as a default framework when seeking to understand the experiences of parents of children with disabilities. Instead, we need to acknowledge the full range of outcomes, perspectives, and interpretations of disability among this group of families. Responses to having a child with a disability are undoubtedly varied (and for some, it may include grief), but they are situated, as I came to understand, in the sociopolitical climates in which we exist. This conceptual shift is long overdue. Second, perhaps we need to ask some critical questions about the ways in which master narratives on disability are communicated, implicitly or explicitly, through language and coursework within particular academic disciplines. In teacher education, despite much interest in the topic of cultivating the dispositions of teacher candidates, there is little discussion on preparing teachers to recognize and disrupt ableism. Surely the "mock journal" assignment to which I have referred in this story, in which I was required to engage in "simulating" the experience of having a child with a disability, emerges as an example of the reproduction of ableism in higher education.

Disability simulation exercises in which people use blindfolds, a wheelchair, or other props in order to temporarily "put themselves in the shoes" of a person with a disability, have long been condemned by disability rights activists who assert that the implications of these are problematic, and the outcomes, misleading at best (Connor & Bejoian, 2007). These activities are objectionable not only because they fail to accurately simulate the lived experience of being disabled by leaving issues of segregation and discrimination unexamined, but also because they systematically reinforce negative stereotypes about disability and reify notions of pity (Brew-Parrish, 1997; Valle & Connor, 2011). Although disability rights activists and scholars have mounted an objection to disability simulations, there is no discussion in the literature about the negative implications of attempting to simulate, for educational purposes, the experiences of *parents* of children with disabilities. From my own engagement in such an exercise, I can say, unequivocally, that it taught me little. Even more troubling, however, is the fact that the exercise only served to reinforce problematic cultural narratives about children with disabilities as burdensome, and tropes about their mothers as irrational, distraught, trudging from one stage of grief to another—arriving, finally, at "acceptance" of the disability. To counter these stock expectations, it is imperative that we provide future professionals in relevant fields (e.g., social work, psychology, medicine, education, and many others) with the necessary tools to critically examine beliefs about people with disabilities and assumptions of negative outcomes for their families. Pre-service training should include multiple opportunities to meet individuals with disabilities and their families, and to meaningfully participate in related community initiatives in order to learn about the wide variety of perspectives and range of issues that may concern this group of parents.

Disability studies scholars invite us to rethink common assumptions about disabilities and urge us to work toward disrupting ableism in society (Campbell, 2009; Linton, 1998). To this end, there is much to be gained from challenging the belief that the source of the "problem" for mothers of children with disabilities can be located solely in their children's impairments, and examining, instead, a cultural and institutional complicity in the reification of the stigmas attached to disability. In doing so, we might come to find our parameters of normative motherhood altered, and our definition of desirable children transformed.

REFERENCES

Bamberg, M. (2004). Considering counter-narratives. In M. Bamberg & M. Andrews (Eds.), *Considering counter-narratives: Narrating, resisting, making sense* (pp. 351–371). Amsterdam: John Benjamins Publishing.

Brew-Parrish, V. (1997). The wrong message. *Ragged Edge Online*. Retrieved from http://www. raggededgemagazine.com/archive/aware.htm

Bruner, J. (1990). *Acts of meaning*. Cambridge, MA: Harvard University Press.

Campbell, F. K. (2009). *Contours of ableism*. Basingstoke, UK: Palgrave Macmillan.

Davis, L. J. (2013). Introduction: Disability, normality and power. In L. Davis (Ed.), *The disability studies reader* (pp. 1–16). New York, NY: Routledge.

Donner, R. (1986). *Social workers' view of parent of children with emotional disturbances: A problem of partner in solution*. Unpublished paper.

Douglas, H. (2014). Promoting meaning-making to help our patients grieve: An exemplar for genetic counselors and other health care professionals. *National Society of Genetic Counselors, 23*(5), 695–700.

Ellis, C. (2004). *The ethnographic I: A methodological novel about autoethnography*. Walnut Creek, CA: AltaMira Press.

Erevelles, N., Kanga, A., & Middleton, R. (2006). How does it feel to be a problem? Race, disability, and exclusion in educational policy. In E. Brantlinger (Ed.), *Who benefits from special education? Remediating (fixing) other people's children* (pp. 77–99). Mahwah, NJ: Lawrence Erlbaum Associates.

Ferguson, P., Ferguson, D., & Taylor, S. (1992). Conclusion: The future of interpretivism in disability studies. In P. Ferguson, D. Ferguson, & S. Taylor (Eds.), *Interpreting disability: A qualitative reader* (pp. 295–302). New York, NY: Teachers College Press.

Ferguson, P. M., & Ferguson, D. L. (2006). Finding the "proper attitude": The potential of disability studies to reframe family/school linkages. In S. Danforth & S. L. Gabel (Eds.), *Vital questions facing disability studies in education* (pp. 217–235). New York, NY: Peter Lang.

Fine, M., & Asch, A. (1998). Disability beyond stigma: Social interaction, discrimination and activism. *Journal of Social Issues, 44*, 3–21.

Friesen, B. J., & Koroloff, N. M. (1990). Family-centered services: Implications for mental health administration and research. *The Journal of Behavioral Health Services and Research, 17*(1), 13–25.

Gergen, K. J. (1985). The social constructionist movement in modern psychology. *American Psychologist, 40*(3), 266–275.

Goff, B. S., Springer, N., Foote, L. C., Frantz, C., Peak, M., Tracy, C., … Cross, K. A. (2013). Receiving the initial Down syndrome diagnosis: A comparison of prenatal and postnatal parent group experiences. *Intellectual and Developmental Disabilities, 51*(6), 446–457.

Goffman, E. (1963). *Behavior in public place: Notes on the social organization of gatherings.* New York, NY: The Free Press.

Gorman, J. C. (2004). *Working with challenging parents of students with special needs.* Thousand Oaks, CA: Corwin Press.

Hahn, H. (1997). Advertising the acceptably employable image. In L. Davis (Ed.), *The disability studies reader* (pp. 172–186). New York, NY: Routledge.

Kroth, R. L., & Edge, D. (2007). *Communicating with parents and families of exceptional children* (4th ed.). Denver, CO: Love Publishing Company.

Kubler-Ross, E. (1969). *On death and dying.* New York, NY: Macmillan.

Lalvani, P. (2011). Constructing the (m)other: Dominant and contested narratives on mothering a child with Down syndrome. *Narrative Inquiry, 21*(2), 272–293.

Lalvani, P. (2014). The enforcement of normalcy in schools and the disablement of families: Unpacking master narratives on parental denial. *Disability & Society, 29*(8), 1221–1233.

Lalvani, P. (2015). Disability, stigma, and otherness: Perspectives of parents and teachers. *International Journal of Disability, Development and Education, 62*(4), 379–393.

Lalvani, P., & Polvere, L. (2013). Historical perspectives on studying families of children with disabilities: A case for critical research. *Disability Studies Quarterly, 33*(3).

Landsman, G. (1999). Does god give special kids to special parents? Personhood and the child with disabilities as gift and as giver. In L. Lane (Ed.), *Transformative motherhood: On giving and getting in a consumer culture* (pp. 133–165). New York, NY: New York University Press.

Linton, S. (1998). *Claiming disability: Knowledge and identity.* New York, NY: New York University Press.

McAdams, D. (2008). Personal narratives and the life story. In O. John, R. Robins, & L. Pervin, (Eds.), *Handbook of personality: Theory and research* (pp. 242–257). New York, NY: The Guilford Press.

Parens, E., & Asch, A. (2000). *Prenatal testing and disability rights.* Washington, DC: Georgetown University Press.

Piepmeier, A. (2012). Saints, sages, and victims: Endorsement of and resistance to cultural stereotypes in memoirs by parents of children with disabilities. *Disability Studies Quarterly, 32*(1).

Rapp, R. (2000). *Testing women, testing the fetus.* New York, NY: Routledge.

Rothman, B. K. (1993). *The tentative pregnancy: How amniocentesis changes the experience of motherhood.* New York, NY: W. W. Norton.

Seligman, M., & Darling, R. B. (2009). *Ordinary families, special children: A systems approach to childhood disability.* New York, NY: Guilford Press.

Skotko, B. (2005). Mothers of children with Down syndrome reflect on their postnatal support. *Pediatrics*, *115*(1), 64–77.

Sooben, R. D. (2010). Antenatal testing and the subsequent birth of a child with Down syndrome: A phenomenological study of parents' experiences. *Journal of Intellectual Disabilities*, *14*(2), 79–94.

Valle, J. W. (2009). *What mothers say about special education: From the 1960s to the present*. New York, NY: Palgrave Macmillan.

Valle, J. W., & Connor, D. J. (2011). *Rethinking disability: A disability studies approach to inclusive practices (A practical guide)*. New York, NY: McGraw-Hill.

CHAPTER 10

Becoming Anahita

A Persian Mother's Pilgrimage to Autism Pride

NEGAR IRANI AND NEGIN HOSSEINI GOODRICH

INTRODUCTION BY NEGIN

This is a story of one mother's journey to understanding autism, narrated by Negar Irani, an Iranian woman residing in Tehran, and translated from Persian into English by myself—Negin Hosseini Goodrich, an Iranian-American disability rights activist and Negar's friend. In addition to directly translating Negar's accounts about, and interpretations of, her life with her son, Ilia, who has autism, I offer my own reflections on her story, situating it within the Iranian socio-cultural context and making connections with the central ideas of disability studies. Additionally, at the start of each of her vignettes, I insert brief preambles about the mythical Persian goddess, Anahita, as a metaphor for the story of her modern-day version, Negar. These are based on representations of the Persian goddess in mythology; however, their content might be more creative than a direct adoption from the original mythology. Persian culture and literature are, in fact, filled with myths about valiant gods and goddesses, capable of accomplishing extraordinary missions. I believe that modern versions of these mythical beings manifest today in individuals, such as Negar, who resist the mainstream and create their own path. Negar's interpretations and evolving perceptions of autism are aligned with many of the principles of the newly formed neurodiversity movement, and with disability studies perspectives of which she has not been aware.

In this narrative, only the authors' names, as well as Ilia's, are real. For the other individuals, pseudonyms are used.

* * *

Reverberating through history's thousands of years, here is a Persian goddess, Anahita[1], the divinity of the waters, the goddess of fertility, healing, and wisdom. She does not conform to patterns but creates a unique passage.

NEGAR'S STORY

"What is autism?!"

I asked the doctor, confused. I had not even heard the word "autism" until then and had no idea what an autistic person may look like. Later, noticing that my 3-year-old son was unable to talk and communicate like the other children of his age, I thought, "this must be autism!"

My name is Negar Irani. I was born in 1979 in Tehran[2] to a family of five. A professor in Chemistry, my father is now retired, and my mother is a housewife. I am their middle child, four years younger than my brother and 5 years older than my sister. I have spent most of my life in Karaj[3]. In 1997, I moved to Qazvin[4] to earn my undergraduate degree in Industrial Management. A year later, I met my future husband, 10 years older, nice and reliable. He had a degree in Law, yet had launched his own private business. We married in 2003, and a year later, on September 27th, 2004, our son, Ilia, was born.

Ilia could sit and crawl when he was 5–6 months old. Two months later, he started walking. By the time he was 11 months old, Ilia was potty-trained. He could hold a spoon at 2 and could say small words like *"ba-ba"* (daddy in Persian) and *"da-da"* (out). Towards his third year, though, some of his behaviors and reactions became different. He could not talk like a 3-year-old boy, nor could he communicate. A month before his third birthday, Ilia was diagnosed with autism. From the first day of his diagnosis, I accepted Ilia's condition with no sorrow. I thought to myself, Ilia is my son and I should embrace him and his autism unconditionally. Instead of feeling depressed because "now my life is different from others," I threw a big party and invited all my friends and their kids to celebrate Ilia's third birthday. I never thought that Ilia had to be excluded from family and friends because he could not communicate with non-autistic children. I thought instead, non-autistic children could help my son interact with all types of people. Ilia was resistant to communication, especially speaking. Sometimes he did not like to see the kids around him, but gradually got along with them. I started taking him to the pool. For almost a year, he only put his feet inside the water—not a huge improvement, but I was very happy about it.

I started searching for information about autism, but it was like being in a desert! No resources, not even a pamphlet let alone an autism center. Qazvin had nothing to offer my son and other kids with autism. In my frequent trips to Tehran, I met two helpful autism experts, Mrs. Raad and Safi, who gave me an Applied

Behavior Analysis (ABA) form to use for Ilia. I knew no one else whom I could ask for help. Not even my educated family could do anything. I realized that I didn't need to wait for any helper or savior. Instead, I had to become Ilia's helper and the very "miracle" many families helplessly awaited. I became my son's first teacher without even having enough knowledge about the job. All I knew was two things: he should be educated continuously, gradually, and patiently, plus, he should never be excluded from society.

My husband gave up sooner than I expected. He used to say, "This boy is a genius and does not need any classes or education!" My mother believed that educating Ilia would only exacerbate his over-reactions, his loud cries and yells. But I did not listen to any of their suggestions. I started working with my son personally. I kept taking him everywhere, as if nothing had happened. I started introducing my son to everyone, identifying him overtly as autistic. I never hid or denied his condition. I proudly displayed his autism in public. He found himself in different places, visiting various people, encountering different situations. Ilia experienced how to live in a society filled with different personalities. I never wanted to isolate him. I never left him behind just because he was autistic.

I am naturally a sociable person and have many friends. Since Ilia's diagnosis, I made even more friends, especially with those who had non-autistic kids. And their kids became friends with Ilia. I used to talk to the children, explaining Ilia's autism and letting them know how they could interact with him and be helpful. Most of the kids would listen and they got closer to my son. One day, I met a lady, Fariba, in a park. She talked about her autistic niece and how she had become her private teacher. Fariba offered help and I accepted. She became my son's second tutor, after me.

NEGIN'S REFLECTIONS

According to the latest reports, 700,000 individuals in Iran live with autism (IRNA, 2018), yet, the actual number of Iranians on the autism spectrum might exceed this number. Disabilities and autism have traditionally been viewed through medical approaches in Iran (Goodrich, 2014). Disability studies perspectives have started to emerge only in recent years, but for the most part, mainstream media have been the sole sources of limited information about disabilities, circulating medicalized knowledge through the traditional, stereotypical lens of ableism (e.g., Billawala & Wolbring, 2014). Therefore, one of the many challenges Iranian parents of children with disabilities encounter is a lack of information and consultation centers, which becomes a source of anxiety among them. Disproportionately impacted are those who reside in small towns and remote areas (Tahmassian, Khorram Abadi, & Chimeh, 2012).

Negar's narrative starts in the early years of the 2000s. A dearth of resources and information about autism, the dominance of traditional beliefs perpetuated by the media, and her own unfamiliarity with autism characterize her initial experience. Although Negar and her husband earned a university degree and were highly engaged in social activities, like the majority of 81,000,000 Iranians, they were unaware of autism and had no experiences related to it until Ilia was diagnosed at the age of three.

Under such circumstances, Negar decided to become her son's "first teacher" by educating herself. Unlike many parents who report initial feelings of shock, bewilderment, anger and depression when their children are diagnosed (Chimeh, Pouretemad, & Khoram Abadi, 2008; Lalvani, 2011), Negar reports having few negative emotions, other than confusion. Instead, she "threw a birthday party" for her newly diagnosed 3-year-old son and didn't think that autism could draw a line between her son and family activities. Negar resists dominant medicalized discourses of disability as well as the segregation and oppression of people with disabilities, and defends "inclusion in work, education and leisure" (Goodley, 2016). In other words, although she acquired no formal knowledge about disability studies, she applied a social model lens, which redefines disability as a sociopolitical construct rather than as individuals' deficit, focusing on the removal of social and environmental barriers and reducing the stigmas associated with disabilities (Baglieri & Shapiro, 2012; Davis, 2002; Goodley & Roets, 2008).

Her husband's reaction, however, was different. In his eyes, Ilia was a "genius" who did not need to go to school. His view reflects a stereotypical belief in which people with disabilities or differences are overestimated or underestimated—i.e., they are considered either super-smart or uneducable. The duality of "dumb/genius"—an inherit of the medical model of disability (see: Kyaga et al., 2011; Roberts, 2012), is a pervasive approach towards people with disabilities and differences in Iranian society. Some parents perceive their children with autism to be "genius", as if ascribing higher IQs to their children would lessen the stigma traditionally intertwined with autism. Goffman's (1963) work sheds light on the stigma associated with disabilities and how the "undesirable mark" of disabilities might be kept hidden by individuals with disabilities and/or their families.

The medical approach to disability in Iran results in the isolation of large numbers of children with disabilities as well as their parents (Kermanshahi, Vanaki, Ahmadi, Kazemnejad, & Azadfalah, 2008). Some families prefer to keep their disabled children inside their homes, sheltering them from people's judgmental reactions. Like a family secret, disabled members are often kept hidden from even close friends and relatives for many years. Negar, on the contrary, seemed determined to purposefully socialize with, and publicize, her son and his autism. Within the context of a society in which the isolation and "hiding" of children with disabilities is common, Ilia's autism does not result in his (or his mother's) detachment from society. Negar mingles with families who do not have a child with autism, takes Ilia to parks and public places, and proudly introduces him as a person with autism. She endeavors to resist dominant perceptions of disability, segregation, marginalization, shame and stigma, and strives for social integration and inclusion for her son.

* * *

Anahita, the Persian goddess, performs the miracles masses long for, and propagates the seeds of fruitfulness. Her wealth is her love which she generously bestows upon all. The goddess of fertility flourishes herself, makes the waters flow and helps make arid desserts fertile. The goddess of perseverance shall not succumb in the face of adversity.

NEGAR'S STORY

Despite my efforts, Ilia's progress was very slow. Disappointment was not even a choice, though. Ilia's speech started to regress at three. He could neither talk nor communicate. By the time he was six, Ilia's reactions were still slow. He could not independently hold a pencil in his hands, refused to follow his teachers, and cried a lot. Resistant to ABA, Ilia would cry and become more dismayed during training sessions. As a result of our social activities, Ilia could understand the dangers in the streets by the time he was four. Without anyone accompanying him or taking his hand, he would react to the dangers. He was also able to take a shower independently (though I preferred to supervise him). Ilia was progressing in his swimming lessons, yet very slowly. It took another year for his swimming trainer to keep him in the water only for a minute. One minute throughout a year was a huge achievement!

I decided to discontinue ABA because I found it useless; I thought it was not to my son's benefit at all. I heard that the school of Special Education in Qazvin had hired a very effective teacher, Mrs. Sadaf. She became Ilia's private tutor and focused on his verbal skills. Along with enhancing Ilia's social skills, we added written tasks, alphabetical comprehension, and math to our curriculum.

After 3 years, Ilia learned how to swim in a public pool. Since I had decided to hire a private teacher in Tehran, I temporarily moved to my parents' home in Karaj to make my daily journeys shorter. I never stopped enjoying my life with my son. We would go everywhere together. For years, Ilia and I used to go to the Park of Women in Qazvin and spend hours there. I wanted him to drain his energy in nature. I would ask my friends and their families to join us, to cheer Ilia up, to interact with him. I felt like the happiest woman on the face of the earth!

Ilia was assessed when he was 8 years old. I took him to an assessment center and emphasized that I did not expect him to get "good grades" but just to communicate and interact with regular kids at school. Since Ilia had a tutor at home and I was working with him, the assessment experts agreed that I should enroll him in a regular school. Convincing the school's principal to enroll a boy with autism was not easy, but Ilia was eventually admitted. As usual, I became friends with the kids first, and talked to them about Ilia and autism. Many of them were friendly and welcoming, and communicated with Ilia very well. Instead of hiring a special needs teacher, I asked a regular private teacher to work with my son. I believed regular teachers would treat Ilia differently compared to their "special needs" colleagues. I usually talk to my son's teachers about autism, Ilia's characteristics, and his needs, to help them balance their expectations. Many teachers knew nothing about autism or had wrong information; I educated them as well. After two years, Ilia started interacting with his speech therapist. When Ilia showed an interest in music, I did not hesitate to buy a variety of musical instruments for him: piano, guitar, keyboard, bass, and drum. Our house soon looked like a studio!

By the time my son was 10 years old, he was able to hold a pencil and could have his hair done without any resistance. Since his focus had gradually increased, he could imitate the environment more and learn better. He was able to get dressed by himself and started progressing in reading and writing. As in past years, we continued going to parks and public places to have fun and experience new things. I never lost a minute to enjoy living with my son!

NEGIN'S REFLECTIONS

Access to education is one of the main challenges for Iranians with disabilities. According to a UNICEF (2013) survey conducted in 13 low- and middle-income countries, "children with disabilities aged 6–17 years are significantly less likely to be enrolled in school than their peers without disabilities" (p. 8). In Iran, in addition to children from low-income and immigrant families (who are mainly from Afghanistan), many children with disabilities are likely to be denied an education, mainly because of inaccessible schools and educational environments (IRNA, 2018).

The Iranian educational system offers both special education schools and inclusive schools to students with disabilities. It is reported that 65,000 students with learning disabilities are enrolled in "regular" schools, whereas 55,000 students with intellectual disabilities study in separate, "special needs" schools (Iran Sepid, 2017). Approximately, 2,000 students with autism also attend the special education schools (*Ibid.*, 2017). No statistics are available to indicate the percentage of Iranian children with disabilities who are deprived of education altogether. Despite regulations in favor of inclusive education, the principals of many "regular" schools reject students with disabilities because of what they refer to as a "lack of trained teachers and educational resources" in their schools (IRNA, 2017). Therefore, many Iranian students with disabilities will be redirected to separate, special education schools for children with disabilities; following professionals' recommendations, many Iranian parents prefer to enroll their kids with autism in these schools.

Negar, a contrarian mother, who advocates for social inclusion of children with autism, resisted his segregation and exclusion, and instead sought to insert understanding of autism in the heart of society, inviting everyone to recognize persons with autism and interact with them. It is worth noting that she purposefully chose *not* to hire a special education teacher to work with Ilia, because she intuitively believed that "regular" teachers would treat her son more like a "regular" student, rather than a person with "special" needs. Her actions are similar to those of many parents of children with disabilities who question professionals' recommendations, and advocate for what they believe to be better solutions (see Lalvani, 2012). Negar also challenged dominant educational approaches to autism, including Applied Behavior Analysis (ABA), which is the first aid most parents in Iran receive, if they are able to find any assistance at all.

A number of disability studies scholars problematize ABA for its ableist view of "recovering from autism" or "recovery [to normalcy]" (Broderick, 2011). In contrast to traditional medicalized views that equate autism with mental sickness to be cured, disability studies aligns with the *neurodiversity* perspective. Coined by Judy Singer, a sociologist with Asperger Syndrome, the term neurodiversity encompasses a view of autism as a human difference to be recognized and valued (Singer, 1999). Proponents of the developing neurodiversity movement during the 1990s, mainly individuals living with autism, rejected the notion of "curing" autism and advocated instead for accepting it as a natural human difference (Robertson & Ne'eman, 2008).

Many parents in Iran are likely to sustain ABA for their children because there are no other alternatives. This is not unlike many parents in Western countries, who accept having their children with autism separated from the mainstream through, for example, enrolling them in segregated ABA schools (Prichep, 2014). This may happen for different reasons, including a need to avoid "courtesy stigma" (Goffman, 1963)—the stigma which affects both disabled individuals and their families (see Lalvani, 2015). Their unfamiliarity with the neurodiversity movement forces many parents to adopt a medical view and relentlessly seek to "cure" autism (Beyzaie, 2015). In the absence of social model based supportive resources, rejecting ABA requires a lot of courage and confidence, and, for a variety of reasons, many parents may be unable, unwilling, or ill equipped to challenge the recommendations of the "experts." Negar's attitude towards her son's autism is incongruous with prevalent patterns in and out of Iran. Rather, her story seems to reflect some elements of the neurodiversity perspective. Resisting social forces, she speaks openly, and with pride, about her son's autism. She does not acknowledge any socially constructed divider between "non-autistic/ us" versus "autistic/them." Instead, she creates an integrating circle into which everyone is invited.

* * *

Infidelity causes Anahita pain, puts her on fire, burns her close to death. Yet, a new phoenix, more gallant, revives, evolves to a stalwart. The goddess arises from her own ashes, spreads her wings and flies into the heavens; she is a proud mother to all her children.

NEGAR'S STORY

Ilia was seven when I learned that my husband was cheating on me. I was shocked. The emotional harm was very difficult to handle. It broke me. In fact, opposite to what people may think, autism did not destroy me, but my husband did. My husband's unfaithfulness brought me sorrow and depression. I had never felt upset or "less" because of Ilia's autism. I loved my son the way he was, and I was always proud of him, yet my husband's infidelity made me feel inferior, worthless, and "not enough." My husband used to say that he loved his family, that he adored me and our son. I believed him, unaware of his private stories. It was the worst thing that ever happened to me. I lost my confidence and energy and became more depressed day after day.

Tolerating the new situation was not easy. I could divorce him but decided to sustain my marriage just because of my son who literally needed his father. Ilia loves his dad. They spend some quality time together. Ilia regularly goes to his dad's store and plays with his dog. He sleeps beside his dad many nights. They have their own father-son nights. Ilia knows his father's friends and shakes hands with them. I thought if we divorced, the rhythm of Ilia's life would be disrupted. Ilia would be the first and the main victim. I did not want it. My husband, in fact, had many affairs when I was traveling between Tehran, Karaj, and Qazvin. I sometimes blamed myself. But I could not stay at home all day to protect my marriage. I had to stick with Ilia's schedule and classes. I could not deprive my son of his social activities. My husband's infidelity marked an epoch, a turning point in my life. It changed many things, including my view of life and myself. In one of those gloomy sunsets, I was sitting on my chair wishing I could do something for all autistic children. I wanted to go beyond my son and assist the other kids and their families. I asked god to show me a way, to give me an opportunity to serve more people.

My father had bought me an Android mobile (cellphone) to help me entertain myself. At first, I thought I was too busy to spend all my time on social media, but something happened which changed my mind. One day, playing with the cellphone aimlessly, tears in my eyes, I noticed a friend had added me to a Viber[5] group. It was set up by an autism specialist who had previously established a center for autism. The more I read the channel's content, the more I learned about families' thoughts and feelings; they were frustrated, anxious, helpless, and with hundreds of unanswered questions. I was shocked to see how much they did not know. I started posting my views, explaining that autism was never a disaster in my life. I wrote about my son's trainings in and out of home. Shortly after that, I was invited to another group for parents with autistic children. I used to read each question and comment and answer them one by one. I shared all my experiences.

This group inspired me to launch my own weblog on which I posted all my experiences. In fact, two of my good friends and mothers of autistic children created a website for me and asked me to categorize my writings, title them, and post them regularly. Soon my weblog content became an online resource for many parents who could not find any reliable material in the Persian language. I also established my own online group with 600 members. Every day and night, I received many questions from members, and spent hours answering them. Since the process was very time-consuming, I asked my trusted specialists and professionals to join my group to answer more technical inquiries. All my services were (and still are) free of charge; I did not even earn one Toman from advising or advertising.

NEGIN'S REFLECTIONS

Mothers in Iran are considered to be the primary caregivers, whereas fathers are mostly the financial providers (Kermanshahi, *et al.*, 2008; Alizadeh & Andries, 2002). Negar's life is aligned with this pattern; she is responsible for raising Ilia and for his education, and her husband is more engaged in activities outside the home while maintaining close relations with his son. Negar expressed that once she realized her husband was cheating on her, she was aware that some people might assume it was because of their son and his autism. This is because many Iranians believe that disabilities cause "invisible mental breakup" and "hidden emotional divorce" among couples (IRNA, 2015). The blame is put on a child's disability, rather than on the lack of supports and resources that aggravate the existing financial and emotional issues for families. Additionally, the rate of family crisis and divorce among Iranians has generally been rocketing in recent years regardless of autism and disabilities (BBC News Persian, 2018).

Negar's story continues through the 2010s—in the era of Internet and social media that helps her to expand her role from being the mother/teacher of her own child to becoming an advocate for a broader community. Social media has enabled many Iranian families to project their voices, and has, in fact, revolutionized the experiences of the Iranian disability community. By projecting authentic narratives, social media are more likely to impact the non-disabled community's understanding of disability. They have reduced the dominance of traditional media, challenging their goal-keeping policies that have historically shaped representations of disability. Social media have given a podium to people with disabilities and their families to represent themselves devoid of any censorship or selective policies that often restrict traditional media in Iran. Nowadays, thousands of Iranians with disabilities, their families, and related organizations have set up their own pages on social media, through which they freely share their stories and experiences. Emotionally wounded but mentally stronger, Negar recruited the power of social media to propagate more progressive ways of thinking about disability and reach more parents. Her social model (Goodley, 2011) voice was aimed at teaching others to find the "issue" not in the individuals with disabilities, but rather in society.

* * *

The challenges are never-ending, and so is the strength of Anahita. Her journey, which began with self-awareness, continues with raising consciousness through propagating knowledge and teaching others. A feminine divinity, Anahita bestows her experiences to those who call upon her to guide.

NEGAR'S STORY

One night in the summer of 2017, Ilia was calmly sitting on the couch when he had a seizure. I was totally shocked, not knowing why and how it happened. I just tried to keep his mouth open to protect his tongue and breathing. I called Ilia's father, asking for help, but could not wait for him and immediately drove to my parents' home to get my brother. We drove to a doctor in Tehran who was kind enough to wait for us at his office until 11 pm. He scanned Ilia's brain, controlled the seizure, and prescribed new medications. The seizure left serious impacts on me; a kind of terror I had never experienced. I needed time to find myself again. I never knew how important it was, as a mother, to be able to drive. I saved Ilia's life because I could drive. Since then, I suggest all mothers should become as independent as possible and be prepared to react appropriately in emergency situations.

Now I have a channel on Telegram App with over 1,340 members. I spend a few hours per day answering the members' questions. The majority of parents are sad and depressed. They prefer to stay at home and hide themselves and their kids. They have high expectations, but they constantly compare their autistic children with non-autistic ones. They set unrealistic objectives and because reaching them is almost impossible, they feel even more frustrated. I get my reward by helping them. A suggestion, a personal story of my experiences, a little guidance, and even my emotional support might make a huge change in their lives. Each day I grow older, stronger, more experienced, mature enough to offer help to others. I grow with my son.

NEGIN'S REFLECTIONS

Iranian women have gradually become more empowered in past decades. Their increasing contribution in development plans (Janghorban, Taghipour, Roudsari, & Abbasi, 2014) have made them more independent and aware of their rights in society and in their families. Higher education is one of the settings in which the Iranian women have now outnumbered men. In the 2017 Universities National Entrance Exam, 213,884 participants out of 378,706 were female whereas 164,822 were male (Tehran Times, 2017).

Like Negar, many Iranian mothers with a disabled child are becoming increasingly aware of the importance of empowering themselves. In her journey towards inclusion and advocacy, the stronger Negar urged other women to similarly gain more control over decisions about their lives and their children. Considering the lack of medical care, especially in small towns and rural areas, Negar encourages mothers to hone their independence, so that they would be able to appropriately react to emergencies and the lack of immediate medical care in some areas.

* * *

Proud Anahita strives to construct a promising future for all mothers and children. She reconceptualizes "fertility" beyond females' physicality—"plant the seeds of knowledge, and you are fertile!" The goddess reaches the highest heavens, enlightened, empowered, and proud.

NEGAR'S STORY

My son is 14 now. He is able to read and write and can do many things by himself. This is my son, and I am very proud of him. These improvements happened, not overnight, but during a long journey in which I learned a lot. It taught me how to think beyond myself and my own child, to expand my world to other people, and to reach those who need to hear my experiences. I learned how to enjoy autism. People may think I am crazy or that I exaggerate, but honestly, I enjoy it! I try to teach it to the other parents, though they do not get it most of the time; their worries do not let them see it the way I do. I choose to see autism as a different way to live, and I try to enjoy every moment with my son. I enjoy his classes. I enjoy waiting for him to come back home. I enjoy going grocery shopping with him. I enjoy taking my son to the parks. I enjoy every moment with him. I'm a proud mother, and I adore my son the way he is!

NEGIN'S REFLECTIONS

Negar's narrative is concluded with her expressing a sense of pride as a mother of a child with autism and as someone who is able to "enjoy" autism. Her "proud" journey begins with learning how to self-educate to become her son's "first teacher" and arrives at a place of autism pride—a perspective in which autism is considered a type of human diversity to be "celebrated rather than eliminated" (Cascio, 2012). Throughout her journey, Negar resists dominant approaches to disability and seeks to make changes by helping other parents reshape their perceptions.

The neurodiversity movement, which utilizes an identity approach to autism (Cascio, 2012), and the notion of "disability pride" are still unknown among the majority of the disability community in Iran. Prevailing medicalized perspectives equate physical and intellectual disabilities with sicknesses to be fixed, generating shame rather than pride. While individualism has been historically and traditionally promoted in Western countries, individualized notions of *self* and *identity* have not been prolifically theorized in Iranian society. Despite this, and unaware of disability studies and/or the neurodiversity movement, Negar demonstrates many elements of social model thinking and practices. In a society where the predominant response to disability is one of shame and stigma, and where women have historically struggled to gain access to equal rights, Negar declares herself to be a proud mother, an autism advocate, and a supportive resource, encouraging others to empower themselves to make changes. Reflecting on her story, I am reminded of the 14th century Persian poet, Ḥāfiz Shirazi, whose verses inspire us to celebrate life and beauty, but also urge us to reimagine life as we know it, and reconstruct new worlds:

"Rose petals let us scatter
And fill the cup with red wine
The firmaments let us shatter
And come with a new design."
(Ḥāfiz Shirazi, 1996)

NOTES

1. For more information about the myth of Anahita, see: http://www.iranicaonline.org/articles/anahid
2. Tehran is the capital of Iran.
3. Karaj is the capital of Alborz Province (32 miles to Tehran).
4. Qazvin is the capital of Qazvin Province (94 miles to Tehran).
5. Viber is a free app that allows users to make free calls, send texts, pictures and video messages to other Viber users (from: https://www.webwise.ie/parents/what-is-viber/). During the first years of 2010s, Viber was commonly used by many Iranians.

REFERENCES

Alizadeh, H., & Andries, C. (2002). Interaction of parenting styles and attention deficit hyperactivity disorder in Iranian parents. *Child & Family Behavior Therapy, 24*(3), 37–52.

Baglieri, S., & Shapiro, A. (2012). *Disability studies and the inclusive classroom: Critical practices for creating least restrictive attitudes.* New York, NY: Routledge.

BBC News Persian. (2018, April 09). *A new record on divorce in Iran in 2018/1396.* [Record-e Talaagh dar Iran Shekast]. Retrieved from http://www.bbc.com/persian/iran-43683683

Beyzaie, S. (2015, May). *Doors towards the light. [Dar-haee be Samt-e Noor].* Retrieved from https://iranwire.com/fa/news/844/6436

Billawala, A., & Wolbring, G. (2014). Analyzing the discourse surrounding autism in the New York Times using an ableism lens. *Disability Studies Quarterly, 34*(1).

Boyce, M., Chaumont, M. L., & Bier, C. (2012). "ANĀHĪD." *Encyclopædia Iranica*, I/9, pp. 1003–1011. http://www.iranicaonline.org/articles/anahid

Broderick, A. A. (2011). Autism as rhetoric: Exploring watershed rhetorical moments in applied behavior analysis discourse. *Disability Studies Quarterly, 31*(3).

Cascio, M. A. (2012). Neurodiversity: Autism pride among mothers of children with autism spectrum disorders. *Intellectual and Developmental Disabilities, 50*(3), 273–283.

Chimeh, N., Pouretemad, H., & Khoram Abadi, R. (2008). Need assessment of mothers with autistic children. *Journal of Family Research, 3*(3), 697–707.

Davis, L. J. (2002). *Bending over backwards: Disability, dismodernism & other difficult positions.* New York: New York University Press.

Goffman, E. (1963). *Stigma: Notes on the management of spoiled identity.* Englewood Cliffs, NJ: Prentice-Hall.

Goodley, D. (2016). *Disability studies: An interdisciplinary introduction.* Thousand Oaks, CA: Sage.

Goodley, D., & Roets, G. (2008). The (be)comings and goings of "developmental disabilities": The cultural politics of "impairment." *Discourse: Studies in the Cultural Politics of Education, 29*(2), 239–255.

Goodrich, N. H. (2014). A Persian Alice in disability literature wonderland: Disability studies in Iran. *Disability Studies Quarterly, 34*(2). Retrieved from http://dsq-sds.org/article/view/4255/3595

Ḥāfiẓ Shirazi. (1996). Ghazal No. 374. As cited in Rashid Abadi, Z. & Khatami, A. (2014). The comparative study of Epicurean thoughts in Horace and Hafiz. *Journal Life Science and Biomedicine, 4*(1), 35–39. Iran Sepid. (2017, December 2). *62,000 Students with Disabilities Study in Regular Schools. [62,000 Danesh-Amouz-e Malool dar Madaares-e Aadi Tahsil Mikonand].* Retrieved from http://www.iransepid.ir/News/12671.html?catid=4&title=تحصیل ھزار دانش آموز معلول در مدارس عادی

IRNA (Islamic Republic News Agency). (2015, September 26). *Autism: The new accused of divorce. Autism, Motaham-e Jadid-e Talaagh.* Retrieved from http://www.irna.ir/fa/News/81773022

IRNA (Islamic Republic News Agency). (2017, September 21). *The educational rights of kids with disabilities. [Hagh-e Tahsili-e Koodakan-e Daray-e Malooliat].* Retrieved from http://www.irna.ir/fa/News/82672133

IRNA (Islamic Republic News Agency). (2018, May 22). *The number of autistic children is increasing. [Tedad-e Koodakaan-e Autism is Increasing].* Retrieved from http://www.irna.ir/fa/News/82922746

IRNA (Islamic Republic News Agency). (2018, September 22). *Left behind education. [Jaa Mandegan az Mehr].* Retrieved from http://www.irna.ir/fa/News/83039261

Janghorban, R., Taghipour, A., Roudsari, R. L., & Abbasi, M. (2014). Women's empowerment in Iran: A review based on the related legislations. *Global Journal of Health Science, 6*(4), 226–235.

Kermanshahi, S., Vanaki, Z., Ahmadi, F., Kazemnejad, A., & Azadfalah, P. (2008). Children with learning disabilities: A phenomenological study of the lived experiences of Iranian mothers. *International Journal of Qualitative Studies on Health & Well-Being, 3*(1), 18–26. doi:10.1080/17482620701757284.

Kyaga, S., Lichtenstein, P., Boman, M., Hultman, C., Långström, N., & Landén, M. (2011). Creativity and mental disorder: family study of 300,000 people with severe mental disorder. *The British Journal of Psychiatry, 199*(5), 373–379. doi: 10.1192/bjp.bp.110.085316.

Lalvani, P. (2011). Constructing the (m)other: Dominant and contested narratives on mothering a child with Down syndrome. *Narrative Inquiry, 21*(2), 276–293.

Lalvani, P. (2012). Parents' participation in special education in the context of implicit educational ideologies and socioeconomic privilege. *Education and Training in Autism and Developmental Disabilities, 47*(4), 474–486.

Lalvani, P. (2015). Disability, stigma and otherness: Perspectives of parents and teachers. *International Journal of Disability, Development and Education, 62*(4), 379–393.

Prichep, D. (2014, June 02). *Do autistic kids fare better in integrated or specialized schools?* Retrieved from https://www.npr.org/2014/06/02/316462407/do-autistic-kids-fare-better-in-integrated-or-specialized-schools

Roberts, M. (2012, October 17). Creativity "closely entwined with mental illness." Retrieved from http://www.bbc.co.uk/news/health-19959565

Robertson, S. M., & Ne'eman, A. D. (2008). Autistic acceptance, the college campus, and technology: Growth of neurodiversity in society and academia. *Disability Studies Quarterly, 28*(4).

Singer, J. (1999). "Why can't you be normal for once in your life?" From a "problem with no name" to the emergence of a new category of difference. In M. Corker & S. French (Eds.), *Disability discourse* (pp. 59–67). Buckingham/Philadelphia, PA: Open University Press.

Tahmassian, K., Khorram Abadi, R., & Chimeh, N. (2012). The effectiveness of behavior management training on parental stress of autistic children's mothers. *Journal of Family Research, 8*(31), 269–278.

Tehran Times. (2017, September 16). *Females outnumber males in Iran's 2017 university entrance exam.* Retrieved from https://www.tehrantimes.com/news/416821/Females-outnumber-males-in-Iran-s-2017-university-entrance-exam

UNICEF. (2013, May 28). *The state of the world's children 2013: Executive summary.* Retrieved from https://www.unicef.org/publications/index_69378.html

CHAPTER 11

Mothering IN THE Panopticon

SUSAN BAGLIERI

She leaned over and placed her hand on my knee. "Here comes the hard part," the teacher with kind eyes and soft voice started. We are sitting side by side, surrounded by piles of papers, children's books, and binders in the small office space. Barbara had completed the task of explaining the program's developmental checklist and showing me samples of work to illustrate what my eldest son—then three years old—had accomplished. The "hard part" for which she was preparing me was the point at which she recounted Jason's problems and struggles, weaving them into a troubling narrative.

* * *

Memory work is slippery work. Stories are shaped in the moments of their remembering, imagining, and telling, as much as they are formed in relation to events originally ordered in space and time. I am conscious of the craft at work in sharing stories of our lives, and mindful of the works of D. Jean Clandinin (2016) and Bronwyn Davies and Susannah Gannon (2006). Each speak of the tenuousness of claims to objective and stable narratives, in favor of the purposeful or collectively meaningful narratives that are cultivated from the messiness of lives lived. The way we recall events and make stories of them are mosaics of our self and others, within innumerable contexts. We become our *selves* in relation to the ways in which life is encountered and later remembered. We are always in the moment of becoming. Each new moment emerges as an amalgam of present and past, of immediacy and memory that shapes the way we act, react, and weave our experiences into the narratives we construct to give order to our lives.

The story I tell here is a reflection on a moment of time and the ways that this moment was shaped in, and continues to construct, my experience of mothering. It is told within a context framed by my professional work in disability studies and education, my family's position of relative privilege, and the tyranny of ability (Parekh, 2017) that pervades mores of contemporary parenting and school practice. In the moment of Barbara placing her hand on my knee and softly intimating the "hard part" about to come, my many selves and positionalities zoomed into focus, laying out a garden of forking paths. To be clear, these are not the curious excursions and jaunty risks imagined by Robert Frost (1916/2002) as roads not taken; rather, these are the paths conjured by Jorge Luis Borges (1998), in which all lose their way amidst infinite futures.

* * *

I knew it was coming and had been gearing up for this conversation for some time. At pick-up time over the past months, Barbara and Isabel would casually ask me questions about how Jason was at home and in his previous childcare program. They would comment on how he didn't like the liquid soap. "Maybe it's the texture?" They warned that he needed to learn to stir his own yogurt because "You wouldn't want for him to go to grade school without possessing this skill." He had committed the ultimate affront of biting a child once while they were rolling around among pillows and plush toys. This conversation occurs in the 11th year of my career first spent as a special education teacher and then as a teacher education professor. It was only a matter of time before I knew we would be officially talking about "sensory issues" and "stimulation" as a culmination of the more casual exchanges we'd been having. And here we were. Barbara hands me a single page of paper with a checklist of the kinds of assessments that can be performed. There is a signature line at the bottom.

* * *

Motherhood, for me, is a constant playing of the decisions and indecisions in which I imagine the impact of my in/actions on my children's lives. "Should I have let them have that juice box?" "Have they had too much screen time this week?" "Should I have kept my youngest out of kindergarten for another year, red-shirting him like I did the first?" "What would have happened if I had pursued evaluation and early-intervention?" Big and small, every decision is imagined and reimagined. My mothering self is constructed by the immensity of love and responsibility through which I experience my children, by the societal advice, blame, and shame targeted at parents that stream across my media feeds, and by my professional life studying disability and education. The decisions of mothering are made within a complexity of contexts. Fierce love and social media mingle with my professional studies in teaching and learning. The headline from *NPR* asking, "Which type of parent are you: A gardener or a carpenter?" pops up in my newsfeed (Gopnik, 2016; Ingber, 2018). "Are you a free range, helicopter, or lighthouse parent?" is clickbait another day. "How Too Much Screen Time Affects Kids' Bodies and Brains," advises *Forbes* (Walton, 2018). I wonder, in remembering sociologist Annette Lareau's (2003) book, how does my social class and culture lead my parenting to reflect a style of "concerted cultivation." In other words, how consciously do I create experiences imbued with intentional learning on how to be middle class and do well in school? Through my present lens as a parent, my memory of Laureau's work has different meaning to me than when I had first read it as part of my professional life.

Sometimes I read the parenting advice pieces about topical issues like screen time; more often I read parenting humor bits that assure me that life with kids is messy—literally and figuratively— and should be laughed about. But I take note of all of it. Every headline is an invitation to judge my parenting. Perhaps taking note is itself a self-flagellation rite that mothers of my place, time, and position endure to alternately atone for our failings and delight in our smugness. Perhaps it is like Jeremy Bentham's imagined panopticon (Foucault, 1977). There is a prison with a tower in the center surrounded by a circle of cells facing toward it. The prison guard sits in the tower and watches, unseen by those in the cells. The gaze of surveillance emanates from the center point. Inhabitants cannot know whether they are being watched, but their lives are lived with constant awareness of the potential of authority's judgmental gaze. The panopticon operates to compel discipline by self-policing. The need for corporal punishment fades as compliance is achieved by each inmate monitoring their own discipline (Foucault, 1977). Sharon Hayes (1996) describes "intensive mothering," in which the mother is positioned to be constantly and actively attuned to her child's intellectual and emotional growth. Annette Lareau's (2003) notion of "concerted cultivation" refers to mothering that is rooted in attentiveness to children and active crafting of their experiences. Each of these approaches to parenting are thought of as morally good (Perrier, 2013) and both are associated with middle-class privilege and affluence. Everything in the world of intensive parenting is a choice made about my children and their futures. Intensive parenting invites constant rumination on whether I have made the correct choice or whether I should have chosen differently. The panopticon is the architecture of a culture that affirms and shames parents based on how "moral" their parenting is deemed. Self-vigilance according to the mores of #Momlife parenting is maintained as I glance at the headlines streaming across my social media every day.

* * *

The paper that Barbara handed to me lists about five kinds of evaluations, with a line that you can check-off next to each if you want them performed. These are the choices. "You can sign it right now and it will all be set up." She is gentle in her suggestion. She wants to help my son. I glance at it, fold it up, and say that I will think about it. I say that I will look it over with my husband and let them know. I do this because I know it will allow me to leave without conflict. Patriarchy provides a convenient escape this day.

"The childcare center has a full team of in-house people who can help. It is a unique feature from which you can benefit," Barbara tells me. Aiming to shift the conversation, I reply that I know the center is committed to being a model of inclusion and that I am sure my son will be supported in the ways he needs in order to grow and learn. I ask how Barbara and Isabel are already supporting him. I don't remember their answers.

* * *

The not-signed paper smolders in my bag. I am certain that I do not want my son assessed, and that I am not going to go down the list of evaluation types and sign it. When my husband, Jason's father, gets home from work I tell him what Barbara described and show him the paper. He is adamant that Jason is not tested, which connects to his own childhood that was lived under the gaze of clinicians and psychologists (but that is not my story to tell). "There is nothing wrong with him," he is certain. "But, what do you think?" My husband defers to me as mother and as a professional who studies disability and education. I think about how I conveniently relied on the patriarchy to make a quick get-away from the meeting. It is so easy to deploy strategies that are politically damaging when there is little threat to the self. I had known all along that this would be my choice, my power to play. "He is fine," I reply. Does my assessment emanate from deep love? Denial? Fear? Is it made based on the gaze of a long-ago self who was trained to see what is wrong with children in special education, or does it reflect the judgement my present self, which is nurtured by studying everything that is right about children, *all* children?

* * *

In *The Garden of Forking Paths*, Jorge Luis Borges (1998) crafts a story in which the protagonist sets out to unravel the legend of an infinite labyrinth in which all lose their way. The labyrinth is the story within the story, in which infinite futures emerge and become simultaneously possible at each fork. As each path is traveled, other paths also continue, posing the possibility for them to interweave and intersect with one another. The stories, for the travelers, are always in the moment of becoming. Are the characters friends or enemies? How do they inhabit and pulse with the potential of both relations at the same moment? I am intensely aware of how my choice to sign or not sign the paper constructs the many possible stories laid before my son and myself. Simply being tasked with making a decision presents a whole branch of pathways that now reside (forever) in my body and mind, constructing possibilities I am now compelled to imagine. All of the possible futures emerge, simultaneously, in the present moment. Whether and how the choice of which forking path to travel will matter is unknowable. What is knowable to me in the moment of decision and indecision is that signing the paper will subject

Jason to what Foucault (1973) calls a medical gaze. The medical gaze favors clinical expertise more than the person being gazed upon. The gaze will view him as bits and pieces, as "behaviors" and "responses to stimuli," and as misfires in the mind. One move toward the compliance signaled by signing the paper and my child is pushed to the center of the cold, gazing light. One move toward resistance and I become the difficult mother or the mother in denial of her child's problems, these tropes common assertions made about parents of disabled children (Lalvani, 2014).

One of my favorite books is Kathleen Collins' (2013), *Ability Profiling and School Failure*, first published in 2003. The second chapter in the book is the dialogue of a school meeting and its aftermath, which was recorded by Jay, a black, 6th grade boy in the Midwestern U.S. He has just attended a meeting with his grandparents and his two White teachers. I have frequently highlighted—when reading this book with students in my teacher education courses—a particular piece of this recording. The tape captures the family's dialogue while in the car going home.

> His grandfather begins, "You gotta clean up at school. Them people, they be lookin' at stuff like that. They think our home probably tore up."
> Jay begins, "I didn't—"
> "Don't say anything," his grandmother tells him. (Collins, 2013, p. 24)

I am not worried about whether, or how, a teacher judges my home. Child protective services is unlikely to be called on my family. Although I live in a racially, economically, and linguistically diverse community in which many families are "the type" that teachers assume "don't care about education" (Lightfoot, 2004), my family does not look like theirs. Mine is a nuclear family with a man and woman head of household. I am of Korean descent, and my husband is of White-European heritage; our children are mixed. We speak English exclusively and are all U.S. citizens. I will be graced with the assumption that I am practicing "intensive mothering" and that I am concertedly cultivating my children to excel in the ranks of the social strata of America. Being on the verge of ability and disability is different for Jay's family than for mine. They will reckon with the convergence of racism and ableism. The experience of being gazed upon and surveilled will not be new to them; this is what it means to be Walking While Black in America. "Them people, they be looking at stuff like that," expresses Jay's grandfather with agitation and deep knowing of how institutions regard families like his own. What privilege it is to be in a moment in which I deliberate over the *choice* of whether to sign a paper that will give explicit permission to usher in the scrutiny, surveillance, and judgement imposed upon families of children with disabilities by professionals who want to help them (Lalvani, 2017). Should I sign the paper and comply with what is supposed to help my child? Or should I explain why I am not signing the paper in resistance and objection to how children's bodies and minds are gazed upon and surveilled in schools?

* * *

I am frozen in place as I sit perched on the verge of what is culturally considered morally good—intensive mothering that concertedly cultivates my child and the maintenance of his class-based privilege—and a choice that is likely deemed immoral, one in which I don't accept the "help" being offered for my son. I choose neither. I decide to stay very still, hoping that the observer at the center of the panopticon will not see me, nor the 3-year-old child standing behind me. I do not move, hoping that the roving spotlight will continue on. I ignore the paper, which is now sitting on a shelf in the kitchen. I do not mention it to Barbara over the next days. After a week or so, she asks me if I have talked it over with my husband and if I have any questions. I tell her that we are still thinking about it. I am averting the imagined discussion in which my certain resistance to the help that is being offered will cause conflict. Yet the paper is a curious artifact still intact in my kitchen. Why have I not discarded it?

* * *

I am staying very still.

Some more time passes, and Jason starts to bring home opened but uneaten yogurt containers. They are sent home in plastic Ziploc bags. I ask my three-year-old why he hasn't eaten his yogurt. He tells me it is because he doesn't like to stir them. I ask him if he asks his teachers for help. He says that I should not put them in his lunch anymore.

The next day I ask Isabel why they are sending Jason's uneaten yogurt home. Isabel explains that he doesn't like to stir the yogurt, so they help him to stir it hand-over-hand. This means they put their hand over his to mix the fruit and yogurt up. But they don't do this unless he asks for help. They send the un-stirred, uneaten yogurt home, she explains, so that I am aware of what is and is not being eaten during the day.

Jason understands what is happening. We are both staying still. Jason has decided he would rather not have yogurt than be "helped" to touch a thing unpleasant to feel. It does not come to me all at once, but I think that I am being punished. Is the silence and stillness of the unsigned paper being met with passive aggressive yogurt messages? I am getting ready to be louder about my resistance as I think of the sadness Jason must feel wanting to eat and it being a tortuous event. I wonder if the teachers are really so inattentive as to not realize what is happening, but I get angrier when I understand that, of course, they realize what is happening. They are demonstrating to me and to Jason how problematic it is for him to not stir the damn yogurt. I ask Jason if he wants me to ask his teachers to stir his yogurt for him. I ask him if he would like me to stir the yogurt before school. To each of these suggestions, he says no, and that he just doesn't want it anymore. He wants to stay still.

* * *

It feels ridiculous and I am embarrassed by how indulgent it sounds to write so much about yogurt, but it is symbolic of the trivial tokens that become emblematic of broader and harder contestations. For some children disability is apparent at their first breaths, or even before birth. Other children are identified as disabled later on, or become disabled as they encounter the institutions of medicine and school. It would not be a stretch to note that the so-called "high incidence disabilities" begin with a teacher noticing how a child holds a pencil or how frequently they fidget. School professionals work and live in contexts that aim to identify problems in children (Graham, 2010; Varenne & McDermott, 1998). The suggestion of disability is ushered into many young lives with the noticing of small things like the not-stirring of yogurt and the avalanche of meaning that then becomes attributed to all things. Once gazed upon, circular reasoning takes over with a logic designed to gather evidence of the suspected malady (Collins, 2003; Reid & Valle, 2004). As David L. Rosenhan (1973) observed, anyone can seem insane when placed in conditions designed for "insane" people; labels in schools—learning disabled, emotionally disabled, attention deficit disordered, and so on—come to serve as filters through which all actions of those labeled and profiled as such are interpreted. Suddenly, the aversion to liquid soap becomes bigger, a reaction to loud noises and hectic spaces loom large, and a biting incident is humongous. Not all parents and children get to choose whether to be assessed, and not all may choose silence and stillness the way that my son and I did in this moment of telling and re-telling. That the outcome of this experience is that Jason no longer brings yogurt to school is an insulting non-outcome when compared to the physical and psychic torture and trauma inflicted upon so many youths in schools. Of this, I am aware. I am writing about #WhitePeopleProblems.

* * *

I have already decided to leave the place as soon as I can secure a new preschool for Jason and his brother. I reach out to two of my trusted friends and colleagues, who, like me, are each mothers and scholars critical of how disability is taken up in education. I tell my story and look to them to affirm my decision to move preschools. They tell me to go with my gut and that it will be different in a place that does not already have the "assessment *apparatus* readily available." (Yes, this is really how my friends talk). In other words, Preschool A, with its full team of on-site therapists and specialists, has its clinical gaze attuned and ready at all times. It is a place at least partially constructed by its skill in seeing problems in children. The set-up predisposes children to be labeled as disabled. Preschool B will not have a form letter with an assessment checklist ready to be printed and signed. The paper remains not-signed as I begin looking for a new preschool.

* * *

Just as the words of Jay's grandfather (Collins, 2003) are indelibly inked in my memories, I also frequently think of Michael's mom, who never stood a chance. David Connor's (2006) poem created from Michael's experience recalls the moment of decision in which this middle school aged, Black young man was placed in special education.

> The way they get your parent …
> *"If you don't sign it, your child's gonna be left back*
> *Coz he can't keep up with the rest of the children …*
> *He'll be more embarrassed to be left back than to be in special ed."*
> She ends up signing the paper.
> You just lost your rights right there. (Connor, 2006, p. 156, stanza 50)

My class and race privilege and professional knowledge enabled me to not sign the paper with Jason's name on it. I doubt a school professional would threaten me in the way that Michael's parent was. I know the research, the outcomes, and I know disability school policy so well I could be an advocate for others. For Jason and me, being on the verge of disablement is a different experience than that of Jay, Michael, and their families. I am about to visit a potential new preschool and whisk my child away. It is so easy to deploy strategies that are politically damaging when there is no immediate threat to the self. Michael and his mom sweated it out in a system that remains largely unchanged. How many privileged parents would it take to force change? Jason and his younger brother will move from one locally touted preschool to another equally touted preschool, leaving the practices of Preschool A unquestioned and unscathed.

* * *

When I visit Preschool B the questions I ask are different than those I asked when I auditioned previous childcare centers years earlier (and there were many). I focus my attention to how structured the daily activities are. I ask if children are coerced to be a part of activities with which they seem uncomfortable. I ask if the staff help the children with their lunch. They assure me in words and by example that children are able to pursue what they want to do for most of the day, that they may play quietly if they do not want to engage with group activities, and that they expect to help children with things like stirring yogurt. My questions on visits to childcare centers previously emphasized play, the number of children, and variety of activities. I am keenly aware that what I am now asking to know about Preschool B is, with what vigor do they pursue compulsory able-bodiedness and able-mindedness of their children.

* * *

Alison Kafer (2003) and Robert McRuer (2006) describe compulsory able-bodiedness and compulsory able-mindedness as the pull of a culture that desires normativity because it is the sanctioned portrait of wholeness and wellness. In the 2013 book, *Feminist, Queer, Crip*, Kafer lays out the assumptions driving the pull toward normativity:

> The first is that disability is seen as the sign of no future, or at least of no good future. The second, and related, assumption is that we all agree; not only do we accept that couples don't want a child with Down syndrome, we know that anyone who feels otherwise is "crazy." (p. 3)

The moral response to disability within this culture is to seek a future in which disabled bodies and minds are eradicated through science, and to devote our energies to tame the unruliness of our unfortunate bodies to be more acceptable in the world (Erevelles, 2000; Overboe, 2008). Kafer recalls an exchange with a professor who thwarted her desire to study cultural approaches to disability that occurred shortly after she became disabled:

> She patted me on the arm and urged me to "heal," suggesting that my desire to study disability resulted not from intellectual curiosity but from a displaced need for therapy and recovery. My future, she felt, should be spent not researching disability but overcoming it. (p. 2)

Rejection of the assumptions about disablement and resistance to the compulsions underlying this exchange sets the framework for Kafer's work toward imagining disabled bodies as present and vital in thinking about futures. What is moral in such a future is imagining disability not as a failure of science or medicine, but as an inevitability of lives. As Kafer notes, "there is a difference between denying necessary health care, condoning dangerous working conditions, or ignoring public health concerns (thereby causing illness and impairment) and recognizing illness and disability as part of what makes us human" (p. 4). Crip futurist thinking is about the construction of worlds in which many bodies and minds are accepted, valued, and anticipated. Social, discursive, and physical environments are designed and navigated in ways that allow us to be and become in relation with each other in public life, in political life. "In imagining more accessible futures, I am yearning for an elsewhere—and, perhaps, and 'elsewhen'—in which disability is understood otherwise: as political, as valuable, as integral," Kafer writes (p. 3). Which of Borges's paths lead to this future? Is Preschool B the "elsewhere" I am searching for, in which my child will have a more accepting present? Where and when may he be viewed as a child who is in need of help *and* who is valuable because of, and not in spite of, himself? Finding words to describe the wholeness of being that is perfectly imperfect is challenging. These are relations among the world, bodies, and minds yet to be found in Kafer's "elsewhen."

* * *

I have shared this story on a few occasions over several years. I am reminded of it more often than I tell it. I think of it in the moment a friend is telling me about her desire to find out how to use public school funding to have her young child assessed because he is not yet wanting to hold a pencil and write. "Occupational therapy can be free for us, and I worry about his being behind when he gets to kindergarten," she intimates. I remember the story during a quick chat with a neighborhood couple I encountered on their way to a school meeting that they called to have their child assessed to see if he can benefit from speech services. Later, they are frustrated that he will not qualify. And later, they pursue a private evaluation.

I was reminded of my story in the course of conducting several interviews and discussions with parents who decided to leave traditional education, and to instead join an educational cooperative in which children lead their own learning in a practice called "unschooling" (Gray & Riley, 2013; Rolstad & Kesson, 2013). The passing mentions during the interviews of "ADD," over-stimulation, and children getting in trouble for moving too much, each bring me back to the choice I made to leave a paper unsigned and then move to a new preschool. These nine families left schools because their children were not allowed to move as often as they needed; because they were not allowed to carry the insulin they needed to stay well; because they were not enabled to eat when their bodies needed; because they could not choose to be in less noisy environments; and because they were being pushed toward or were escaping from the disablement occurring in special education. Some left when special education failed their children and others left school when they were confronted with entering into it. There are many reasons that the families I interviewed described for joining the cooperative, but it is clear that nearly all left school to avoid the gaze or at least gain control of how it is directed at their children. They escaped professional scrutiny and compulsory able-bodiedness and gained solace and support in finding other families making similar choices to leave schools.

To actively seek the "help" provided by professionals in education is a response to the compulsion of normativity. To resist the "help" being offered at schools by leaving them is another response. While not available to all, privilege and confidence in personal liberty connected to social class, to color, and to location, enables choice. Privilege enables the choice to leave schools. It is deployed when seeking early intervention to maintain school advantage. It is exercised when the family is able to pay for multiple evaluations until the desired outcome is achieved. Each of these choices are enabled by the possession of knowledge and power, most often associated with class and racial privilege. Yet, with our choices—especially those that resist— comes uncertainty. The intensity of the panopticon looms large as we are gazed upon with moral judgement, the primary threat being guilt over the influence we have wielded on our children's destiny. To have complied with professional advice is to be blameless, no matter the outcome. To resist is to forever question and be questioned. That Jason "is fine" and will always be fine because I am taking care of him is a testament to my privilege. Still, I am ever aware of the pull of compulsory able-bodiedness and compulsory able-mindedness as its force forges a fork in the paths before me and before the others with whom I talk about parenting and education. Many parents perceive the verge of disablement, some leaping toward it; others leaping away from it. We deliberate upon and choose directions in practice of intensive mothering, and our motherhood is constructed within and by these decisions. Motherhood, for me, is wandering through Borges's labyrinth as I live and imagine the simultaneous presents and futures that unfold each time I remember the moment Barbara rested her hand on my knee.

REFERENCES

Borges, J. L. (1998). The garden of forking paths. In J. L. Borges (Ed.), *Collected Fictions* (pp. 119–128) (A. Hurley, Trans.). New York, NY: Penguin Books. (Original work published 1941).

Clandinin, D. J. (2016). *Engaging in narrative inquiry.* New York, NY: Routledge.

Collins, K. M. (2003/2013). *Ability profiling and school failure: One child's struggle to be seen as competent.* Mahwah, NJ: Lawrence Erlbaum Associates.

Connor, D. J. (2006). Michael's story: "I get into so much trouble just by walking": Narrative knowing and life at the intersections of learning disability, race, and class. *Equity & Excellence in Education, 39*(2), 154–165. https://doi.org/10.1080/10665680500533942

Davies, B., & Gannon, S. (2006). *Doing collective biography: Investigating the production of subjectivity.* Berkshire, UK: McGraw-Hill Education.

Erevelles, N. (2000). Educating unruly bodies: Critical pedagogy, disability studies, and the politics of schooling. *Educational Theory, 50*(1), 25–47.

Foucault, M. (1973). *The birth of the clinic: An archaeology of medical perception.* (A. M. Sheridan, Trans.). London; New York, NY: Routledge. (Original work published 1963).

Foucault, M. (1977). *Discipline and punish: The birth of the prison* (2nd ed.). (A. M. Sheridan, Trans.). New York, NY: Vintage Books.

Frost, R. (2002). *The road not taken: A selection of Robert Frost's poems.* New York, NY: Macmillan. (Original work published 1916).

Gopnik, A. (2016). *The gardener and the carpenter.* New York, NY: Farrar, Straus and Giroux.

Graham, L. J. (Ed.). (2010). *(De)constructing ADHD: Critical guidance for teachers and teacher educators* (Vol. 9). New York, NY: Peter Lang.

Gray, P., & Riley, G. (2013). The challenges and benefits of unschooling, according to 232 families who have chosen that route. *Journal of Unschooling and Alternative Learning, 7*(14), 1–27.

Hayes, S. (1996). *The cultural contradictions of motherhood.* New Haven, CT: Yale University Press.

Ingber, S. (2018, May 28). What kind of parent are you: Carpenter or gardener? *NPR.* Retrieved from https://www.npr.org/sections/goatsandsoda/2018/05/28/614386847/what-kind-of-parent-are-you-carpenter-or-gardener

Kafer, A. (2003). Compulsory bodies: Reflections on heterosexuality and able-bodiedness. *Journal of Women's History, 15*(3), 77–89. https://doi.org/10.1353/jowh.2003.0071

Lalvani, P. (2014). The enforcement of normalcy in schools and the disablement of families: Unpacking master narratives on parental denial. *Disability and Society, 29*(8), 1221–1233. https://doi.org/1 0.1080/09687599.2014.923748

Lalvani, P. (2017). Gatekeepers of normalcy: The disablement of families in the master narratives of psychology. In M. Rembis (Ed.), *Disabling domesticity* (pp. 287–308). New York, NY: Palgrave Macmillan. https://doi.org/10.1057/978-1-137-48769-8_12

Lareau, A. (2003). *Unequal childhoods: Class, race, and family life.* Berkeley, CA: University of California Press.

Lightfoot, D. (2004). "Some parents just don't care": Decoding the meanings of parental involvement in urban schools. *Urban Education, 39*(1), 91–107. https://doi.org/10.1177/0042085903259290

McRuer, R. (2006). *Crip theory: Cultural signs of queerness and disability.* New York, NY: New York University Press.

Overboe, J. (2008). Disability and genetics: Affirming the bare life (the state of exception)*. *Canadian Review of Sociology/Revue Canadienne de Sociologie, 44*(2), 219–235. https://doi.org/10.1111/j.1755-618X.2007.tb01135.x

Parekh, G. (2017). The tyranny of "ability." *Curriculum Inquiry, 47*(4), 337–343. https://doi.org/10.1080/03626784.2017.1383755

Perrier, M. (2013). Middle-class mothers' moralities and "concerted cultivation": Class others, ambivalence and excess. *Sociology, 47*(4), 655–670. https://doi.org/10.1177/0038038512453789

Reid, D. K., & Valle, J. W. (2004). The discursive practice of learning disability: Implications for instruction and parent–school relations. *Journal of Learning Disabilities, 37*(6), 466–481. https://doi.org/10.1177/00222194040370060101

Rolstad, K., & Kesson, K. (2013). Unschooling, then and now. *Journal of Unschooling and Alternative Learning, 7*(14), 29–71. Retrieved from https://jual.nipissingu.ca/wp-content/uploads/sites/25/2014/06/v72142.pdf

Rosenhan, D. L. (1973). On being sane in insane places. *Santa Clara Law Review, 13*(3), 379–399. Retrieved from http://digitalcommons.law.scu.edu/lawreview/vol13/iss3/3

Varenne, H., & McDermott, R. (1998). *Successful failure.* Boulder, CO: Westview Press.

Walton, A. G. (2018, April 16). How too much screen time affects kids' bodies and brains. *Forbes.* Retrieved from https://www.forbes.com/sites/alicegwalton/2018/04/16/how-too-much-screen-time-affects-kids-bodies-and-brains/#4ce478d11549

CHAPTER 12

Karma, Dogma,
AND THE Perfect Child

MONIKA TIWARI

Starry-eyed, secretly dreaming of a future life with a perfect husband and perfect children, I was a young girl living in the beautiful valley of Dehradun in India—"Doon" as the locals fondly call it, a small paradise at the foothills of the Himalayan mountain ranges. It remains one the most sought after destinations for tourists because of its pleasant climate, picturesque landscapes and easy proximity to Mussourie (the "queen of hills"), Haridwar (a religious pilgrimage destination), and Rishikesh (the land of yogis and ashrams). Life in Doon was charming and peaceful, untouched by the hustle and bustle of city life; surrounded by lush forests and natural springs and brooks, it was the fascination of most people. My reminiscences of Doon include memories of sleepy summer days, picking juicy lychees and mangoes from our backyard trees. The air, filled with the sweet aroma of these fruits, intoxicated the mind, body, and soul. The neighborhood uncles and aunties enjoyed our excitement as we playfully climbed the trees to pick the delicious treats. During Holi, the festival of color, we celebrated by showering colored powders on each other, and on Teej, another holiday, we celebrated the season of showers itself. The festivities included adorning ourselves with green glass bangles and jingling silver anklets, and we'd show off our henna tattoos, sing and dance. Even today, I can close my eyes to instantly travel back in time, and I am filled with nostalgia. Amidst this carefree world I grew, and so did my dreams of my future life—a *perfect* life. As strange as it now seems, my dreams never had anyone with a disability in them. I had never thought about disabilities, and believed that I did not know anyone with a disability. This says a lot about the society, culture, and environment in which I was raised. Did disabilities not exist when I was growing up, or was it just kept hidden? How is it that in a school of almost 1,000 students, I do not remember anyone with a disability? Why did I not notice them at all?

Now, when I think harder, I do remember a boy in a wheelchair during my early elementary years, and there was also a "handicapped" boy, as he was called, in my class. Additionally, the brother of my close friend had Down syndrome, and yet I did not think I knew anyone with a disability. A decade later when my daughter was born and diagnosed with Down syndrome, I was clueless about what it meant. Considering that the brother of my close friend had Down syndrome, I should have known much more about it. But alas, this was not the case. As a teenager, whenever I visited my friend at her home, she would quickly ask her little brother to go away after greeting us. Maybe it was just something any big sister would do, or maybe she was not comfortable. I would say hello to him, but had no other interactions. I did not spend any time thinking about him. Was it because I didn't see the disability at all? Or was it because nobody ever mentioned or talked about it? I dig deep into myself and make an undesirable discovery: it was because I didn't think of him as being worthy of much and did not value his opinion. That was part of my social conditioning. When I was growing up, people didn't talk about disability at all, and "staying away" from them was generally found to be the best and most hassle-free approach. Often, they were kept hidden because of the shame that families felt. So, during my first 25 years of life I had encountered just three people with a visible disability; those with invisible disabilities were just considered "weird." More recently, I was sitting with my mom on a snowy December morning in our home in New Jersey, sipping a cup of tea and talking about our life in the past, and whoa—I could now recall so many people whom we had just termed as "weird" back then out of ignorance. They were different, and so they seemed outside of my world. A feeling of guilt comes over me. I know I was probably kind to them, but did they need only my kindness? Sadly, I missed every opportunity to interact with them.

A BEAUTIFUL GIRL

Life drastically changed after my childhood. The young dreamy girl did find her "perfect" husband and left India to join him in the USA. Everything seemed just right! Newly married, basking in the glory of love, I began my new phase of life in my new country—a country of dreams and opportunities. One morning soon after, I called my husband, excitedly, to tell him it was time to go to the hospital to welcome our first little bundle of joy, our baby girl! Now was the time when all of the young girl's dreams were about to come true. Filled with excitement, we left for the hospital. But things soon started to take a different turn.

It all began with the obstetrician in the operation room. Seconds after the delivery, I inquired if everything was fine. The doctor, hiding what she knew then, said that all was fine, the baby had just passed meconium, that was all. The pediatrician then said, "Trisomy 21." My husband understood it immediately, but I did not. My doctor probably thought that it was the most devastating news and that is why she tried to shield me from it. She just left the room and didn't return until two days later. Then, instead of giving me information about Down syndrome, she talked about how my daughter was probably my dad reborn, and that all of this had occurred because I still had dues to pay toward him, and therefore, I must fulfil my karma! (It is necessary to mention that my obstetrician is also from my Indian community; like me, she was raised in a culture that strongly believes in the power of karma.) She left, adding, "Wait for the results of the blood test, as miracles do happen." In that moment, the world was spinning around me. I was stunned. So, having a child with disability was a result of my bad karma? I should wait for a miracle because what happened was such a nightmare?!

In Hinduism, the most commonly practiced religion in India, it is believed that all beneficial effects are the result of good deeds done in the past (including our past lives), whereas all harmful effects are because of bad deeds committed in the past. These good or bad deeds are called the karma of a person. A popular Hindi expression is, "jaisi karni waisi bharni"—in other words, you reap what you sow. The belief is so deeply rooted that people go as far as blaming their actions in a previous birth if they can't find any good reason for the things that happen in their present life. Everything from diseases to losing a loved one to injustices in society can be blamed on someone's karma. I recall a distant relative who, thinking I needed consolation for giving birth to a baby with Down syndrome, tried to offer me solace by giving me a candid talk on how my karma got me into such a difficult situation. I was amused, but also angry. Another elderly relative thought that she could put my fears to rest by saying, "do not worry, such children do not live long." This ended my belief in the notion that wisdom comes with age!

Filled with fear and surrounded by talk about "bad karma" and offers of condolences, we began taking care of Aarya—our baby girl. We were afraid for her future. I had fears about my daughter's acceptance, her marriage, and her life after I passed away. If I had grown up in an inclusive society, an inclusive school, and had friends with all kinds of abilities, I may have known how to react to the situation differently. My mom, who was with us during this time, confessed that she prayed that our newly born daughter should only live if her disability is not a major one. Such were the perceptions of everyone around us. They offered us a long list of suggestions for remedies. Some people suggested prayer and performing rituals; others suggested alternate treatments like homeopathic medicines or that we visit a place in South India where it was claimed that Down syndrome could be cured. A priest advised us to make sure our daughter worships Lord Shiva every day to make her "normal." Horoscopes were written and read by astrologers who recommended we observe a fast on holy days in order to bring health and prosperity to our child. My obstetrician cursed her own fate—one in which god had chosen her to deliver a child with Down syndrome. A dear relative thought Aarya was actually a part of god, and another person expressed her hope that if my daughter could not live a "normal life," she might as well not live at all. This is how I began my journey as a first time mom—surrounded with the message that something terrible had happened.

Some family members, assuming that we were aware of the condition prenatally, were bewildered about why we did not abort the fetus (and some of them continue to be bewildered). During my pregnancy, a triple screening test had actually given some indication there might be a chance of a genetic condition, but I had never followed up with any further testing and had put it out of my mind. Some thought us to be fools and expressed this. They just could not understand why we continued with the pregnancy if there was an indication of a genetic defect, or why we didn't have further tests done to find out about any abnormalities. In Indian middle-class society, abortion is often considered to be the obvious choice whenever there is any sign of an "abnormality." Almost everyone who came to visit us post-delivery had that one important question to ask, "Did you know of the baby's diagnosis during your pregnancy?" One visitor was very perplexed and even raged about it, asking why we didn't just travel to India to end the pregnancy if it was difficult to get a late-term abortion in the USA. In their minds, getting invasive tests done and aborting seemed very natural and the right approach; anyone that did not fit the mold of normal/perfect could be easily eliminated.

In a new world, among new people, we began our journey as parents with a promise to make our beautiful daughter the focus of our life. At every step, there were people who made us feel like we belonged to a different world—a separate world of disability. But I also started to find people who opened, for me, new ways of thinking. I call them my angels. Maybe some will think it is a bit too much to call them "angels" but, for me, there does not seem to be any other word more appropriate; they guided us so that we could move in the right direction. You will read about these angels throughout my story.

My first angel came in at a time when we were hopeless and thought our world had shattered in just one moment. A couple of days after our Aarya was born, there was a phone call from my nephew who was a resident doctor at that time. He was really cheerful on the phone and congratulated me! He reacted to the news of Down syndrome in a very natural way. At that time, I found it strange that the news was not devastating for him. This was the first time someone had reacted in this way, and I realized that maybe it isn't so terrible to have a child with Down syndrome. For the first time, I started to wonder why people were making me believe that something terrible had happened and that we needed to live with sadness for our whole life.

The next three years were spent adjusting to our new life, getting acquainted with the disability world, joining family support groups, and beginning early intervention sessions for Aarya, inside and outside of the home. We had wonderful therapists who helped us create a new vision for our daughter. Confusion and fear started to change into new hopes and desires. Our daughter was blossoming and flourishing each day. Unaware of the negative perceptions of those around her, she was growing up with a strong mind and personality. Each day I looked at her and gained strength. She didn't care what the world thought of her; all she cared about was our love, our belief, our trust in her. How could I let her know that our beliefs were weak; we were not sure we even knew how to be good parents to her. She had the most beautiful smile and her laughter brightened up the whole room. I marveled as she danced, sang nursery rhymes, read books, and played on the playground. We felt immense joy as she spoke her first words, "bubbles... bubbles," in the sweetest voice. We were such proud parents!

SPECIAL PLACES FOR SPECIAL KIDS

Our first encounter with special education professionals was at an early intervention center and school for children with Down syndrome. I had made friends with many new moms and professionals there. They helped us break free of the negative views that had surrounded us. Our hopes rose! However, we felt like we were living in a parallel world, separate from the rest. Aarya was growing up beautifully, but we could only take her to a few places where people would welcome her; the rest were meant for "typical" children. We felt restricted. By now, we had a vision, high hopes, and a promise to support our daughter to be anything she wants to be, but it seemed this was to be achieved in a parallel world of disability. The therapists, teachers, and administrators were veterans in their field, and did wonders teaching kids with Down syndrome, but they believed in educating them in a *special* school. They believed that only specialists could work with my daughter in these separate, "special places" reserved for people with disabilities. They expressed a view that "regular" schools would be too distracting, difficult, and fast-paced for our kids.

Aarya was now three and it was time for her to start preschool. We thought that we were very aware, knowledgeable, and competent as we went into the school for our first IEP meeting. The early intervention specialists had prepared us well, and we were able to face the team of professionals feeling confident. We walked out of the meeting triumphant; the district explained that they had placed Aarya in just the kind of program she needed: a very experienced special education teacher, a nice big classroom with a smart-board, a very small group of students, and three paraprofessionals in addition! It was a separate class for "special" children. Oh, how thrilled we were that she would be receiving such fancy, specialized services, only to find out later how ignorant we actually were.

FINDING *BODH GAYA* IN A DISABILITY STUDIES CLASS

As Aarya began school, I, too, found time to go back to school. I enrolled in an Inclusive Education Program at Montclair State University. On my first day of class in a disability studies course, I felt very excited and a bit more qualified for the program than the other students, as a mother of a child with "special needs." At this moment, professor L.—the second angel in my life, entered and everything changed. I sat there on that first day of the class bewildered and confused as she talked about the history of disability, inclusion, and segregation. As I continued to attend her classes, my whole perception and thought process towards disability took a 180 degree turn. Trying to make sense of it all, I questioned everything I knew. So, an inclusive environment is good for Aarya? And it is possible? Really? What? How? This was my *Bodh Gaya*— my place of enlightenment. Bodh Gaya, situated in India, is a significant place for Buddhists; Buddha is said to have attained enlightenment under a particular Banyan tree here at this spot. Well, Buddha may have attained his enlightenment at Bodh Gaya under a tree, but I found mine in a disabilities studies class! This is where the transformation began in myself and my husband. The class used to end at 10:45 p.m. every week. We did not have a second car so my husband used to pick me up from the university. I remember those night drives home; sipping coffee in the car, with Aarya sleeping in the back seat, we would discuss what had transpired in that night's class and the prospects of getting Aarya included in a general education classroom. If I had not attended Dr. L.'s class, our lives would have been very different today.

From there began my advocacy to get Aarya included, and to start educating others in the process. It took us one year to convince the child study team at Aarya's school, with endless meetings, emails, and videos. That year was filled with moments of shock, disbelief, and hopelessness at many times, and rage at other times. Again and again, I hit a wall. We were, once again, surrounded by people who were trying to convince us that a separate classroom with only students with disabilities in it, taught by a special education teacher, is the best way to educate our child. Apparently, my preschool child was incapable of learning anything from anyone else. Whenever we brought up the matter of Aarya being separated from her "typical" peers, we were dismissed. The head of the special education department stated that she had concerns about placing Aarya in a general education classroom because "it might scare the other students." Thinking of this statement sends shivers through my body even today. During one IEP meeting, when I inquired about my other options besides the recommended self-contained option, the school psychologist informed us that there was no other option, and that we could take our child wherever we wanted and come back when she turns five. Even as I write this many years later, I am still in disbelief. What made them think that they could tell us these things? Didn't they know that it went against special educational laws? We were also blamed for disregarding, or going against, the opinions of the professionals. One professional gently suggested that we should stop fighting for inclusion because "it's just a buzz word floating around." They suggested that we should look at our daughter's individual needs instead of buying into "some inclusion theory."

The fight continued on, and simultaneously, I continued my program at the university. In my courses, I learned the language and concepts I could use in responding to the ableist reasoning for self-contained classrooms presented by professionals, and make an argument for inclusive education based on current educational laws and research. I learned about strategies and teaching practices for including children with disabilities in general education classrooms. But even as I continued to transform my thinking, I kept getting push-back from the professionals. They told me that I would shatter Aarya's self-esteem and confidence, and that I would be doing her a disservice if I pushed to have her in a general education class. As my advocacy for inclusion continued, so did their adamant reasoning for self-contained classrooms.

In my next semester, I come across my third angel—professor B. One night after class, feeling helpless, I approached her and asked to speak with her for a couple of minutes, but before I knew it, it had been an hour. At the end of that conversation, I asked if she would come with me to the next IEP meeting as I felt helpless in convincing the child study team that my daughter had the right to be treated and taught like her peers. It is disheartening that we should have needed to prove that my daughter was worthy of learning alongside her typical peers. She had never even been given a chance to be with them. Dr. B. agreed, and at the next IEP meeting, we were finally able to get Aarya into a general education classroom. Aarya was now included and sat with her peers in school! Strong supports and advocacy were needed to keep her included. However, I continued to feel that I was being judged by professionals as doing a disservice to my daughter. It's an irony that I had to explain to educators that it was my daughter's right (just like all children) to be with everyone else.

My story cannot be complete without the mention of one other angel, Dr. E.—a professor I encountered in my third semester. She gave me the confidence to never underestimate my own power. She made me believe that I can advocate on my own, and not just for my own child but for many others. She showed me the importance of passing on the knowledge to others and empowering other people through sharing my experiences. These days, I am doing just that; I am involved in my local special education parent advisory group, sharing information, and helping parents to come together make changes at our schools.

A "PERFECT" CHILD

Something else magically happened as we treaded along the path of life. There was a transformation, not just in us, but also in the people around us. Before becoming Aarya's mom and dad, we were products of a very conservative and narrow-minded society. We were molded, conditioned, and trained to judge others through the lens of *perfection* that society has created. Aarya broke that lens for us. I also started to notice that my mother's perceptions became transformed. This is significant since she was raised in an even more conservative environment than I was, and all her life she has been immersed in very traditional culture. In India, people do not even need to be scientists to think that they can make perfect babies! They rely on horoscopes and astrology to make decisions about marriages, to predict if the couple would have babies, and whether the babies would be intelligent, healthy, etc. Since ancient times, the practice of match-making based on horoscopes has been aimed at trying to create a perfect couple, perfect children, a perfect family, and a PERFECT world. The Indian astrologers can give Western scientists a run for their money! To see my mom breaking through these barriers, taking the opportunity to learn and to change her way of thinking, at her stage of life, was incredible. Today she is a strong advocate for people with disabilities, and my pillar of strength.

Outside of our family, too, I saw a lot of people transforming. Their ideas about what Aarya could or could not do has changed. However, even now, when they see her succeed and blossom, they give credit to us (her parents) for it—instead of attributing the credit to her. Some in my family call her a "miracle child," and while it is intended at showing their love for Aarya, it also reflects that their expectations for her were extremely low. I also noted a transformation in the professionals in the child study team at Aarya's school; their perceptions towards disability have changed greatly. I no longer go into the IEP meetings feeling fearful of "losing inclusion" for Aarya.

Fast forward to 8 years later. I found out that I was pregnant again. We were delighted! Aarya was ecstatic to know that we would soon have a little baby at home. My husband and I had decided that, no matter what, we would welcome the new baby with excitement and happiness. Sadly, many around us still came back with suggestions of doing prenatal testing to find out if the baby was going to be "perfect." They had endless love and boundless caring for us, but it seemed that, even after 8 years, the perceptions of some people around us had not changed at all. Their views were still constricted. They did not see that we already had a perfect child.

CHAPTER 13

Mother Is Wise

How Disability Constructs Maternal Identity

LINNÉA FRANITS

My mother was 38 years old when she gave birth to me, and I was 38 years old when she passed away. I noticed this numerical curiosity when reflecting about the timeline of our lives, and found it interesting that I arrived in her life at the chronological midpoint that neatly divides her days into those without me and those with me. Using the same logic, I might identify the present time in my life as my days without her, but that would not be accurate as she is still with me in many ways, including the ways in which I am wise about disability. I use the term "wise" in the manner that Goffman (1963) introduced it in his classic work on stigma, and specifically as it applies to living with disability. That is, "being wise" is having intimate knowledge of a person's lived experience of being marginalized and stigmatized because of disability (Cochrane, 2014; Goffman, 1963). This knowledge is indirect, or what Cochrane (2014) terms a vicarious narrative, and is unique to those in close proximity to the person with disability. In this sense, my mother and I both became *wise* because of my sister, Annalise, who was a woman with disability.

I was born into a disability story that had already begun to unfold, as my sister's neurological malfunctions predate my birth by two years. Thus, I always knew my mother as one who navigated around disability with a skill set untested in the lives of the other mothers I knew in our community. I modelled much of my own response to disability on the attitudes she nurtured in our household. Our family activities were not curtailed by my sister's medical fragility, and the tempo of our life together was set by my parents' seemingly effortless inclusion of her in all that we did. For example, we went on long car trips and lived abroad for a year. We went to restaurants regularly, went to church several times a week, and practically lived at the local beach in the summer. I am fairly certain, in retrospect, that it was not effortless and that my mother, in particular, might have strategized in ways that I just did not see as a child. At the time, I didn't get the impression that my mother did anything differently because of my sister's disability, and she seemed to presume that the places we went to, or the people we spent time with, would be just as inclusive as we were. But there were also moments of insecurity and tension around my sister's impairments when we grappled with contexts that could not, or would not, be accessible to her. In these moments we understood that some differences are embraced by society as representative of the beauty of diversity, while others trigger feelings of shame and stigma. As I have established somewhat of a critical distance from my birth family and have started to examine the evolution of my thinking, I wonder to what extent dominant cultural tropes about disability infiltrated my mother's perspectives. Where did she establish points of resistance to the grand narratives that persist about disability? And, what did she knowingly or unknowingly pass down to me?

My interest in my mother's response to disability is piqued by my exploration into my own identity as a mother of a son with autism and a congenital heart defect, and my musings about how his disabilities have helped to construct my motherhood. Our mothering narratives, imbricated and nested, interact with each other in ways that are not easily teased apart; yet, as I analyse the construction of my own maternal identity, I discover points of resonance and dissonance with her mothering as seen from my viewpoint. I must be mindful that all of this is from my viewpoint and what I refer to as her mothering is, of course, my interpretation of her mothering, without the benefit of her weighing in on my perspective, as she passed away several years ago.

Although I intend to interrogate these narratives of maternity and disability using autoethnographic research methods (Jones, Adams, & Ellis, 2013; Kim, 2016), I must also recognize that my recollections of growing up with a disabled sibling are evolved and reconstructed memories. That is, time, growth, and the retelling of stories tends to alter them in various ways (Bochner & Ellis, 2016). Even as I call these stories up from my memory, I construct them yet again as I bring in new perspectives gained from my scholarly pursuits and my experiences as a mother of a child with a disability. I cannot present my sister's narrative of disability, nor can I present that of my mother. However, I can re-present their stories as observed from my own perspective, both as a child and through my present identity, which I mindfully and reflexively examine with methodological discipline.

DIGGING IN: AUTOETHNOGRAPHY AND PHOTO-ELICITATION

Autoethnography, which is a form of life-writing, is a natural fit for an exploration into identity and disability, as it intends to observe cultural phenomena through the lens of personal narrative (Jones *et al.*, 2013; Kim, 2016). Ellis describes that she chose autoethnography for her work because "what was happening extended beyond me and could yield insights about culture, social structure, relationality and communication" (Bochner & Ellis, 2016, p. 197). Autoethnographic products are, therefore, both interior explorations as well as vehicles for examining a variety of contexts and critiquing cultural practices (Boylorn & Orbe, 2014). My explorations require that I "zoom in" to my own experiences and then turn the lens to "zoom out" to reveal the contexts within which those experiences are situated, particularly the cultural tropes related to disability.

I often use prompts for my autoethnographic reflections, and family photographs are particularly effective for this exercise. Researchers who use family photographs within inquiry (Baxter, 2009; Hirsch, 1997; Kuhn, 2002) elicit narratives from others or themselves that help to describe and contextualize the images within the sociocultural spaces they inhabit. My application of this method is to use family photographs as prompts to interrogate disability as a constructive force, specifically as it impacts, and is impacted by, maternity.

AN ORDINARY PHOTOGRAPH

Figure 13.1. My sister (L) and me (R) on our parents' laps.

Source: Linnéa Franits, personal photos.

I chose this particular family photograph (Fig.13.1) as a prompt, because it includes my mother, my six-year-old sister exhibiting a marker of her impairment, my father, and my three-year-old self. The photograph was taken in Sweden, where my family lived for about a year while my father was on a sabbatical. Our trip was demarcated by my sister's unexpected hospitalization, brain surgery, and recovery, and many of my memories of that time relate to that dramatic alteration to our itinerary. But even more powerfully encoded are the ordinary days leading up to her medical internment, as well as the days of recovery in our temporary home following that episode.

In the photograph, taken before her surgery, my sister sits on my mother's lap with a broad grin that reveals a missing tooth as her left eye deviates from her focused gaze at the camera. One of the symptoms of the recurrent tumor, an astrocytoma lodging near her cerebellum, was this "crossed eye" that became particularly noticeable when she tried to converge her visual fields on a point such as a camera lens. The juxtaposition of the iconic gap-toothed grin of a typical first-grader and the significantly atypical twist of her eye that signalled pathology, is an apt metaphor for how my family-my mother in particular, built an understanding of disability. The ordinary and the extraordinary coexisted in ways that both resisted and supported dominant formulations of living with a disability.

The ordinariness of our lives in the midst of this medical crisis was primarily dictated by adherence to routines and what seemed to be my parents' general optimism and faith that all would work out for good. I never got the sense that events were any different than what my parents had planned all along, and even though my sister's hospitalization was not something that they could have anticipated, it felt like a slight detour rather than a major upheaval in our lives. As a three-year-old, I could not go with my parents to the hospital to visit Annalise, but rather stayed with my grandparents who had joined us for a visit to their homeland. This amended schedule was simply the way it was, and there was little drama in its execution. In these early days, my parents presented my sister's medical situation, as well as her resultant impairments as just another chapter in our family's life.

But our year living abroad was also an extraordinary thing, and, as we travelled to visit relatives around Sweden, I often felt like we were dignitaries who were feted and celebrated in each home. We represented the success story of a prior generation who had immigrated to America, and our tales of suburban paradise bestowed an aura of celebrity that we all enjoyed. But at some point in these glad gatherings there would be a hushed tone conversation between our hosts and my parents, most often my mother. I didn't understand much of the language, but I could tell from my mother's voice, her leaning in to the listener, and the listener's horrified expression, that she was describing the reason my sister's balance was impaired and her eye wandered. I recognized the inevitable look of pity that they would give my sister, as they understood that she would soon undergo brain surgery. Our shiny family narrative had a blemish on it and it took the form of disability. This photograph then is "… precisely in the space of contradiction between the myth of the ideal family and the lived reality of family life" (Hirsch, 1997, p. 8). The stigma associated with disabilities, particularly neurological impairments, was certainly ensconced in the 1960's when the American dream was blossoming and diseases such as polio were being eradicated; disability was not a part of the picture. Families that included a person with a disability were outside of this tableau and bore a mark of abnormalcy. Being a mother to a child with a disability often means "perceived inferiority and exclusion" (Jones, 2013, p. 10) in a society that still considers disability as tragedy and in which individuals with disabilities and their families are marginalized. Although mothers of children with disabilities can have very positive lives within their families, the lack of support beyond the home and stigmatizing attitudes in other contexts often bring greater challenges than the impairments themselves (Home, 2002).

The narrative that grew around our time in Sweden took the shape of concentric circles, emanating from the hub of my sister's health issues, and broadcast primarily by my mother. Upon our return to the U.S., and for years hence, the stories about our life in Sweden were told and re-told, ever echoing back to the dramatic point where a Swedish neurosurgeon saved my sister's life. My mother's identity as Annalise's primary caregiver, advocate, historian, and protector grew out of this narrative, as well, and it became the template upon which future stories were plotted. All other neurology visits, diagnostic tests, send-offs to surgery, as well as the more ordinary activities of daily living with a person with cognitive impairments became a familiar routine for my mother and, eventually, for me.

THE NARRATIVE ARC OF MOTHERHOOD

The tenets of narrative identity formation presume that individuals construct their understanding of who they are by crafting a storyline that incorporates memories of past experiences and expectations of future happenings into a cohesive tale that works to make meaning of life events (McAdams & McLean, 2013). These storylines are situated in contexts that, acknowledged or not, powerfully shape them; individual identities emerge within grand narratives embedded in current sociological ideologies (Cochrane, 2014; Couser, 2012). In my mother's case, her identity narrative was likely to have been dictated, in part, by the imposed societal definitions of what motherhood is, but even more powerfully, by society's assumptions about what it means to mother children with disabilities (Lalvani, 2011; Landsman, 2005). I, in turn, have constructed my own identity as mother of a child with a disability informed by observations of my mother in that role, as well as the different contextual circumstances in which I find myself and buffered by insights from my scholarly enterprises in disability studies.

An early chapter in my mother's life included a bout with tuberculosis, which stalled her opportunities to marry and have children at the time when her contemporaries were busy doing so. She used to tell me that the joy of finally falling in love with my father, when she had already accepted her lot as an unmarried woman, was only surpassed by her quick pregnancy and subsequent settling into the charmed suburban life for which she had longed. When the fairy tale was truncated by the news of my sister's first brain tumor, bursting into her toddlerhood, my mother had to rewrite the narrative again. One of her key beliefs, that surely must have informed the way she framed her circumstances as well as determined the trajectory of her extended maternal role, was the proverbial idea that the sins of our forefathers are paid for by future generations. I wonder if my mother thought her own or her family's "sins" to be a reason for my sister's neurological insult and subsequent disability. Although she believed in a merciful and forgiving God, I wonder if perhaps she might have needed a way to explain the unexpected circumstances in which she found herself. The rhetoric to which she was exposed in the church where she was deeply connected likely contributed to her internalized rationale to take care of my sister "until her dying day," as I remember her saying. I grapple with the idea that my mother may have made some caregiving decisions because of the guilt she carried about somehow causing my sister's disability, and that I may have also internalized this notion which I express in my own mothering.

The construction of disability as a marker of sin is an ancient trope (Kebaneilwe, 2016; Longmore, 2003; Otieno, 2009), which has projections in modern interpretations of sacred texts such as the Old and New Testaments of the Bible. In her comprehensive catalogue of Biblical passages that associate physical and mental impairments with immorality and/or disobedience, Otieno (2009) suggests that in sum these passages point to the stigma that disability brings upon an individual as well as that individual's family. The rhetoric that presumes that spiritual health is expressed in physical health or appearance abounds in contemporary texts about healing and cure as the dominant ideology related to disability in the family (e.g., Autism Speaks, 2018). One of the themes that Landsman (2005) identified in her study of mothers of young children with disabilities was her participants' reiteration of the common belief that disability was often a consequence of bad decisions that mothers had made before or during pregnancy (Landsman, 2005). Popular culture is rife with examples of disability as punishment or outward expression of moral failing, and this has long been a narrative in fairy tales and major motion pictures alike (Longmore, 2003).

My young adulthood was marked by neither the health concerns nor the suburban dream that factored into my mother's story. And yet, having grown up in an atypical family, I longed for a semblance of ordinary life that included marriage and eventually a child. Because we could, my husband and I waited nearly a decade before we tried to get pregnant. My mother automatically interpreted this delay as fear on my part that disability would affect my own offspring. I explained to her that it had more to do with our desire to travel, establish a home and the tenure clock, but she maintained that I had been somewhat scarred by living so close to disability and that it had prevented me from bringing a child of my own into the world. In one particularly tearful conversation in her kitchen, she apologized to me for my sister's disability and said that the physicians had assured her there was no chance that my children would have the same neurological issues as my sister. I remember being shocked that she had even considered that my sister's disability could be realized in my offspring, but given her theological arithmetic, I understood why she said that to me. I was equally surprised when I did finally become a mother and revealed to her that our infant son had been diagnosed with a life-threatening congenital heart defect, and she said through her tears, "I knew it! I just had a feeling that something would be wrong." It seemed that, despite her earlier assurances to me, she had continued to harbor a narrative that included more drama to come in the form of disability. Although she didn't explicitly state this, I wonder if her emotions about my son's perilous health status were further intensified because she felt culpable for passing on impairment to her only grandchild. Did she somehow feel responsible, not only for my sister's fraught medical conditions, but also for those identified in the next generation?

I can somewhat relate to her maternal guilt as I have often retraced the months of my pregnancy and catalogued the risks I took, wondering if any of my behaviors did, in fact, change my son's developing cardiac anatomy. Was it the red wine I had before I knew that I was pregnant, or could it have been something I breathed in at the steel mill that I walked through in my first trimester? I've scoured the evidence online and perused support group posts to see if there is something I can pinpoint as the cause of my son's battle with mortality. In no way do I believe that his cardiac defect is a punishment for past sins, but am I reiterating my mother's narrative and reifying cultural expectations by wanting to take the blame for my child's pain? Landsman (2005) describes the grand narrative of "diminished motherhood" that mothers of children with disabilities are thought to experience. However, this seems to be more a product of societal stigma related to disability than a response to the impairments; perhaps this is the experience of those *wise* to disability. Perhaps my mother was speaking more from the grand narrative about the so-called "tragedy" of disability in families rather than her own experience, which I never heard her describe as tragic.

MY SISTER'S WORDS AND THE CONUNDRUMS OF FREEDOM

Annalise's baby doll was named Margie and mine was Lulu, and as girls we spent countless hours acting out what we thought mothers of babies did. We enjoyed the endless outfit changes, imaginary bottle feedings, and proud promenades around our suburban neighborhood pushing plastic prams. Of course, our dolls never presented the challenges that real parenting can bring such as colic or croup, teething or tantrums. Diapers were dampened only by the water that mysteriously made its way from the machine-stamped mouth hole to the same shaped hole in our dolls' nether regions. Our role-play activities with our rubber-headed charges were as far from real mothering as playing with a Matchbox car is from driving NASCAR. While my sister would never become a mother, she would play an integral role in my learning how to be one. Lulu contributed less to my realistic maternal tutelage than the practice I got while mothering my sister as her needs dictated. As the younger sister, I initially looked to Annalise as the more competent and knowledgeable one, but quite early on, that dynamic shifted as I realized that I was surpassing her in achieving academic as well as social milestones. Rather than switch places with her and take on the mantle of the older sibling, I maintained my status of little sister but adopted a caregiving persona modeled after my mother's way of being with her. I was her "big, little sister" (Garvin, 2010, p. 188).

One of the earliest maternal habits that I adopted was interpreting my sister to others. It is a relatively common experience for mothers to understand their toddler's first attempts at language when others hear gibberish, and so they become expert translators of their child to the rest of the world. This can become a protracted stage when the child has a disability and thus needs interpretation far beyond toddlerhood. Although my sister had great language skills for most of her life, her extreme difficulty with short-term memory and her overdeveloped desire to please often led to her misinforming her listeners, which could be charming but also problematic, so my mother would tend to speak for her. During my sister's frequent hospitalizations, my mother was her primary translator, lest she misreport some critical piece of information such as a symptom or status. Not only did I observe someone other than my sister relaying accurate information to nurses and doctors, but I began to adopt the view that my mother and I had a broader, more complete understanding of my sister's physical needs than she did herself. While this was ostensibly a positive and important advocacy skill that ensured appropriate care for my sister, it was easy for this attitude to slip into a belief that we could represent my sister to the world better than she could represent herself in any context. We were quick to speak for her in medical settings, but also in mundane settings such as restaurants and shoe stores.

The act of speaking for another individual can lead to assumptions about that individual's competence, or lack thereof, and can be a strong contributing force that constructs disability for that individual (Biklen & Burke, 2006). While some of her cognitive impairments made it difficult for her to make decisions, it was also a lack of practice exerting her agency that disabled my sister more than she might have been. This seeming acceptance of dependency on my sister's part was sometimes maddening to me as a teenager. As she observed me grow up and out of childhood, relishing the freedoms and independence this brought, and then surpassing her as I achieved milestones that she would never be near, she sometimes became sad, but most of the time seemed to be happy for me. I wanted her to desire to be more independent! As my sister grew through adolescence she sometimes (rightly) resisted us speaking for her as she began to recognize her agency. But these points of resistance were simultaneously coupled with her deep gratitude for my mother; I know this, because later in life she spoke of our mother's consistent love exhibited in her ever-presence, particularly when decisions needed to be made. I realize now that the binary of dependence and independence is a false one, and from my present perspective, I better understand that the delicate balance that she and my mother established was more of an interdependence.

One skill that my sister learned later than most was how to ride a bicycle. Although we were speedsters on our tricycles when we were small children, Annalise's recurrent need for neurosurgeries and a mild balance impairment throughout her childhood eliminated, for a while, the ordinary two-wheeling activity from her repertoire. At one point, though, my mother understood my sister's strong desire to master the skill and recognized it as an occasion for her to explore the world in a way hitherto unavailable to her, as an independent seeker of adventures. The sessions they spent together every night after dinner were heartbreakingly poignant, as my middle-aged mother jogged behind the bicycle and supported my not-tiny, pre-adolescent sister just enough for her to maintain her upright stance as she dutifully pedaled. It was an ordinary scene, set in the context of the extraordinary, as the older, neurologically impaired tween finally gained the kinesthetic sense that it takes to ride a bicycle. That bicycle was literally the vehicle that established Annalise as a bonafide citizen in our neighborhood and made her known to all. Her daily rides after school and after dinner became part of our neighbors' routines too, and her affable nature made it easy for her to become friendly with folks that she would see on a regular basis along her route. Although I was somewhat embarrassed at the time, watching my mother during these nightly lessons and wondering if it wouldn't have been easier to consider that riding a bicycle is not something that people with brain tumors do, I now believe that my mother's persistence in this activity was somehow restorative to her. What did it feel like when she was finally able to lessen her firm grasp on the Schwinn's saddle, when she felt my sister's body respond to the momentum of the wheels and she could finally let go altogether? And how much did she understand this to be an apt metaphor for her hopes that Annalise could one day be on her own, go into the community, and find her own adventures?

One day, when my parents were out grocery shopping and I was sitting in geometry class, my sister had some sort of an accident while she was out riding her bike. While we will never know the details of that event, the subsequent hospitalization, coma, surgery, and year of rehabilitation that my sister endured are not easily forgotten. My parents came home from the store to find a police officer at their front door who wondered if this young victim could be their daughter. Grief-stricken, my mother perseverated about being responsible for the accident because she had allowed my sister this freedom and had even provided her with the tools to exert it. Once again, the mother-blame rhetoric resurfaced, and my mother could only imagine being judged for not adequately protecting her impaired daughter. Even if my mother had finally come to a point of not feeling guilty for my sister's early neurological problems, this accident was, in her mind, clearly something for which she could be blamed. She asked me more than once if I thought that people thought that she had been irresponsible in allowing my sister the freedom that bicycling alone brought. My attempts to reassure her that she had given my sister an immeasurable gift in teaching her this skill, and that nobody would blame her for that, seemed to quell her anxiety, at least for a time.

SISTERMOTHER

Figure 13.2. My sister and I during her final hospitalization.

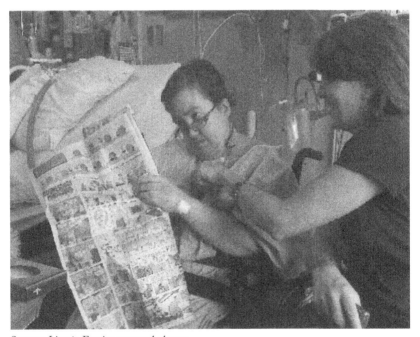

Source: Linnéa Franits, personal photos.

My sister was lying on a gurney in a hospital hallway, awaiting a CT scan of her head, which would reveal the cause of the recent onset of frightening seizures she was having. The transport aide had parked us outside the suite of nuclear medicine testing bays and I nervously chattered as we waited for her turn to be wheeled through the cavernous entryway into the dim tunnel. She didn't seem to be too anxious as she enacted the familiar role of obedient, supine patient, and obligingly answered my inane questions. She had been in this position dozens of times before and thus had a certain practiced calm about her as she stared up at the acoustical tile. But then she turned her head to me and said in a plaintive tone, "Oh, Linnéa–Mom." I recognized this shorthand but wanted to give her a chance to elaborate on what she meant. It would have been too convenient for me to supplant whatever she meant with what I wanted her to mean, knowing that she could be easily swayed. Instead, I probed a bit and asked her what she was thinking about our mother, who had passed away a short time before. She went on to describe how Mom had always been with her when she was in the hospital and would be the one to accompany her to scans, therapies, and operating rooms. In fact, this was a frequent topic of conversation when she reminisced about our mother, and how she had embodied love through her omnipresence whenever Annalise was hospitalized. Her realization at that moment outside of the CT room was that I was the one to be at her side now, and that the role of chief advocate had been bequeathed to me. Although I was well aware of the caregiving tasks in which I was engaged at the moment relative to her hospitalization, I had not yet made so clear a distinction of the motherly duties that were now mine. This shared epiphany left us both somewhat wonderstruck, but our rumination was interrupted by the scan room doors yawning open as my sister was wheeled in for her turn.

The next few years gave me ample opportunities to accompany Annalise to doctor's appointments, diagnostic tests, and further hospitalizations as her neurological status continued to decline. Because she could so clearly articulate how important my mother's presence had been to her in years past, I was compelled to follow suit and "be our mother" for her when she was hospitalized. In part, I was taking on the familiar role of interpreter, so that her impaired short-term memory, growing language deficit, and partial deafness would not result in inaccurate conclusions or mistakes on the part of the medical staff. But the more important role I served was related to meeting her basic and emotional needs. Having observed my mother in the preceding years, I was well-acquainted with the kinds of help I would need to provide Annalise in her hospital room. The routine included setting up her meal trays, navigating the bedpan and bathroom adventures, and providing general entertainment to help pass the time. But simply being present was clearly what she desired and judged to be an expression of the deepest love.

During her final hospitalization, I moved more clearly into the role of guardian as many medical decisions needed to be made about my sister, including the most difficult and ultimate decision to take her off life-supporting technologies. My mother never anticipated that I would be in that most undesired position, as she had been clearly told that Annalise wouldn't live past adolescence. Even as she accrued a list of health concerns of her own, she would never relinquish her maternal duties related to my sister, and repeatedly told me that she had no expectation that I would take over caregiving for my sister. But, just as the leading lady does not anticipate getting sick, my mother did not foresee her own mortality and relatively early departure. When she died, I, her understudy, stepped into the role for which I had been preparing all of my life.

AND SO THE STORY GOES

Figure 13.3. Bike riding lesson.

Source: Linnéa Franits, personal photos.

The photo of my son on a bicycle, with me walking closely behind, (Fig.13.3) is ostensibly an ordinary scene of a mother engaged in an iconic activity that is still a rite of passage in this particular time and place. He wears a helmet and relies on training wheels to maintain his balance, but the uneven sidewalk and unreliable angles of the training wheel mount make falling a very distinct possibility, and therefore I hover nearby. Falling off a bicycle goes with the territory of learning how to ride one, but for my son, once this possibility became a certainty he could not bear the risk. He became so afraid of a potential fall that he abandoned the challenge altogether, shortly after this photo was taken. As I examine this image today, I can identify a spectrum of emotional responses I have to it, and recognize the common ground I share with my mother in this role as fierce protector. I was somewhat relieved at Aidan's decision as it meant that he wouldn't wind up with a fall-related injury and would be safe. But I was also disappointed, as I strongly desire for him to explore activities that other children his age like to do, and want him to broaden his repertoire to include these typical and fun experiences. It would have delighted me if he had worked through his anxiety to get to a place where he could be proud of his perseverance and new skill, and I do feel somewhat guilty for not pushing him more to shake off any bump or bruise that he might have experienced from a fall. But as I reflect on my reluctance to facilitate his own version of independence. I wonder if it is due to my deep-seated fear that he could have had a more significant injury as that which had befallen my sister.

Like my sister, my son has had several life-saving surgeries for, in his case, a significant congenital heart defect, and I have channelled my mother's bedside persona to get through those toughest days in the ICU. In a strange way, I am grateful for having had such a model that made the existential angst that accompanies such a life event a familiar state. Yet I struggle to walk the same tightrope that my mother navigated between poles of being over-protective and pushing my son into the world to fend for himself. There is judgement about either extreme and peril below, so I must be diligent to keep my balance.

Unlike my mother, but not unlike countless other mothers, I have had to fight for appropriate inclusive public education for my autistic child and have been schooled in the diplomacy required at IEP meetings through experience. When my sister attended regular classes at our public school, she was just naturally included without a mandate in place. I recognize that this was not a universal practice in the 1960's, that vast numbers of children with disabilities were excluded altogether from public school, and am grateful for the contexts that enabled my sister to thrive in typical classrooms. Another difference in our experiences has been the level of overt mothering advice offered to me from all corners, most of the time from people who do not have an autistic child. In both of our cases, though, there has been a sense of judgment about our mothering decisions. My mother lived with guilt about allowing Annalise to ride a bicycle on her own, and I live with guilt about not helping Aidan push through his anxiety to learn to ride that bicycle. Although it differs in points of attachment, the power of stigma around disability hasn't changed much despite the half-century that separates our mothering. The narrative that I have constructed about myself as one who is *wise* about disability is richly informed by my mother's legacy, as well as my own experiences of having a son with a disability. The ways in which disability has constructed each of our motherly roles in ordinary and extraordinary moments are clearly connected as my story has grown out of hers, intertwining at times yet veering off in its own direction beyond the future that she anticipated. While I mindfully interrogate the forces that shape my narrative, I must also recognize that there are deep recesses, yet unknown to me, where my mother's story still dwells. As I continue to leaf through old photo albums or scroll through the images I capture these days on my phone, I seek to understand how agency, interdependence, and maternal guilt are complicated by grand narratives about disability and motherhood. My commitment to deconstructing those oppressive ideologies will enable me to resist writing my own story in ways that match a narrative that is not emancipatory.

As our children's protectors, at times overzealous (Jarman, 2012), we mothers of children with disabilities sometimes face difficult decisions about the most ordinary things that have the potential to make our lives extraordinary. Have I been too protective of my own son because of his disability or do my actions mirror my mother's complicated feelings around my sister's independence? Landsman (2005) posits that mothers act as "intermediaries between children with impaired bodies and a society that discriminates against them" (p. 18), and that it is when we inhabit this liminal space that we are perhaps most apt to enter a state of interdependence with our impaired children. Even though we adopted different styles, my mother and I have both been judged by a society that has yet a different narrative around mothering and disability than the ones that either of us have enacted. It is that grand narrative by which we are both measured, at times even by each other. If my mother were here today, I might ask her about what it's like to teach a child to ride a bicycle, to have her succeed, to go off on her own, and to make a name for herself in the community. I would also ask her about how to deal with the fear of letting go of the seat, sensing a wobble, and predicting a crash. She might say that because we mother in a society which pities us, and in which our children are excluded and rejected, that we are interdependent. She might say, because of our experiences, we are privileged. She also might say that we are wise.

REFERENCES

Autism Speaks. (2008). About us [*web blog*]. Retrieved from https://www.autismspeaks.org/about-us/mission

Baxter, K. (2009). *Reflections of family photographs from five generations: The role of narrative and reflexivity in organizing experience.* Saarbrücken, Germany: VDM Verlag Dr. Müller Aktiengesellschaft & Co. KG.

Biklen, D., & Burke, J. (2006). Presuming competence. *Equity and Excellence in Education, 39*(2), 166–175. doi: 10.1080/10665680500540376

Bochner, A., & Ellis, C. (2016). *Evocative autoethnography: Writing lives and telling stories.* New York, NY: Routledge.

Boylorn, R., & Orbe, M. (Eds.). (2014). *Critical autoethnography: Intersecting cultural identities in everyday life.* New York, NY: Routledge.

Chang, H. (2009). *Autoethnography as method: Developing qualitative inquiry.* New York, NY: Routledge.

Cochrane, L. (2014). *Telling disability: Identity construction in personal and vicarious narratives* (Doctoral dissertation). Retrieved from ProQuest LLC (ED568344).

Couser, T. (2012). *Signifying bodies: Disability in contemporary life writing*. Ann Arbor, MI: University of Michigan Press.

Ellis, C., & Bochner, A. (2000). Autoethnography, personal narrative, reflexivity: Researcher as subject. In N. Denzin & Y. Lincoln (Eds.), *Handbook of qualitative research* (2nd ed.; pp. 763–768). Thousand Oaks, CA: Sage Publications.

Garvin, E. (2010). *How to be a sister: A love story with a twist of autism*. New York, NY: The Experiment.

Goffman, E. (1963). *Stigma: Notes on the management of spoiled identity*. New York, NY: Simon & Schuster.

Hirsch, M. (1997). *Family frames: Photography narrative and postmemory*. Cambridge, MA: Harvard University Press.

Home, A. (2002). Challenging hidden oppression: Mothers caring for children with disabilities. *Critical Social Work, 3*(1). Retrieved from http://www1.uwindsor.ca/criticalsocialwork/challenging-hidden-oppression-mothers-caring-for-children-with-disabilities

Jarman, M. (2012). Disability on trial: Complex realities staged for courtroom drama-the case of Jodi Picoult. *Journal of Literary and Cultural Disability Studies 6*(2), pp. 209–225.

Jones, M. M. (2013). The othered sister: Family secrets, relationships and society. *Review of Disability Studies: An International Journal, 9*(2–3). Retrieved from http://www.rds.hawaii.edu/ojs/index.php/journal/issue/view/6/showToc

Jones, S. H., Adams, T., & Ellis, C. (2013). Introduction: Coming to know autoethnography as more than a method. In S. H. Jones, T. Adams, & C. Ellis (Eds.), *Handbook of autoethnography* (pp. 17–48). Walnut Creek, CA: Left Coast Press.

Kebaneilwe, M. (2016). Disability as a challenge and not a crisis: The Jesus model. *Journal of Disability & Religion, 20*(1–2), 93–102. doi: 10.1080/23312521.2016.1152939

Kim, J. (2016). *Understanding narrative inquiry*. Los Angeles, CA: Sage Publications.

Kuhn, A. (2002). *Family secrets: Acts of memory and imagination*. New York, NY: Verso.

Lalvani, P. (2011). Constructing the (m)other: Dominant and contested narratives on mothering a child with Down syndrome. *Narrative Inquiry, 21*(2), 276–293. doi: 10.1075/ni.21.2.06lal.

Landsman, G. (2005). Mothers and models of disability. *Journal of Medical Humanities, 26*(2–3), 121–139. doi: 10.1007/s10912-005-2914-2.

Linton, S. (1998). *Claiming disability: Knowledge and identity*. New York, NY: New York University Press.

Longmore, P. (2003). *Why I burned my book and other essays on disability*. Philadelphia, PA: Temple University Press.

McAdams, D., & McLean, K. (2013). Narrative identity. *Current Directions in Psychological Science, 22*(3), 233–238.

Otieno, P. (2009). Biblical and theological perspectives on disability: Implications on the rights of persons with disability in Kenya. *Disability Studies Quarterly, 29*(4). Retrieved from http://dsq-sds.org/article/view/988/1164

CHAPTER 14

Typicality AND THE (Br)other

DIANE LINDER BERMAN AND DAVID J. CONNOR

Dear Adam,

I am writing this letter to you because I want you to know what I've learned from having you as my son. You, my Adam, are a radiant boy with an incandescence that can light up a room. You have wisdom, intelligence, talent, and dedication, and yet, somehow, you feel that your gifts are not quite enough. I want you to know that dedication and a drive for perfection are good traits, but remember that one deserves to feel content, not only with accomplishments that eclipse most expectations, but also with those that do not meet any.

Expectations. There we have our first problematic word. You, my love, were born into a world where your dad and I were grappling with that word. Our first days, weeks, months, and even years together were a time when we were trying to sort out how to deal with expectations about children's development. Your brother, Benny, as you know, was in the midst of a sea of evaluations. It seems there are expectations even of babies in our society, and when your brother "failed" to meet those defined as normal and valued by society, we entered a whole new world. As educators, we had been trained to constantly measure the achievements of children, and so, at the time, we did not question our responsibility as parents to work tirelessly to make sure your brother met the constantly increasing and changing expectations put forth by the teams of specialists that streamed in and out of our home.

I remember looking at your big brown eyes one morning. You were five months old. I held you to my breast as I signed off on papers describing your brother's skills. You had such questions in your eyes as I looked over the weekly report on your brother's progress; it seemed you had an awareness of something that I did not yet understand. At 2 years of age, your brother was assigned many "goals." When he repeatedly failed to meet them, you saw your dad and I get stressed and argue. Even as you slept in my arms, you surely felt the tension in my body. It seems you were always sensitive beyond imagination. I remember the day, when you were ten months old, before you had words, you crawled right up to Benny's therapist's knees and looked deeply into her eyes. She looked down at you and then told me how lucky I was that I had one child who was typical. She went on to reassure me that one day you would care for your brother when your daddy and I were dead. I fired her that day, though inside I allowed her toxic words to soothe some of my own anxieties.

This particular therapist was one of many that continually saw Benny as only a product of weakness and failure. To counter this attitude of viewing Benny as the sum of his deficits, daddy and I made a conscious choice to celebrate his every breath because we feared that if we did not, he would have no chance in this world. In the energy it took to do this, I fear we did not always celebrate you as we should have, and for that, I will always have regrets.

Time passed, and daddy and I started to realize how wrong things were in this new world we had entered with hopes of "curing" your brother of his multiple disabilities. It seemed as if therapists and evaluators were taking over our lives. They told us which toys to hide and suggested we limit Benny's time playing with certain other toys because he seemed "too fond of them." They cautioned us about the dangers of "perseveration." When Benny enjoyed spending hours playing with his musical toys, they saw his interest in music as "stimming." They offered us full-time Applied Behavior Analysis (ABA) therapy, and chided us when we refused it, suggesting we were "in denial" at best and neglectful at worst. I soon noticed that even though we were opposed to that approach, they were utilizing it in their interactions with him. After watching your brother deteriorate, we switched to a new team with a new approach, one where therapists accepted him for who he was, and used his interests and strengths to guide them. This was progress, but we were not yet where we needed to be as parents.

At the time, it was hard to see the two of you together without comparison. There's that second problematic word—comparison. It was hard to watch your tremendous strengths unfold (so effortlessly, it seemed) right beside your brother who was struggling to meet a milestone he should have met years before. We did not yet know how to celebrate each of you as individuals. How to really enjoy your first words—"helicopter" and "garbage truck" at 13 months—while simultaneously celebrating your brother who had no words at 3 years old, but who had his own ways of communicating. We did not know how to undo that horrific culture of comparison we practiced so many times as educators. And so we downplayed your achievements, feeling guilt in acknowledging or celebrating them.

When you were four and your brother six, we relocated to find a school district that was committed to full inclusion. Prior to this, Benny was in a self-contained program in New York City. Even in a so-called "special class" with multiple teachers, he did not seem to be making progress. The school administrators wanted us to accept placement within what is known as District 75 (D75), a citywide superintendency that is primarily composed of separate schools and classes for severely disabled children. In other words, significantly restrictive environments. This made no sense to me, and so, despite being told repeatedly by school officials that I was "refusing to accept Benny's limitations," daddy and I decided to find another option.

We relocated to a district just outside of NYC so that Benny could be educated in a general education kindergarten. We bought a home nearby. In this school, we believed Benny would have a chance at being included. (Many families would not have this option to just be able to pick-up and move; I am constantly aware of that). At this new school, we watched, with awe, as teachers were able to find ways for you and your brother to grow and develop, each at your own pace. We saw Benny find strengths we never knew he had. As his new peers helped him learn to speak, or learned to communicate with him in other ways, and his teachers created strategies to teach him to read and write, he began to participate as a true member of his school community. Simultaneously, we saw you develop into a child we never knew we had. You became an expert on the devil sticks, and began to play piano, violin, and cello. We learned that you also had a passion for dance and acting. It was such a joy to watch you light up the stage all through elementary school. We finally found we could celebrate you both, and it felt delicious. By watching the model of inclusion at this school, we began to learn how to be the parents you both needed. We learned that expectations that come from outside are meaningless. Steeped in education theory, we were used to finding answers through research and from experts, but we learned that sometimes the answers had to come from within ourselves and from our children.

Over the years, Adam, you have continued to grow into a spectacular young man. Your talents continue to develop as we watch you take on lead roles in many shows and sing with such beauty in so many choral groups. After we moved to Vermont, just days after you began school, teachers were reaching out to me when I entered the school, telling me how much they enjoyed your contributions to the class. Yes, you are a student with deep intelligence and a curiosity about almost everything. There is no subject that does not excite you, and no task you are reluctant to try. But it is more than that. Your eyes are always radiant, seeking to understand and connect. Your understanding of the true meaning of inclusion, and the way you appreciate everyone, makes you a person who enhances every community. You have a wisdom that goes far beyond your 13+ years. I am sure some of it has roots in your early years when you watched society exclude and marginalize your brother.

Sometimes, I notice that self-doubt clouds your eyes. Sometimes you feel that you have not achieved enough. I fear that this desire for perfection and, as you yourself say, your need to "feel special" comes from these early years before we knew how to parent. I could lay the blame on society, but I must take responsibility, as well. Your first years were spent watching us measure your brother against a myriad of expectations. You observed a series of obstacles our family faced, that were not the result of your brother's disabilities, but rather, the result of society's approach to his disability and my initial inability to recognize this.

You had to internalize that somewhere. I want you to remember, though, that we finally threw away the books that told us what to do, and all of the lists of behaviors we wanted to encourage or extinguish, and we began to celebrate your brother for who he was at the time. It was then that things fell into place; our family became happy again and your brother, Benny, began to flourish into the talented and intelligent young man he is today. Your brother, as you know, still has multiple disabilities, but now we see that they do not constrict his life at all. And you, Adam, are a young man who has so many talents. I hope I can help you define your goals in terms of your own strengths and not against arbitrary measures that society creates.

Adam, you know what most do not know, because you grew up alongside Benny, and, for you, disability is a natural part of life. Additionally, when we relocated, you were educated alongside students with a range of disabilities like autism and Down syndrome. To you, this is what a "regular" classroom looks like! I remember that in elementary school, when the students with more severe disabilities were taken to another room for part of the day, you said you felt sad. In middle school, when you saw that some students with disabilities spent all day in a separate classroom, you were angry. Adam, to some people you represent the "gifted child in the inclusion class" who, they fret, may not reach his potential. But you also stand for the so-called typical children who have the power to include or exclude.

Adam, you have seen your brother grow into a spectacular young man. He is excelling in college prep chemistry and algebra 2. I recall that you brought him into theatre and performance arts, where he found that he has great talents. He now sings in a choral group and has been in four plays this year with the local community theatre. In many ways Benny is achieving all that he wants to achieve, but you also see he is often alone. While the kids talk to him in school, they rarely reach out to him outside of school. Even when he reaches out, he is often ignored. Perhaps your observations of how your brother is often socially on the outside—in the margins—have shaped you. Perhaps this is why you are the person who reaches out to your classmates with disabilities. Perhaps it is because disability is normal for you. You know how to talk to everyone, and you know that those who are quiet or reluctant to talk can still be a friend.

Adam, you know that disabilities are not limiting. I admire the way you are able to appreciate and value people, whether they have disabilities or not. I am not there yet; sometimes I see weakness when I see disability, while you see only strength and diversity in all people. You are one of the only people in the world who can get Benny to laugh and interact with such a full and rich voice. Your ability to build bridges will take you far in this world. Your vision is valuable; people like you have the power to change the world. So, Adam, I want you to know that while you will not be responsible for your brother, as he has skills to function in the world, your sensitivity and insider-knowledge bestow on you a responsibility to continue to open doors to all, and to educate others by your own example. The possibility of a future world that is inclusive to all people rests on the shoulders of young people, like you, who can recognize the value of differences, who see strength where others see weakness, and who can imagine a community that is expansive. There is nothing you need to do, other than to keep being you— I just thought you should know what a difference you have made, and will continue to make, in this complicated and beautiful world.

I love you always and forever,
Mom

When I saw the call for chapters for this book, which was to be about the experiences of mothers of children with disabilities, it seemed a natural fit. I had already written two books about my experiences parenting Benny (Berman, 2009; Berman & Connor, 2017). I wanted this chapter to be different, though. This chapter would be about my other son, Adam, my "typical son," who is far from ordinary as typical might imply. Adam has always been the child that surprises me. This surprise stems from his own way of taking risks, as well as the distraction I faced when he was small, battling the world to create a place for Benny to flourish. I recall, one morning when Adam was just 2 and Benny 4, after Benny boarded the bus to his preschool, I looked down at Adam and felt a flood of warmth that took my breath away. My eyes raced from his shiny curls to his ruddy cheeks already damp with sweat, and I felt as if I was seeing him for the first time. Our hands were intertwined as if they knew each other well, but my eyes and mind had not focused enough on this child before me. He bent down and picked up a leaf, held it to the sun, and told the world that it was shaped like a parallelogram. The math teacher in me swelled with pride. That morning, we ran through the park; I followed his lead and we found a myriad of rocks and leaves, and I watched in awe as he classified them in all different ways. We sat in the mud and rolled in the grass. The mother in me wondered where I had been all the other days up until this one. It did not take me long to realize where I had been. I was on the phone with agencies, battling for the services I knew Benny needed, or rejecting Applied Behavioral Analysis (ABA) and other services I did not want. I was listening to social workers tell me I was "in denial," and doctors telling me I was wasting time.

I was also writing a book. I felt the world had to hear our story. They needed to hear the extent to which we struggled to access inclusive education for our son, even though we came to the table with great advantages. I self-published the work and donated a handful to a local parenting group. It was there in the parenting group that the book fell into the lap of David Connor. He contacted me, introducing himself as a professor at Hunter College in the Department of Special Education. David was interested in my experiences, both professionally and personally. I was new to the world of special education and flattered that he even read the book. Although I was basically a mom, and he was an accomplished professor of education who was not a parent, we found we had a kinship. Paving the way for potential collaborations which at the time were far from view, a friendship naturally developed and took root.

Our collaboration is an interesting one because we approach similar questions from different vantage points. David offered me a part-time position as an adjunct instructor at Hunter College, where I have now taught for 6 years. He encouraged me to thread my personal story into a course on inclusive education. At first, I was uncomfortable about sharing my story, but as the years went by, I became bolder about what, and how, I share. Today, I do not know how I would teach the class *without* connecting it to my personal story. There is power in the personal story; it touches students in a way that a traditional text cannot. Although my story usually centers on Benny, each time I share it I notice that it ripples outward, touching on more and more related issues, such as the experiences of my other son, Adam. So, I have started to ask myself, how can I incorporate Adam into the story I tell?

I shared this letter with Adam, and he appears to have taken comfort from it. I wrote it because I want him to know that the "problem" did not reside with Benny's disability but with society's definitions of normality, and the pressure this puts on all of us to conform. But now, I am gradually coming to see that perhaps there is more to be learned from understanding inclusivity through Adam's lenses. Adam learned about inclusivity and acceptance first-hand because he grew up alongside his brother. This brings me to wonder, how can we bring this awareness and understanding to other kids who are not as fortunate to grow up beside a person with a disability? How can parents and teachers alike learn from personal stories, such as this one, to undo the negative effects of comparison and to resist arbitrary ideas about what is normal? We spend so much time in schools focusing on the person with the disability. However, what can we, as educators, learn about disability and community—this time, not from *Benny's* story, but rather, from *Adam's*? I turn to my friend and colleague, David, with these very questions.

REFLECTIONS FROM A COLLABORATIVE RESEARCHER AND TEACHER

I, David, admit to struggling a little, at first, with this chapter, convinced that in this collection of mothers' stories, Diane's voice would be sufficient. And of course, it is. However, Diane encouraged me to collaborate as we have developed a rhythm in exchanging thoughts about so many aspects about inclusive education—so we agreed, why not this topic, too? Among other things, Adam is symbolic of the "typical" children in classrooms—children who have not been categorized as disabled.

I think it worthwhile to share my account of how Diane and I came to what I see as a symbiotic professional relationship that is also somewhat personal in the form of being friendly colleagues. Diane's original book had piqued my interest because it was from the point of view of a mother who was also a teacher, someone who saw the value of advocating for inclusive classrooms—even in the face of formidable institutional challenges. The text was in accessible language, so other parents could read and understand what is essentially a common story about a family's response to a child who didn't fit the proverbial mold of societal (read: school) expectations. As a teacher educator who seeks to incorporate multiple perspectives of parents, I found Diane's observations and ideas invaluable; therefore, I requested copies of the book whenever I was involved in parent events. I also used portions of it when teaching graduate classes, so teachers could come to see the challenges parents sometimes face in trying to negotiate our professional structures that inhibit authentic parent voices. As an educator supporting inclusive practices, I was also intrigued by the (ongoing) story of Diane's quest for inclusion. I had always seen inclusion as a matter of principle, a human right. Not all students in my classes agree, nor do I expect them to. That said, one day when teaching my graduate Inclusion class, I was taken aback by a cynical student who asked, "Do you have children of your own? How can you advocate for such things with certainty if you're not a parent?" I was shocked by her directness, yet quickly found my footing by referring to my own extended family in which many of my relatives have disabilities. Still, her question hit me hard, and opened up a door for thinking about: Do you have to have children (deemed disabled or not) to advocate for, or support, inclusive education? Once the door was opened, I was always able to justify a "no" in my head. This disposition of being an advocate for—and an ally of—those with marginalized identities and working toward their increased access to all aspects of society is related to the broad notion of social justice, and to our roles as educators in shaping the world we seek.

Since becoming an educator, I'd valued working with parents and learning from them. Generally speaking, I had formed good relationships with most parents of the high school students I had taught, recognizing the strength of knowing students' families. As it happened, in the very same Inclusion graduate class attended by the cynical student, I'd planned a panel presentation by parents that turned out to be memorable for multiple reasons. Three mothers were willing to talk about their children, the educational choices they had made, and relate it to the complexities of inclusive education across varying contexts and concerns. I had deliberately chosen the participants such that their narratives would compare and contrast, revealing many shades of gray rather than presenting inclusive education in black and white.

The first mother was the oldest of the three and aunt of my co-instructor. She told the story of her now middle-aged daughter. It was a tale of exclusion, describing limited options for education presented to her when her daughter was a child, and of society's expectation that children with intellectual disabilities be kept apart from others. It was also the first time she had spoken about this topic in public; she expressed how she wished the world had been configured differently, and her regrets that she had not fought more for her child who still remains largely cut off from the world, save for a few family members. In her genteel and poignant observations, she wished there had been inclusive education a generation or two earlier and shared how her family still lives with the repercussions of exclusion.

The second mother was a college professor who worked in the field of education and had a daughter, now in middle school, with severe and multiple disabilities. She had strongly advocated for her daughter to be in an inclusive program, believing her daughter benefitted. That said, once her daughter had reached a certain age, the mother had decided a specialized setting was more beneficial. In sum, this mother's tale was about choice, exploring the pros and cons of options, along with what services different settings supplied. At the same time, it is worth considering how this scenario illuminates difficult choices parents are forced to make because existing systems are not always sufficiently inclusive. Ironically, while their own dispositions may have previously sought inclusive settings, parents can eventually become worn down by trying to make inclusion work within a limited system, and disenchanted with a lack of *belonging* their child feels in what are sometimes inclusive classrooms in name only.

The third mother was a former graduate student of mine, whose daughter with a learning disability was in high school. The mother's first words were, "*I can be a cunt.*" I asked myself, "Did she just say what I thought she said?" The look on fifty faces confirmed my fear. The bold statement served as a prelude to how the mother talked about being a fighter for inclusion and accommodations for her daughter at every step of the way, even if it meant appearing big-mouthed or being viewed as "a difficult parent." Whereas the other two panel participants had conveyed middle-class genteelness, this mother was talking "street," complete with a pointed finger stabbing the air between herself and the class full of teachers.

I share this story as I think parents' perspectives have been as important to me as those of labeled students—who were also on a panel presentation later in that same course. Both panels were cited in course evaluations as being the highlights of the class. I may not have children of my own, but as an educator, *I want to know* both student and parent insights based upon their thoughts and experiences. I think every educator should keep parents in mind when doing their daily work, particularly parents' desires around inclusive education for their child with a disability. Teachers can be major players at IEP meetings, and can potentially swing the balance between what psychologists or educational evaluators recommend and what parents actually want for their child. When I was a teacher attending numerous Individualized Educational Program (IEP) meetings, I saw how well-intentioned but unthinking "experts" can limit parental input. As a consumer of research, and a professional with a disposition largely informed by Disability Studies, I have been impacted by Jan Valle's work with parents of children with disabilities as she has verified discrepancies of perspectives between parents and teachers about many aspects of schooling, including the IEP process, "diagnosis," and placement (see, for example, Valle, 2009, 2016; Valle & Aponte, 2002; Valle & Gabel, 2010).

But let's make sure I return to the topic of this chapter. It is different from previous collaborative works between myself and Diane, because here, the focus is on Adam as the (br)other. This focus reminded me of an important moment in the documentary film *Including Samuel* (Habib, 2007) when Isaiah, Samuel's non-disabled brother says, "I'm here, too," asserting his presence in a family that sometimes appeared consumed by his disabled sibling's needs. And yet, I recognize that sibling rivalry, in its many forms, exists in almost all families. Bearing that in mind, I do think it is important to point out that, like Isiah, Adam's sensitivity, maturity, and general humanity that is so apparent has been shaped, in part, by a relationship between non-disabled and disabled siblings. In brief, Adam is a far cry from the pity-based stereotypical notion pervasive in our culture that readily casts non-disabled siblings as personally "damaged" by having a disabled sibling. On a personal note, the phenomenon of being a non-disabled sibling within a family, and how that position impacts a person has also intrigued me personally, having several branches of my own family tree that have children with disabilities. Like Adam's, their life experiences strike me as having been deeply informed, and enriched, by their relationships with disabled siblings. Additionally, as I have come to know Diane over the years, I have visited both her family home and the school of her children, so have met both Adam and Benny, as well as their father, David.

I share the information above as it all inevitably shapes my reflections on Diane's open letter to Adam. Focusing on Adam is an unexpected—yet in many ways, necessary—shift, as it allows us to concentrate on the topic of non-disabled siblings through an assets-based lens that is underdeveloped in professional literature. As a result of writing her letter to Adam and foregrounding his experiences, Diane has, within this chapter, asked me if I'd address a series of questions she poses about: how we can bring Adam's type of awareness and understanding (about the value of inclusivity) to other kids who are not as fortunate to grow up beside a person with a disability; how parents and teachers alike can learn, like Adam, to undo the negative effects of comparison and resist arbitrary ideas about what is normal; and what can be learned about disability and community from non-disabled students—in other words, not from *Benny's* story, but *Adam's*? In the following section, I endeavor to answer these questions from the perspective of a teacher educator focused on inclusivity, knowing that any response can only be the start of a deeper exploration of the topic.

Let me begin by stating that I think the degree of success with inclusive classrooms depends upon how it is framed by the person who is teaching it. For example, in the late 1980s, inclusive education was viewed as placing children with disabilities in general education classrooms. It was a shift in thinking about *where* they should be educated. For some people, this original understanding is definitive. However, this understanding of inclusivity is reductive, as it primarily views inclusion as a technical, programmatic, bureaucratic endeavor, rather than a philosophy—a way of thinking about students. For other people, inclusive education signifies *all* students, including those deemed Gifted and Talented; who are immigrants; learners of English as another language; who self-identify as lesbian, gay, bisexual, transgender, questioning (LGBTQ); and so on, as well as those identified as disabled. What is missing from much of these discussions of children who have been historically marginalized in schools are the children who are often referred to as "typical." The typical students are also thought of as "normal," as they do not have a label in school. The "normal" child is in the mind's eye of society but is rarely explicitly defined. As Disability Studies scholars have pointed out, the taken for granted notion of a "normal" child is more usefully viewed as a myth (Baglieri, Bejoian, Broderick, Connor, & Valle, 2011; Brantlinger, 2004; Dudley-Marling & Gurn, 2010). I, therefore, think that considering all children equally, yet knowing their needs can be very different, is a good starting place. Classrooms are always about balancing, and *kids with and without labels* need to be planned for, be engaged, have multiple learning activities, develop strengths, practice areas of need, be assessed, and so on. Using a Universal Design of Learning (UDL) approach with Culturally Sustaining Pedagogy (CSP) helps teachers develop a disposition of striving toward supporting and including all students (Waitoller & King Thorius, 2016). Ultimately and ideally, classrooms should be a place where students are first thought of by their names rather than their disabilities or their perceived differences from a norm. On a related note, teacher education programs continue to reify a man-made divide between disabled and nondisabled students. Instead of certification solely in general education, or in special education with general education, why not have all teacher education programs address the needs of all students? The issues Diane raises can be discussed within any teacher education classroom and can likely result in a meaningful discussion.

From my perspective, Adam has always been woven throughout the larger story that Diane has chronicled in different publications. He has appeared in different renderings and episodes, sometimes in relation to Benny and sometimes in relation to himself. However, I think centering Adam purposefully, and how his own experiences have given rise to some of the questions that Diane has about when, where, and how, do we teach about—and challenge—"typicality" is worth exploring. And while Adam is what many folks may consider a typical kid (or invoke the label of Gifted and Talented), his identity is shaped, in part, by being Benny's brother, and by seeing how Benny moves in the world and how the world reacts to Benny. I am curious to know how Adam's knowledge supports or contrasts with existing research and related literature, particularly the possibility of something new coming out of Adam's story that can inform teachers.

In fact, some of the most compelling research features personal stories, so centering them can be very powerful. Plus, every graduate student comes with personal stories that we do not always fully tap into. Everyone has family members with disabilities. From my perspective, we need to get culturally responsive in terms of disability. By this, I mean asking about what we can learn by discussing and analyzing how families have responded to their members with disabilities. How might intersections with nationality, gender, race, age, and so on, influence how family members—and perhaps, in particular, siblings—come to understand what constitutes disability and the place of people with disabilities in all aspects of the world? There exists some related literature that can be used in teaching—there's a genre of memoirs written by siblings of individuals with disabilities, for example, *Riding the Bus with My Sister* (Simon, 2002), and collections such as *Special Siblings: Growing up with Someone with a Disability* (McHugh, 2002). There also exists a number of books written for children and youth about having a sibling with a disability such as *Just Because* (Elliot, 2014) and *The Sibling Survival Guide* (Meyer & Holl, 2014). Additionally, there are examples of collaboration between disabled and non-disabled sisters, such as Doris Fleischer and Freida Zames' (2011) classic, *The Disability Rights Movement: From Charity to Confrontation*. All of these, and similar sources, can be unpacked in a critical manner, and be potentially brought into conversations that explore the topic of disability from multiple perspectives.

For Adam, like many of the siblings in the suggested texts, disability is not a big deal, but is, in fact, normal. Perhaps this phenomenon is an outcome of Diane's parenting, including the schools that she chose for him to ensure he had shared experiences with Benny in the form of curriculum, teachers, social events, and so on. He has seen how structures and attitudes can present very real obstacles for his brother to have access to all aspects of the world that "typical" kids have. Adam sees how some structures are unjust and doesn't quite "get" the fuss about disability, annoyed at the limiting terminology used in educational discourse. With age, I suspect his appreciation for what he knows, that is, disability is "normal," will only deepen and manifest in good ways we can't yet foresee. What can we learn from Adam's response? Perhaps, when students are afforded the opportunity to meaningfully interact with all kinds of children, they don't see the man-made line of disability, making human differences "no big deal."

The fact that the school where Diane works is structured to be integrated is a good start but, as all should know, assumptions can't be made about whether that will be enough for "typical" students who do not have a sibling with a disability, and therefore we need to facilitate conversations, activities, and learning experiences. One way is to include disability as integral to how we conceive of diversity at large. Some of the best suggestions have come from kids themselves in the book, *Listening to the Experts: Students with Disabilities Speak Out* (Keefe, Moore, & Duff, 2006). Students with disabilities talk about approaches toward better understanding who they are and their place in the community, and their nondisabled friends talk about ways in which they have challenged existing boundaries and came together in new ways. I also think there is a way to learn from the Gay-Straight Alliance movement within schools across the country, and cull from students on both "sides" who are interested in challenging historical associations with stigma and creating an environment that honors equality across human differences.

ON PROFESSIONAL REFLECTION AS A FORM OF CULTURAL HUMILITY

My intent in contributing to this chapter as a professional working with a mother of a disabled and a non-disabled son, was to take an approach that DasGupta (2008) calls "narrative humility" (p. 980). The concept of narrative humility evolved in the discipline of medicine and seeks to actively dismantle the idea of practitioners being all-knowing "experts" by asking them to locate themselves, rather, in a position of humility. By first acknowledging the need to know more information, a doctor should enter a dialogue that evolves with the patient. DasGupta explains:

> Narrative humility acknowledges that our patient's stories are not objects that we can comprehend or master, but rather dynamic entities that we can approach and engage with, while simultaneously remaining open to their ambiguity and contradiction, and engaging in constant self-evaluation and self-critique about issues as our own role in the story, our expectations of the story, our responsibilities to the story, and our identifications with the story—how the story attracts or repels us because it reminds us of any number of personal stories. (p. 980)

These suggestions encourage cultivating a disposition that allows professionals to habitually question what we currently think we know, and why we think we know it. More importantly, professionals are asked to listen to other ways of understanding a situation that are deeply personal and contextual, and therefore this approach has the potential to yield new and insightful knowledge. In other words, professionals are requested to always be open to potentially new ways of knowing, relinquishing the idea of themselves as sole keepers and distributors of knowledge. Furthermore, they are asked to consider these alternative ways of knowing, alongside of, and informing, their own current ways of knowing. For professionals, much of what we know—our "area of expertise"—has been developed and shaped through a body of academic knowledge that is mastered (with practical applications) and evaluated by professionals, and is then, in turn, manifest in academic degrees that lead to professional certifications, where people now become sanctioned to evaluate others.

I am aware of the irony of utilizing a conceptual tool from the field of medicine, a discipline that has a long history of oppressive practices to people with disabilities (Fleischer & Zames, 2011; Foucault, 2009; Stiker, 1999; Terry & Urla, 1995) and one whose authority scholars in Disability Studies in Education (DSE) have questioned (Danforth & Rhodes, 1997; Gallagher, 1998), along with offering new ways of conceptualizing human differences and "doing business" in education

(Baglieri, 2012; Cosier & Ashby, 2016; Danforth, 2014; Gabel & Connor, 2014; Lalvani & Polvere, 2013; Valle & Connor, 2010). However, it is precisely because narrative humility has evolved within the field of medicine with a view to changing that field's formidable internal dynamics of power, that I see its potentially immense value in infiltrating the discourse of special education that is historically one of medicalization (Kauffman, Anastasiou, & Maag, 2017). For example, if we take out the word "patient's" from DasGupta's explanation above and replace it with either "mother's" or "student's," we see the prospective value in accepting the idea of needing to adopt a stance of narrative humility. Therefore, I ask: What might be the benefits of a more humbling professional stance within education in general, and special education in particular? DasGupta (2008) asks us to consider how:

> ...humility is a central aspect of many spiritual traditions, whereby the stance of humility is one that enables not only personal growth, but is a hallmark of some degree of spiritual enlightenment—whereby the most learned monks are the most humble, recognizing how much they have left to learn. (p. 981)

Furthermore, adopting this stance would not mean relinquishing existing professional knowledge, but rather, creating a dynamic space in which a professional educator engages with the reality of a mother or a student, with view to synthesizing *all* knowledge available.

In *Including Samuel*, Dan Habib asks the question, "Where does inclusion occur?" and Douglas Biklen responded, "In families... all of the time." Diane's letter to Adam requires us to think in terms of a whole family, and in particular, parental relations to different siblings. Hearing a parent's perspective, and *why* a mother's experiences—both in life, and in the field of special education, specifically—have informed her thinking provides a counter-narrative to college classroom discussions in which parents are often discussed as being "in denial" or "not caring" (Valle, 2016). Diane's lived experiences capture her shift in understanding disability, from following the narrow scripts offered by special education personnel, to one in which she eventually trusted herself more than psychologists, therapists, and teachers. This type of parental knowledge should have a place as a central theme within teacher education.

CLOSING THOUGHT

Diane shared with me that Adam did not like the word "typical." I am aware of its implications and limitations, and suggested Diane ask him why he did not like the word. Adam's response was:

> I do not like the word typical because you are using it to compare me to Benny, and no one should compare us—at least not in that way. We are different, but not in that way. You shouldn't describe a person as disabled or typical because that does not make you who you are.

According to Diane, "All said while chowing down chicken, pasta, and a salad at dinner. With very little thought, these words just roll out of his mouth." And there you have it, a brother rejecting othering. Simple as that. Now, how can we get more educators to do the same thing?

REFERENCES

Baglieri, S. (2012). *Disability studies and the inclusive classroom: Critical practices for creating least restrictive attitudes.* New York, NY: Routledge.

Baglieri, S., Bejoian, L., Broderick, A., Connor, D. J., & Valle, J. (2011). [Re]claiming "Inclusive Education" toward cohesion in educational reform: Disability studies unravels the myth of the typical child. *Teachers College Record, 113*(10), 2122–2154.

Berman, D. L. (2009). *Beyond words: Reflections on our journey to inclusion.* Harrisburg, PA: White Hat Press.

Berman, D. L., & Connor, D. J. (2017). *A child, a family, a school, a community: A tale of inclusive education.* New York, NY: Peter Lang.

Brantlinger, E. (2004). Confounding the needs and confronting the norms: An extension of Reid and Valle's essay. *Journal of Learning Disabilities, 37*(6), 490–499.

Cosier, M., & Ashby, C. (2016). *Enacting change from within: Disability studies meets teaching and teacher education.* New York, NY: Peter Lang.

Danforth, S. (Ed.). (2014). *Becoming a great inclusive educator.* New York, NY: Peter Lang.

Danforth, S., & Rhodes, W. C. (1997). Deconstructing disability: A philosophy for inclusion. *Remedial and Special Education, 6*(18), 357–366.

DasGupta, S. (2008). The art of medicine: Narrative humility. *The Lancet, 371*, 980–981.

Dudley-Marling, C., & Gurn, A. (Eds.). (2010). *The myth of the normal curve.* New York, NY: Peter Lang.

Elliot, R. (2014). *Just because.* Oxford, UK: Lion Hudson.

Fleischer, D., & Zames, F. (2011). *The disabilities rights movement: From charity to confrontation.* Philadelphia, PA: Temple University Press.

Foucault, M. (2009). *The history of madness.* New York, NY: Routledge.

Gabel, S., & Connor, D. J. (2014). *Teaching and disability.* Mahwah, NJ: Lawrence Erlbaum.

Gallagher, D. J. (1998). The scientific knowledge base of special education: Do we know what we think we know? *Exceptional Children, 64*(4), 493–502.

Habib, D. (Producer & Director). (2007). *Including Samuel* [DVD]. Available from http://www.includingsamuel.com/home.aspx

Kauffman, J. M., Anastasiou, D., & Maag, J. W. (2017). Special education as the crossroad: An identity crisis and the need for scientific reconstruction. *Exceptionality, 25*(2), 139–155.

Keefe, E. B., Moore, V. M., & Duff, F. R. (2006). *Listening to the experts: Students with disabilities speak out.* Baltimore, MD: Paul H. Brookes.

Lalvani, P., & Polvere, L. (2013). Historical perspective on studying families of children with disabilities: A case for critical research. *Disability Studies Quarterly, 33*(3).

McHugh, M. (2012). *Special siblings: Growing up with someone with a disability.* Baltimore, MD: Brookes.

Meyer, D., & Holl, E. (2014). *The sibling survival guide: Indispensable information for brothers and sisters of adults with disabilities.* Bethesda, MD: Woodbine House.

Simon, R. (2002). *Riding the bus with my sister.* New York, NY: Grand Central Publishing.

Stiker, H.-J. (1999). *A history of disability.* Ann Arbor, MI: University of Michigan Press.

Terry, J., & Urla, J. (Eds.). (1995). *Deviant bodies: Critical perspectives on difference in science and popular culture.* Bloomington, IN: Indiana University Press.

Valle, J. (2009). *What mothers say about special education: From 1960s to the present.* New York, NY: Palgrave Macmillan.

Valle, J. W. (2016). Learning from and collaborating with families: The case for DSE in teacher education. In M. Cosier & C. Ashby (Eds.), *Enacting change from within: Disability studies meet teaching and teacher education* (pp. 243–264). New York, NY: Peter Lang.

Valle, J., & Aponte, E. (2002). IDEA and collaboration: A Bakhtinian perspective on parent and professional discourse. *Journal of Learning Disabilities, 35*(5), 469–479.

Valle, J., & Connor, D. J. (2010). *Rethinking disability: A disability studies guide to inclusive practices.* New York, NY: McGraw-Hill.

Valle, J. W., & Gabel, S. L. (2010). The *sirens* of normative mythology: Mother narratives of engagement and resistance. In C. Dudley-Marling & A. Gurn (Eds.), *The myth of the normal curve* (pp. 187–204). New York, NY: Peter Lang.

Waitoller, F. & King Thorius, K. (2016). Cross-pollinating culturally sustaining pedagogy and universal design for learning: Toward an inclusive pedagogy that accounts for dis/ability. *Harvard Educational Review, 8*(3), 366–389.

CHAPTER 15

Confessions

OF AN Inept Supermom

CAROL ROGERS-SHAW

Like Julie Kaomea (2005), I, too, felt "from the moment my daughter was cut from me, our separation was sudden, harsh, severe" (p. 81), undoubtedly influencing our journey forward. Kaomea described seeing her daughter six hours after birth, "in her fish-tank-like incubator, with a mess of wires hooking her up to a series of monitors, an intravenous needle in her bandaged arm" (p. 82). I, too, remember that image, captured in a Polaroid photograph now tucked away in a pink chocolate cigar box, along with a hospital bracelet and newborn bib emblazoned with a bright yellow and turquoise stork. The photograph, showing my daughter in her incubator a few hours after her birth, was taken as I lay in a dimly lit treatment room with my own intravenous needle pumping burning magnesium sulfate through my veins to treat postpartum preeclampsia. I remember sobbing because I couldn't see my daughter, hold her, kiss her. A nurse, recognizing my misery, took the Polaroid snapshot and brought it back to me, but like Kaomea, all I could think was, "How did this happen, what did I do wrong?" (p. 82). As I look at the photograph now, I see a beautiful baby girl that I've always loved with fierce protectiveness and pride, and I still feel the pain. Not the pain from the cesarean surgery, but from the overwhelming sense of not being good enough.

As a diabetic, the complications from my pregnancy and delivery set me up as a failure in the eyes of my doctors and the nurses. It was not until later that I realized they set me up as a failure in my own mind, too. My excessive weight gain did not fit the model of what doctors called a "normal" pregnancy. My C-section five weeks before the due date was not "natural." The need for my daughter to be whisked away immediately to the neo-natal intensive care unit did not reflect a "typically healthy" birth, and my inability to cuddle with and nurse my baby precluded the opportunity for "traditional bonding." My daughter was not even a day old and already we were "different." I wonder, in these circumstances, when does one begin to be a parent?

Kaomea (2005) described her experiences as a mother whose child was perceived to be at risk even before she was born, because she was indigenous within Western health, social, and education systems. Her traditional Hawaiian knowledge of motherhood was neither recognized nor valued, so no matter what she did, she felt like she was "always already" failing (p. 77). As a mother whose disability affected the birth of her child, I started out with a sense of failure. Later, I couldn't control the difficult conditions my daughter, who has a learning disability, faced in school. I felt I was *always* failing, having *already* started behind myself. I use Kaomea's ideas as a lens through which I view my own (m)othering. Kaomea also reclaimed the indigenous tradition of storytelling and shared her personal narratives, calling upon others to share their stories. I answer her call, agreeing that "[w]here there is one, there are many" (p. 80).

Goodley (2011) argued that "[a] key site of the oppression of disabled people pertains to those moments when they are judged to fail to match up to the ideal individual; when they are categorized as embodying the failing individual" (p. 78). At the moment of my daughter's birth, I began failing as a mother because I did not live up to the ideal. This was continually reinforced through conversations with medical personnel and other young mothers in which they extolled the virtues of stress-free natural deliveries, breastfeeding, and the importance of immediate maternal bonding—experiences denied to me because of health complications. Their assumptions and surety that they were doing motherhood the "right way" chipped away at my confidence. Immediately, I knew I had to make up for my dismal start. I had to "save" my child from a lifetime of suffering at the hands of her inadequate mother!

My identity as a mother has been undoubtedly shaped by my own disability. Additionally, the messages I received from an ableist society led me to view myself as *less than*, as physically deficient. In my senior year of college, I received a diagnosis of Type I diabetes, called juvenile diabetes at that time. I don't remember a defining moment when I recognized my disability because perhaps, at the time, I saw diabetes as a disease to be treated rather than a disability with which I live. Even today, I feel somewhere in between disabled and diseased. Neither label provides any comfort. Legally, the Americans with Disabilities Act Amendments Act (ADAAA), signed in 2008, considers diabetes a disability, and it often seems that every moment of my life is affected by my body's inability to process glucose, whether it's from checking my blood sugar levels, counting carbs, managing exercise, ending up in the hospital due to complications, or being a mother. Certainly having a diagnosis of a disability is nothing like having a fatal disease; I'm living a meaningful and fulfilling life despite my diabetes, but the feeling of being disabled is still hard to accept. For one is not disabled in a solitary world, but in a society full of individuals without the same disability--a society in which we are measured against the models that are held as ideal. Watermeyer (2009) argued that the medical, rehabilitation, public discourse, and media representations of disability "remain firmly attached to the construct of disabled life as incomplete and lacking, with a constant awareness of what has been lost or was never had" (p. 92). It is difficult to resist internalizing this view of disability, particularly when it intersects with the discourses on mothering.

After my initial diabetes diagnosis, I experienced grief; suddenly, I could no longer control my own body. That same feeling crept in again during those post-partum days. My daughter, Bri, was immediately placed in the neo-natal intensive care unit where decisions about her care were made by medical professionals, and I was unable to participate. This sense of feeling helpless played a significant role in my experience of parenting. I wish my pregnancy and delivery could have been more ordinary.

In this chapter, analyzing vignettes from my life, I examine the dominant cultural and institutional discourses and practices surrounding disability that have shaped me as a mother. I reflect on the sense of loss of control I experienced, first as a new mother whose child's birth did not meet the established norms of society, and then again through the imposed constraints of schooling after my daughter's diagnosis. I highlight the role of ableism in creating otherness in both myself and my child, as we did not meet mainstream medical and educational standards for a mother and a student. However, my narratives are not passive tales about being shaped by society's expectations; they are stories of fighting back. As a young d/Deaf child draped in a red cape and looking for a superpower, Joseph Michael Valente (2011) decided he was going to be a "Saver" like Superman who saves Lois Lane, and that words were going to be his superpower. His stories would become a way to resist the constraints he faced within educational, rehabilitative, medical, and discursive contexts. By creating a superhero version of himself, Valente (2011) wrote a counter-narrative of disability where his particular superpower was a unique understanding of the lived experience of d/Deaf children oppressed by the structures of schooling. From the moment of Bri's birth, I, too, wanted to be a "Saver." First, I wanted to save my daughter from what I believed to be my own failings, and later, from the oppression she faced as a student with a disability.

Inspired by Valente's idea of wanting to "punish perpetrators with superpowerful stories that move people to act, to push ... back .... [against] destructive social structures and their processes that systematically harm children whose bodies and minds do not conform to narrow-minded cultural scripts of dis/ability" (p. 110), I want my stories to show mothers that by disrupting the imposed narratives on normative motherhood, we can fight back. And so, borrowing Valente's metaphor, I invent a superhero narrative; the superpower I have is that of storytelling, and the "villain" is the prevailing discourses and practices related to disability. But unlike a superhero, I have self-doubt. I am vulnerable and unsure. I resist labels, I struggle against the definitions of normalcy constructed by our society, and I make many mistakes. Sometimes I get it right and sometimes I do not. My inner superhero is complicated and often conflicted, as is motherhood itself. Sometimes I am donning my superhero costume as I head to school to fight for classroom accommodations for my child, and at other times, I am driving in the car discussing the importance of being kind and generous with my daughter buckled up in the backseat. Playing the roles of "Saver" and mother aren't simple. Both parts of me must find a way through an intricate maze with multiple dead ends and passages to clarity.

LOOK ... IT'S A TEACHER! IT'S A MOTHER! IT'S SUPERMOM!

As a child, I was a reader. Stories have always been important to me. I can still hear my mother's voice saying "Read a book," any time I expressed the slightest degree of boredom. Nancy Drew books were my favorites. I spent many nights reading by flashlight under the covers, getting lost in her adventures rather than going to sleep. I envisioned myself by her side, along with Bess and George, a band of super sleuths. It's no wonder that I became an English teacher; I wanted to share my own passion with others and help them to experience literature as I had. Then I had a daughter with a reading disability, and I didn't have control over how she would experience school, how she would experience reading. Just as Kaomea (2005) "found [her] self-confidence and [her] ability to take care of [her] child rapidly eroding, [I too] was transformed from a confident [teacher] to an anxious, guilt-ridden, unfit ... mother of a[n]... at-risk child" (p. 84) who was unable to recognize what was causing her daughter's difficulty in communicating and unable to find a solution to help her.

I remember a late summer day when Bri was two and a half years old. Although it was mid- afternoon, the kitchen was dim as only limited light filtered in through the single window whose view was blocked by trees. The beige counter tiles, old wood floor, and neutral-colored wallpaper made the room feel indistinct, yet confined and suffocating, as if we were caught in a vaguely sensed dust storm. My attention was acutely focused on the sobbing toddler standing in the middle. She was wearing a dress with tiny purple flowers on a white background, and her blond hair curled under and framed her small face which was streaked with tears. She kept repeating "Eeee" "Eeee" "Eeee" as I kept guessing "Do you want cheese?" "Does your knee hurt?" "Do you want to watch T.V.?" "Do you have to pee?" I couldn't understand what she was trying to say. She was in distress and didn't have the means to communicate effectively.

At that moment, I knew my daughter could not express herself clearly, but I did not know the reason why. I did not recognize that Bri's problem with speech sounds might actually be an indication of a learning disability and that she might need help to communicate in another way. What I did recognize was that Bri was so frustrated by her inability to make her desires and needs known to me that it was causing her a lot of distress. I, too, felt a lot of anxiety and often became frustrated because I couldn't meet those needs or desires. Again, there was the nagging sensation that I was failing. I wasn't being a good mother. As Caplan (2013) stated, the myths of good mothers "set standards that no human being could ever match, such as that mothers are always, naturally, one hundred percent nurturant" (p. 100) or that mothers instinctively "know everything they need to know about mothering" (p. 101), but in reality there are times when we are angry or disappointed or sad, and there's certainly a lot we don't know. The burden of trying to live up to these unrealistic standards constructed by society leaves women feeling guilty when they can't meet those mythical and gendered expectations of motherhood.

KRYPTONITE IN THE CLASSROOM

Shortly after my first inklings about Bri's learning differences, her nursery school recommended she be tested for a hearing deficit and begin speech therapy. They identified her as lagging behind her classmates who communicated with clearer words, better pronunciation, and complete sentences. It didn't matter that Bri was clever and funny and observant. Her ability to communicate through gestures, facial expressions, or actions was not enough; as far as they were concerned, she didn't meet school-defined norms and standard ableist benchmarks. Campbell (2001) defined ableism as

> beliefs, processes and practices that produce a particular kind of self and body (the corporeal standard) that is projected as the perfect, species-typical and therefore essential and fully human. Disability then, is cast as a diminished state of being human. (p. 44)

Procknow, Rocco, and Munn (2017) described ableism as "the belief that being without a physical or cognitive disability, impairment, or chronic illness is the norm…. People of able-body/-mind construct the world, language, culture, and belief systems to maintain this norm" (p. 365). Within schooling, there are expectations that marginalize learners with disabilities. Students are constantly measured to determine if they are performing at, above, or below grade level, and if they are below grade level, they are determined to be at risk, separated out, and provided with instruction that will make them more "normal."

When her pre-school teachers did not understand Bri's communication, once again I received the message that I had failed as a parent. I hadn't prepared her for the school environment, and I couldn't solve the problem myself. I needed an outside source to "fix" what was wrong. Like Kaomea's child, my daughter was "starting behind even before [she began her] formal schooling in kindergarten" (p. 88). It didn't matter how many books I read to her, how many educational games we played, how many enrichment activities I planned; I was *always already* failing.

A few years later, I found myself in a second grade classroom, bright with fluorescent lights and noisy with parents chatting as they looked for their child's name on the brightly colored folder placed in the middle of each small table that served as the student's desk. I sat in the chair at Bri's spot, opened the folder, and began to look through the pages of lined elementary school paper with awkwardly shaped letters written in pencil, her stories, as the teacher talked about the writing process and invented spelling. I understood the concept of young children using invented spelling. As Chomsky (1979) explained, "the ability to write in this way, representing words the way they sound, precedes the ability to read" (p. 3), but the words I saw written under pictures of a school classroom, of a rose, of Santa Claus with gifts, of a little girl walking a dog, had no correlation with the sound of the words that would describe them. I found imagination and creativity depicted in the crayon drawings above the scrawled text. Yet, it was clear that Bri was unable to write, and likely also to read, in the manner of the students sitting around her each day at school, and that written work was the tradition-bound basis for judging her knowledge acquisition.

These memories clearly point to my increasing understanding that Bri was different and that, in the school setting, it was not judged to be a *good* different, or even an *okay* different—it was a deficiency. The school recommendation for testing led to a diagnosis of dyslexia and auditory processing disorder, and a treatment plan involving intensive phonics training and accommodations. However, she did not simultaneously receive the option to choose alternative ways of expressing herself that were equally valued in a welcoming environment. She was put in a special class for reading and had to attend summer school to "catch up." The school's response was aimed at trying to "fix" Bri, forcing her to read and write like the students who represented the norm, rather than recognizing that perhaps the school's way of evaluating her abilities needed to be fixed. The accommodations she received were in the form of extra time on tests, but all that meant was that when the testing session ended and the class went out to recess, she was allowed to stay behind and keep working. These accommodations only served to mark her as *other*, as a failure who couldn't manage to finish the test in the allotted time and therefore had to forfeit the fun of recess. No wonder Bri did not like school.

In an environment of ableism, "we have difficulty imagining that learning to read could be anything other than good or not learning to read could be anything other than tragic or disastrous" (Boldt, 2006, p. 280). Furthermore, Boldt (2006) explained, "children who struggle with learning to read experience most keenly the fact that learning to read is a *demand* and not a choice" (p. 273), a demand that can feel like "an assault to [a child], infused with danger, threat, and loss" (p. 279). Bri's reaction to this demand not only shaped her psyche, but it also provoked a physical reaction; she vomited most days on the way to school. Her grandmother drove her to school each day when I was at work, and she always brought a bath towel in the car. Frequently, she would pull over so Bri could throw up. I felt so much anguish knowing that school was such a miserable place for Bri that it made her sick, but I couldn't make it better despite putting notes or toys in her backpack to provide encouraging surprises and reminders that she was loved no matter what happened in the classroom.

The environment and demands of school can be extremely frustrating for students who learn differently, and parents who want to help their children be successful in this setting feel anxious and helpless. Instead of traditional assessments that heavily rely on written text content, perhaps those that allowed for oral or graphic responses, or content acquisition through multimedia means could have offered Bri a way to be included and to demonstrate what she knew. Instead, the school's response to Bri's differences was more traditional, based on the medical model of disability that sees a problem that must be diagnosed and then treated with a specific plan of corrective action. The effects of schooling constraints are clear; as Goodley (2011) pointed out, "[p]eople with learning difficulties, who fail to meet developmentalist stages, are discarded from mainstream educational systems because of their lack of fit with educational prerogatives" (p. 79). Bri was segregated in a special reading class and isolated for testing. We were pushed to spend years trying to overcome the problems—to make Bri more like other learners through tutoring and accommodations.

As Hehir (2002) noted, "in the eyes of many educators and society, it is preferable for disabled students to do things in the same manner as nondisabled kids" (p. 3) despite the fact that there can be various ways to acquire knowledge, to demonstrate an understanding of it, to use it. In contrast, the social model of disability, which focuses on environmental barriers, demands that educators examine the way they teach and alter their methods to meet the needs of students with disabilities. Perhaps Bri would have benefitted from alternative teaching strategies rather than being segregated in a special reading class and isolated for testing. Had she, for example, been given the opportunity to create a video of her favorite book rather than write a book report, she might have excelled. Instead, both Bri and I felt the emotional distress and frustration of her inability to be as successful in school as her high intellect warranted because, at the time, we did not recognize that maybe her difficulties stemmed not from her differences but from rigid school structures and practices. Today, when I see her achievements in her career in digital media, I imagine how much more successful and happier she would have been had she been offered opportunities for alternative and creative means of expression in school.

TRYING TO LEAP TALL BUILDINGS IN A SINGLE BOUND

Early in high school, Bri asked for teacher or classmate notes for lectures to compensate for her auditory processing issues. Her request was denied; she was told it was against the Honor Code, as it would give her an unfair advantage. When she came home and told me the school's response, I seethed with anger. And I fought back. I set out to become a warrior parent and used every weapon I could find. I bought study guides; I borrowed teacher's editions from colleagues at my own school; I copied their lecture notes; I highlighted the important sections of related articles; I did everything I possibly could to give her a fighting chance. The response Bri received from school illustrates a lack of comprehension of learning disabilities. The teachers, operating on ableist assumptions that hold all students to the same standards, did not understand that providing her with accurate class notes would diminish the disadvantage she experienced, not provide her with an advantage. In this instance, Bri's experience was typical of students with learning disabilities who are "regarded as intellectually inferior, incompetent, lacking effort, or attempting to cheat or use unfair advantages when requesting accommodations. The phenomenon of being misunderstood ... lead[s] to devaluation and marginalization" (Denhart, 2008, p. 484).

When a superhero feels under siege, she takes the stance of a fighter, ready to deflect the blows. There is a body of literature that suggests that parents of children who are marginalized in school often find themselves in the position of "fighting a battle" to secure access to educational resources; they use the weapons available to them and take on different roles on this battlefield, from "squeaky wheels" to "mothers from hell" (Lalvani & Hale, 2015). The constant vigilance needed in this struggle requires superpower strength and sometimes the subtlety of disguise, like the mild-mannered nature of Clark Kent.

For me, the role was that of Supermom—the "Saver" striking out to find justice in the form of a fair education for my daughter. However, I was a privileged Supermom—a well-educated, economically-advantaged, white woman whose career as an educator provided her with vast knowledge of learning disabilities. My social, educational, and economic advantages enabled me to understand both the policies of special education and the structures of school bureaucracy. I could be an effective advocate for my daughter because I had the language and could therefore "talk the talk." And, ultimately, I could pay for private school where my daughter might not have been protected by certain public laws and policies, but where the environment was conducive to meeting her unique needs. I was a paying customer who could make some demands. My superpowers cannot be disentangled from my privilege.

Within educational discourses, this is an ugly story. There exists the popular trope of the "ranting" parent of a child with a disability making "unreasonable demands" on the school. As a teacher, I am aware that appropriate accommodations can sometimes seem unreasonable to school personnel. I remember one particularly tense meeting with my daughter's principal. Bri's seventh grade English teacher insisted on giving weekly spelling quizzes that were multiple choice--three versions of a word spelled incorrectly and one spelled correctly. This type of assessment sets a child with dyslexia up for failure. I had requested an alternative test for my daughter, to no avail. After a few rounds of recriminations, the principal and I were eventually able to come to a solution that would work for Bri. At this meeting, I was able to make effective arguments on my daughter's behalf. As I was leaving, the principal told me that she expected nothing less from a parent than to fight for her child. But, I wonder, why should a fight be necessary? Moreover, what about parents who are not in a position to "fight"? What happens to their children when the changes required to address their needs don't happen unless there is a "battle" and the parent "wins"? Minoritized parents "experience many more obstacles to successfully navigating school bureaucracies and contending with professional authority than their more privileged and culturally-attuned counterparts" (Lalvani & Hale, 2015, p. 34). I left that conference feeling that maybe it wasn't about being a "good" or "bad" mother after all. Maybe it was about being what Winnicott (1953) referred to as a *good enough mother*. I did not have to be perfect. I would not be able to eliminate every obstacle placed in front of my daughter by an ableist society, but I could win some battles. I could make mistakes and still raise a confident, happy child. My privilege allowed me to be a "good enough mother."

FROM ANOTHER STAR

Before graduation at Bri's high school, a senior class photograph is taken. Students arrive at school on this day wearing a sweatshirt from the college they will be attending; a photograph is taken and then used to market the school and loudly proclaim its success in meeting its elitist norms. Just as it became clear at Bri's school "that the position of 'reader' is better than the position of 'not reader'" (Boldt, 2006, p. 285), so was it upheld that the position of "college student" was much better than the position of "not college student," although Ellen DeGeneres, Anna Wintour, and Steve Jobs, for example, might disagree. Bri spent the stressful college application process receiving the message that she didn't quite measure up; her first choice schools (all large state schools) were demeaned by other students as mere "safety schools" of last resort. Our last stop on our final college tour, with a decision made, was the campus bookstore to find a sweatshirt with the school name emblazoned in the largest letters possible. Bri wore it with pride on photo day, and despite being asked to shift further to the back row, she refused to move from a front and center spot when the picture was taken. Bri was angry at that moment. I imagine it was a cumulative hostility for a school that continually made her feel less worthy, a school that epitomized ableist ideology and devalued her accomplishments as a learning disabled student. Even today, she feels that resentment. When we first talked about my writing a story about these experiences, she was excited at the thought of "revenge research." She wanted me to include the name of the school to shame them for their treatment of students with learning disabilities. Like Valente (2011), she wanted this story to "punish" the perpetrators. When I think about Bri's successes as a student, I recognize an element of resistance, of fighting back.

Bri's college graduation, a moment of celebratory success, was the culmination of strength built through years of struggling to find ways to compensate as a student with a learning disability. The distance between that long-ago afternoon in the kitchen and her graduation from college reflects an incredibly arduous and exhausting journey that required tremendous cognitive effort on her part, to meet the rigid requirements of traditional learning. Kaomea (2005) argued that we must stop viewing difference as "a problem—a detriment to be compensated for rather than a source of strength and knowledge to be supported and built upon" (p. 89). I wish her differences had not been viewed as challenges to overcome. I wish we lived in a society that valued her uniqueness; it would be a better place.

Although I've critiqued the ableism in schools, I now turn to the ableism in my own thinking. I'm not sure that, as a parent, I did enough to recognize and celebrate the resourcefulness of my daughter who found ways to handle the challenges she faced. My dilemma is described succinctly by Bridgens (2009) in her quote and explanation of Landsman's (2003) work as:

> the mother's paradox of thinking both "I love you as you are" and "I would do anything to change you." This paradox causes parents to veer between medical and social models, choosing, as their only practical recourse against prejudice, to help the child fit into society, which constrains choices they or the child may make (Landsman, 2005). Living with these contradictions is not easy—with every choice there is some loss, either having to deny the impairment or not fit into society. (p. 755)

I experienced this paradox throughout Bri's schooling. For example, when she was struggling at the beginning of high school, I knew I could love her and accept her choices if she decided to take a gap year, attend a specialized school like a culinary institute, or find employment after graduation. School had always been difficult, and more than anything, I wanted her to be happy. I recognized that might mean no more schooling. Yet, I also wanted her to fit in. I didn't want her to be scorned; I wanted her to succeed at what was deemed "normal" at that school—graduating and going to college. So I searched for the best tutors, argued for accommodations, helped her with her schoolwork. Sometimes I wanted her to take the easy courses or focus on her art and athletics; other times, I wanted her to meet the challenges of rigorous academic courses which often translated to stress and pressure. There were also times when tutoring sessions took the place of playing with friends, and even though they helped lessen her load, I wish I had more frequently chosen fun over schoolwork.

This paradox becomes evident in stories where mothers of children with disabilities describe their experiences. Their narratives "interweave in a sometimes contradictory fashion that defies any attempt towards rigid categorization… suggest[ing] mothers' understandings of their child's disability are constantly open to renegotiation and flux" (Fisher & Goodley, 2007, p. 76). I can write many stories of my repeated struggles with the teachers and administrators of her school as I advocated for Bri to get the acceptance and support she needed. However, I can now look back at my own journey and identify moments of ableism in my own responses, such as feeling relief when Bri's difficulties in communicating had a label and a proscribed way forward. I didn't always recognize the importance of celebrating the advantages of her differently thinking brain.

EDUCATION, JUSTICE, AND A WAY FORWARD

Sitting on the shelf in Bri's closet is a copy of Norman Mailer's *The Executioner's Song*. It's 1,136 pages long, and multicolored post-it notes are still sticking out of those pages, marking passages underlined in blue ink with comments written in the margin. In junior year English, Bri wrote a ten-page analysis of this book, the longest one on the list of suggested titles; she earned an A. And yes, there seems to be a bit of "I'll show you I can do it" in the choice of book. It's easy to fall into the trap of wanting to present a triumphant ending to our story—the "overcoming" narrative. I want to resist that urge, so I'll include her confession, when we talked about my writing this chapter, that she didn't actually read a lot of that book! It seems, she'd found a way around ableist expectations. There were certainly many moments of triumph throughout Bri's years of schooling, and while it's healing to focus on these, it is also dangerous for me to present these as "success stories," as that would perpetuate the myth of progressive narratives and serve to further marginalize learners with disabilities.

When I consider my memories of Bri's childhood, I see some irony in the fact that some of those I cherish the most involve reading books, considered to be the bane of existence for children with dyslexia. I recall the time, after a day spent touring Westminster Abby in London, taking photographs with Big Ben in the background and strolling through Regent's Park, that we sank down against bright white pillows on a soft bed, and Bri snuggled at my side as I read the ending to *Harry Potter and the Sorcerer's Stone*. A few days later, we dashed through the doors of Shakespeare and Company on Rue de la Bûcherie in Paris to find a copy of *The Chamber of Secrets*, to begin reading on the cross Atlantic flight home. Then, years later, as we sprawled on the yellow gingham couch in the family room, sunlight streaming in through the panes of the French doors, we reached the end of *Harry Potter and the Deathly Hallows*. I read the entire Harry Potter series aloud to Bri, beginning in elementary school and ending in high school. We anxiously awaited each installment and lived together in that magical world.

Even before our children are born, stories swirl in our heads; we envision our child, ourselves as mothers, our lives as a mother-child unit. But those are not always the stories that play out in real life nor the stories that others tell about us. I am a mother whose identity has been influenced by my own disability as well as my child's disability. I have many stories to tell, some that I'm proud of and some that I'm not, some that I'm happy to share and some that I'd rather keep hidden, some that make me laugh and others that bring tears. While I may have started out with the perception of failing because I couldn't immediately meet the standards demanded by society—those that produced the "good mother" label, I now see the power in my stories. And so, for those who believe they are mothers whose stories begin with failure, we can redefine our motherhood if we insist on writing the stories ourselves. The concept of an *always already failing* mother is not indicative of who I am now. It's taken a long time for me to recognize that I am a *good-enough supermom*.

REFERENCES

Boldt, G. (2006). Resistance, loss, and love in learning to read: A psychoanalytic inquiry. *Research in the Teaching of English, 40*(3), 272–309.

Bridgens, R. (2009). Disability and being "normal": A response to McLaughlin and Goodley. *Sociology, 43*(4), 753–761. doi: 10.1177/0038038509105419

Campbell, F. (2001). Inciting legal fictions: "Disability's" date with ontology and the ableist body of the law. *Griffith Law Review, 10*(1), 77.

Caplan, P. (2013). Don't blame mother: Then and now. In M. Hobbs & C. Rice (Eds.), *Gender and women's studies in Canada: Critical terrain* (99–106). Toronto, ON: Women's Press.

Chomsky, C. (1979). Approaching reading through invented spelling. In *Conference on theory and practice of beginning reading instruction* (p. 44). Pittsburgh, PA: Learning Research and Development Center. Retrieved from http://files.eric.ed.gov/fulltext/ED155630.pdf

Denhart, H. (2008). Deconstructing barriers: Perceptions of students labeled with learning disabilities in higher education. *Journal of Learning Disabilities, 41*(6), 483–497. doi. org/10.1177/0022219408321151

Fisher, P., & Goodley, D. (2007). The linear medical model of disability: Mothers of disabled babies resist with counter-narratives. *Sociology of Health & Illness, 29*(1), 66–81. doi: 10.1111/j.1467-9566.2007.00518.x

Goodley, D. (2011). *Disability studies: An interdisciplinary introduction*. London, England: Sage Publications.

Hehir, T. (2002). Eliminating ableism in education. *Harvard Educational Review, 72*(1), 1–32.

Kaomea, J. (2005). Reflections of an "always already" failing Native Hawaiian mother: Deconstructing colonial discourses on indigenous child-rearing and early childhood education. *Hūlili: Multidisciplinary Research on Hawaiian Well-Being*, (1), 77–95. Retrieved from http://uploads. worldlibrary.net/uploads/pdf/elib/collect/hulili05/index/assoc/d0.dir/book.pdf

Lalvani, P., & Hale, C. (2015). Squeaky wheels, mothers from hell, and CEOs of the IEP: Parents, privilege, and the "fight" for inclusive education. *Understanding and Dismantling Privilege*, 5(2), 21–41.

Landsman, G. (2003) 'Emplotting Children's Lives: Developmental Delay vs Disability', Social Science and Medicine 56(9): 1947–60.

Landsman, G. (2005) 'Mothers and Models of Disability', Journal of Medical Humanities 26(2–3): 121–39.

Procknow, G., Rocco, T. S., & Munn, S. L. (2017). (Dis)Ableing notions of authentic leadership through the lens of critical disability theory. *Advances in Developing Human Resources*, *19*(4), 362–377.

Valente, J. M. (2011). *d/DEAF and d/DUMB: A portrait of a deaf kid as a young superhero*. New York, NY: Peter Lang Publishing.

Watermeyer, B. (2009). Claiming loss in disability. *Disability & Society*, *24*(1), 91–102.

Winnicott, D. W. (1953). Transitional objects and transitional phenomena: A study of the first not-me possession. *International Journal of Psychoanalysis*, *34*, 89–97. Retrieved from https:// pdfs.semanticscholar.org/a56f/ba056a21039574e5b2371f4ad01728b54366.pdf

"Tell Me About When I Was Born"

(Mostly) True Tales About How We Became a Family

PRIYA LALVANI

The past is always up for grabs.
—McAdams & Adler (2010)

"Tell me a story," my son, Amiel, would say to me each night when he was younger. Some of my favorite memories of his childhood involve our bedtime rituals. I would tuck him in bed after a game (usually one that we had invented out of things that were around), and then we'd tell stories. Sometimes I'd read stories from books, but often we made up our own; there was one about five superhero children who repeatedly saved the world, another about a pair of butterfly siblings who could only eat cake, and a story about two brothers, Amielie and Bedielie—one of whom always made the right choice while his brother, though well-intentioned, kept getting in trouble but always managed to find his way out in the end. One of Amiel's favorite stories was about the night he was born and the rather strange events that apparently transpired.

It is not unusual that a child should inquire about his birth. Children seem to have a fascination with their birth story, and telling it is enjoyed by many mothers. However, when I attempted to relate to my little boy his birth story, he added to the narrative an unusual twist. This is how it went:

Amiel: Tell me about when I was born.
I start to tell the story. It is not a particularly remarkable one. So, for the benefit of a three-year-old boy, I try to dramatize parts that might be of interest. I describe how his dad and I were at our favorite Mexican restaurant with friends when I went into labor, and I wouldn't leave because I didn't want to miss out on the fun. And how, at the hospi-

tal, the doctor tried to speed things up by saying: "Come on, push harder, don't you want
to have your baby on Valentine's Day?!" Despite my attempts to add some action to this
otherwise unremarkable story, he is not impressed. These details do not seem to entertain.
Amiel: No, no! That's not the story!
Me: What do you mean? Yes, that's exactly how it happened. I'm sure of it.
I forge on with my story, inserting more details that might delight a child.
Me: Dad was so nervous when the doctor asked him to cut the cord. He didn't want to
mess this up!
Amiel: Noooo! Tell the real story. You know, the REAL story.
Me: (Confused): Oh, you mean about how daddy and I got to have a baby? (I'm thinking,
maybe he's seeking some information on the whole "birds and bees" thing.)
Amiel: No. Not THAT story! The REAL thing that happened when you and daddy went
to the hospital and had a baby. And I was ANOTHER baby in the hospital. And I was
in the crib next to your baby. And so I JUMPED right out of my crib, and I JUMPED
in that baby's crib, and I TOSSED him in my crib.
Me (Incredulous): Wait a minute. So, you switched places? You switched babies?
Amiel: Yes.
Me: How come?
Amiel: Coz I wanted to come home with you and daddy. That's what happened. And
then I came home. And now we all live right here.

The story sticks. After this, each time Amiel said, "Tell me about when I was
born," we'd make references to the infamous switcheroo. Over time, we all allowed
this to become our family's private story of his birth. We had an understanding that
this is just "our make-believe story"; nevertheless, this was the one he enjoyed. At
first, despite secretly finding it amusing, I wondered if I should be alarmed. It was
certainly creative, I thought to myself, but what were my son's reasons for inventing
this dark story of how we became a family—one in which he ostensibly left his birth
parents, stole the boy we actually birthed ("tossed him in my crib"), and implanted
himself into our lives ("jumped in that baby's crib"). Moreover, in this fictitious
account of kidnapping and baby-swapping, it seems I played a complicit role.

Around this same time, Amiel also enjoyed the book: *Are you my mother?*
(P.D. Eastman, 1960), and I would read it to him frequently. In this story, a baby
bird, finding its nest empty (the mother bird has gone to find food), spends the entire story scouring the area trying to locate its mother. Not knowing what "mother"
might look like, the baby bird approaches many animals or inanimate objects (e.g.,
cow, dog, and steam shovel) and asks, "Are you my mother?" One day, upon reaching
the end of the book where the baby bird finds its actual mother, Amiel remarked,
"Just like me, when I jumped into the crib!" It occurred to me then, that possibly,
for him, the make-believe account of what happened after his birth was not really
about baby-switching after all; it was about choosing. Perhaps it was about belong-

ing—finding your place in your community. Or, maybe it was about having a sense of control in an otherwise random universe. In Amiel's story, his dad and I didn't *just have* a baby; instead, he had us!

Of course, I cannot know any of this for sure, and I will always wonder about my son's reasons for inventing this mythical tale, as well as my own reasons for readily adopting it. Undoubtedly, what I've written here is my subjective interpretation of what he might have meant, and there are just as likely a hundred other interpretations. Still, I like to think that by telling us that he "jumped in our crib," perhaps he was trying to say that he would *choose* to be in our family.

BIRTHING A STORY

Storytelling might well be the most ubiquitous human activity, existing across time and cultures (McLean, 2015). However, as McLean explains, it is not merely an activity done for its own sake. It is a social practice in which humans engage to find meaning, and a social tool through which we craft our *selves*. Although we inherit many aspects of our being, which may become central to our identities, storytelling is the process through which we make sense of these; through the stories we tell, and the ones we choose to leave out, we actively engage in interpreting the world around us, and positioning ourselves within it (Bruner, 1990; McLean, 2015). As such, our identities are purely social, i.e., they do not simply emerge, nor are they constructed in isolation; rather they are co-constructed through the hearing and narrating of stories (McAdams & Manczak, 2015; McLean, 2015).

If identities are purely social, then so, too, are stories. Stories are fundamentally social acts, for they are told *to* someone or *for* someone; storytelling necessarily requires an audience—whether real or imagined. Additionally, just as identities are neither inherited nor constructed in isolation, our life stories, too, do not reflect any individual person's recollection. In order to construct a meaningful self-story, individuals narrate accounts about their lives to others, and retell the ones they are told (McLean, Pasupathi, & Pals, 2007). Through their telling and retelling, the stories evolve, taking on new meanings. In this way, we engage in continually shaping our identities and simultaneously constructing the nature of social realities. The idea that our identities are narrated or constructed may seem threatening, because it suggests that they are, to an extent, fictitious (McLean, 2015). However, McLean explains, people don't latch on to stories on a whim; we choose to hang on to those that resonate with us or help us to communicate our inner understandings about ourselves to the world. Furthermore, she explicates, we don't just hear stories, we *make stories* out of raw experiences; we possess a uniquely human ability to engage in meaning-making about the nature of events.

Family stories, in particular, are co-constructed narratives through which we come to understand who we are as a group. Through public and private communications, members of a family come to define their collective unit; family stories are therefore an important site of identity construction. Many family stories are initially inherited. Take, for example, our birth stories, which are, at first, necessarily someone else's story. We hear our birth stories multiple times before we narrate it as our own; literally, our understanding of the first moments of our own existence is defined by the stories told by others (Baddeley & Singer, 2007). Gradually, children start to initiate reminiscent conversations, add to, or create, their own narratives, and thus influence the collective narratives in the family (Baddeley & Singer, 2007). My son's imaginative tale about how he "jumped in" our crib is, for our family, more than just a quirky story. It feeds into our family identity. Perhaps it is nothing more than our mutual appreciation of the absurdity of the myth that unites us. Over the years, we have continued to make references to it. I suspect that my son, now in college, probably doesn't find it as amusing any longer, but he indulges us anyway. The story, for whatever reason, has persisted.

I embarked on this book project to highlight just this: events, by themselves, do not shape us. Rather, it is the meaning that humans assign to the events that matter; it is our interpretations of our experiences that will influence us the most. For this reason, I have been intrigued by, and therefore solicited for this book, the stories that mothers tell and their interpretations of their stories in the context of the environments in which they exist. Unlike my son's account of how he came to join our family, the autoethnographies in this book are *not* fictitious. However, like my son's fabricated tale, they are indeed endeavors through which we position ourselves within a broader society.

It is fair to say that many mothers (including myself) enjoy telling stories about their family. But the stories we tell do not exist in a social vacuum. Every story of motherhood is, at its core, an act of meaning-making about personal identity within the parameters of what is socio-culturally defined as acceptable or *normal*. And so, when disability enters the stage, our stories often take an unexpected turn. Act two, scene one. The scenery changes. The new backdrop is ableism. We may find ourselves going down the metaphorical rabbit hole where we are likely to encounter a cast of characters who claim to "know best." Or we may find ourselves navigating spaces that confine—our choices restricted, our judgements suspect. Through our journeys we re-examine what we had believed to be true, and we begin to re-narrate our family stories.

BIRTH STORY: REDUX

Fast forward a few years. Our second child, Minal, was now three years old. One night, when I was putting both children to bed, this following conversation took place:

Amiel: Tell the story about when Minal was born.
(Good grief, I think to myself, here we go again!)
Me: You mean how she jumped out of her own parents' crib and into ours? (I imagine he
wants to bestow upon his sister the same narrative of choosing our family).
Amiel: NOOO. That's silly. That's not what happened. Tell the REAL story.
Me: Um…okay… I'm not sure which one. Tell us what happened.
Amiel: When you and daddy were having a baby, you went to the hospital, and the doctor
showed you all of the babies they had at the hospital. And the doctor said, "Do you want this
baby?" And you said, "No." And then the doctor showed another baby and said, "Do you
want THIS baby?" And you said, "No, we want OUR baby!" And then you saw Minal
sleeping in a crib, and the doctor said, "Do you want THIS baby?" And you and daddy
shouted, "YES!" And then, Minal came home and lived right here with us.
Me: (Stunned. Not sure what to say). Oh, yeah…that's it.

I should offer some context for this second birth story. When Amiel was four years old, his sister was born and, soon after, diagnosed with Trisomy 21 (Down syndrome). From the very beginning, Amiel was immersed (at least in our home) in conversations which positioned disability as a natural human variation. For him, his sister's differences were simply a part of life—another aspect of our family's diversity, much like the presence of different racial or ethnic identities and religious backgrounds within our family. At the dinner table, conversations about disability and disability rights were common. Amiel joined in his sister's early intervention sessions, considering such activities to be a part of what families just do. Their relationship and interactions seemed similar to what one might expect of any other sibling pair.

However, despite our efforts to position disability in a positive way, Amiel was probably also picking up on the ableist messages we all received at the time. He had likely noticed how his parents bristled at the condolences that were constantly sent our way, the looks of shock or pity when we told others about her diagnosis, and the unrelenting questions about whether we had known about "her condition" prior to her birth, or why we had chosen to *not* find out. We had an alternative narrative about disability within our home. Still, dominant views on disability that centered on "tragedy" and "devastation" surrounded us, and surely informed my son's understanding of how his sister's birth was viewed in society.

Around this same time, a favorite book of both children, one that I'd frequently read to them, was: *Mama, do you love me?* (Joosse, 1991). In this book, an Inuit child poses a string of questions about whether she would be loved by her mother even if she transgressed the rules by committing certain acts, such as putting glue in her mother's shoes. The mother in the story reassures her daughter, calmly and repetitively after each question, that even if she is angry or displeased about her daughter's actions, the child will still be loved. The underlying theme in this beloved book about a child testing the limits of unconditional love and acceptance is one that would resonate with many parents, and is at the core of many children's questions about the nature of family relationships. I have since wondered if Amiel's story about how Minal came to be in our family was somehow related to this same question: what are the limits of our acceptance as parents? What kind of child would be desirable to us? In the second birth story he invented, one in which his dad and I pick a baby out of a line-up of candidates, a child does not strategize or plot to choose her parents. Rather, in this story, the focus seems to be on what kind of child we—the parents—would desire. Through this imaginary account of his sister's birth, Amiel (knowingly or not) participated in the co-construction of our re-emerging family identity—one in which disability is positioned as yet another form of diversity. Rejecting a narrative in which we merely "welcome" or "accept" his sister as part of our family, he replaced it with a more empowered narrative—one in which we actively sought her out. Indeed, in his story, we affirmatively *chose* her to join our family.

IDENTITY, FAMILIES, AND DISABILITY

Storytelling is an important means through which families share meaning about themselves and position themselves within the broader universe (Huisman, 2014). Family identities continually evolve as members jointly adapt and reconstruct their stories in response to events and experiences. When something unexpected occurs, we engage in a higher degree of meaning-making, focusing on details we choose to remember, and shading experiences in ways that create coherence out of chaos (McLean & Morrison-Cohen, 2013). As Bruner (1990) asserted, one of the primary uses of narratives is to make sense of the noncanonical. Humans need to appraise events, and ultimately, their appraisal may be more consequential than the event itself, for it is one's interpretation of whether an event is negative or positive that will prompt specific meaning-making processes to different degrees (e.g., deRoon-Cassini, de St. Aubin, Valvano, Hastings, & Horn, 2009; Park, 2010). However, the appraisal of any event can only occur within the context of what that event is culturally understood to be; identities are constructed within socio-culturally defined parameters of normalcy and acceptability. For this reason, as Galvin (2006) argued, the family stories of individuals with non-dominant family structures, or who have family members with marginalized identities, tend to be counter-narratives, which respond to, or resist, oppressive cultural discourses.

Perhaps Amiel's story about how his sister came to be a part of our family was his counter-narrative in response to cultural definitions of normalcy among families, which were implicitly, and often explicitly, communicated to us. Perhaps it reflected his emerging understanding that, as a unit, we exist within a society that considers us "atypical," and one in which his sister is assigned lesser value. Resisting dominant narratives that center on *grief* and *tragedy*, his story seemed to challenge common assumptions about disability. In it, we were cast as a normative family, and his sister, as a desirable child.

ACTS OF RESISTANCE

Just as Amiel's story about his sister's birth was his way of making meaning, the authors who have contributed to this book have responded to master narratives in which they are positioned as "other." Their autoethnographies are based in lived experiences at the intersection of motherhood and the politics of *normal*. From different vantage points, they shed light on how normalcy is constructed, its boundaries fiercely guarded by its gatekeepers. In some chapters, we learn of the ways in which reproductive technologies shape the expectations and experiences of motherhood, lending support to Gabel & Kotel's (2018) claim that mothers who would choose to give birth to children with disabilities are often viewed as transgressing cultural norms. In others, we are given a glimpse into a world in which mothers must confront institutional power structures or engage in a "battle" in order to gain access for their children. They explicate the many ways in which mothers endeavor to build inclusive communities when they don't already exist, and do the work of establishing allies for their marginalized family members—whether it is their child or an elderly parent. Some stories highlight the complexities of decisions surrounding the classification of children in schools, parents' understanding of the stigmatizing power of labels, and the social hierarchy of identities. Others compel us to consider the ways in which race, ethnicity, gender identity, and social class intersect with dis/ability within a power structure. We encounter the stories of mothers who draw from their cultural or economic capital when seeking inclusivity or resources for their family members, and the (very different) stories of mothers who are not in possession of the same amounts of capital, revealing the extent to which the experience of having a child labelled with a disability is linked with socioeconomic privilege. Collectively, these autoethnographies illustrate "the power of the trope of the good mother" (Gabel & Kotel, 2018, p. 191) and the constructed hierarchy of acceptable children. They call attention to the patriarchal surveillance of mothering. They create a dissonance by questioning who gets access to the category of *mother*, and who should decide.

Ultimately, these are stories of resistance. Throughout this book, a central idea echoes: humans are not passive in the construction of identity. Bamberg (2004) asserted that when positioned malignantly through hegemonic discourses, individuals produce counter-narratives that assign new meaning to psychological and social phenomena, and thus, redefine their identities. Consistent with his assertions, our autoethnographies illustrate the many ways in which individuals, refusing to submit to notions of otherness, exercise agency. Through our stories we enact our resistance to, and rejection of, dominant narratives that are not consistent with the ways in which we define our own families and selves. Through our counter-narratives we push back. Not only are these stories *about* resistance, but the writing of these stories *are* acts of resistance.

There is power in the counter-narrative. At the beginning of this book, I stated that stories are not just passively influenced by contexts; they, in turn, have the power to change contexts. I revisit this idea here at the close of this book. Richey (2011) argued that counter discourses should not be locked in research conversations, but "legitimized through activism and institutional change" (p. 185). In this same spirit, it is my hope that the stories we told in this book may open or further dialogues across academic disciplines and professional practices toward the goal of social change. Perhaps they may spur educators to rethink unquestioned assumptions about disability, and about "these" mothers as unrealistic, irrational, or making unfair demands in the context of their children's schooling. Additionally, moving away from medical model-based special education practices that seek to sort, segregate, and remediate, we might begin to understand inclusivity in schools as a practice related to democracy, educational equity, and social justice (Slee, 2001; Ware, 2003). Consistent with Campbell's (2009) invitation to invert the traditional approach to disability, we might shift our collective gaze to the "production, operation, and maintenance of ableism" in schools (p. 4). By gaining an awareness of the ways in which decisions pertaining to the education of students with disabilities are linked with socioeconomic privilege, we can act to disrupt practices that lend institutional support to the marginalization of students with disabilities, and to the disablement of their families. It is only then that genuine professional-family partnerships can occur in the context of education.

Our counter-narratives invite medical and mental health professionals to question biologically deterministic and universal definitions of disability. Perhaps our stories might urge medical professionals to rethink the ways in which a diagnosis of a child's disability is communicated to family members, or to approach their interactions with mothers who receive a prenatal diagnosis of a genetic variation with a better understanding of how their own language and affect can shape mothers' experiences. Thus, they might begin to disrupt practices through which negative or biased interpretations of disability are upheld, and consider, instead, the need to provide more balanced information to families, which necessarily includes the perspective of those with lived experiences of having a disability and of parenting a child with a disability.

Ferguson, Gartner, and Lipsky (2000) caution us against making assumptions about outcomes for families of children with disabilities, drawing attention instead to the wide range of responses, interpretations, and resiliency that exist among them. Their claims resonate throughout this book. Perhaps then, it is time for mental health professionals to make a paradigm shift, moving away from expectations of lifelong grief or "denial" among this group of families and towards an understanding of parents' responses to their children's disabilities as agentic and purposeful. In order to do this, they should first deeply examine their own beliefs about disability and consider the ways in which they might be complicit in the oppression of this group of families through professional discourses in which the stigmas associated with disability are perpetuated, and in which parents of children with disabilities are pathologized.

From a disability studies perspective, disability is understood as a constructed phenomenon, its meaning situated in sociopolitical contexts (Linton, 1998; Oliver, 1990). Disability studies scholars and activists call on us to retract our collective gaze from impairments and refocus it on institutionally sanctioned ableism and the marginalization of those with disabilities. The authors who have contributed to this book have heeded this call. Their narratives challenge all assumptions about the familial experience of disability and dismantle any definition of normative motherhood. Their stories reveal the multiple ways in which interpretations of motherhood, disability, and, indeed, normalcy itself, are mutually negotiated between individuals and societies.

A good story is supposed to have a beginning, a middle, and an end. But our stories are evolving; our identities are continually in flux. Each chapter in this book is a life story in progress; even at their conclusion, they are unfinished stories—they are not done.

* * *

The other day, my daughter, Minal, now 16 years old, asked me to explain what I am writing in this book. So, we engaged in a conversation about what I have written and what I hope to communicate through it. Lately she has become very interested in the topic of disability and is increasingly participating in negotiating and narrating her own identity as a young woman with Down syndrome. We frequently talk about what this means to her. On this occasion, the conversation turned to the topic of her birth, and she asked me to tell her the "real story" of what happened when she was born. No, she was not referring to her brother's story about selecting her out of a line-up of babies—a story which she now finds a bit silly. She was referring to (in her words): "What happened after I was born, and the doctor told you that I have Down syndrome? What did you actually say?!"

And so I begin to tell another story.

REFERENCES

Baddeley, J., & Singer, J. A. (2007). Charting the life story's path: Narrative identity across the life span. In C. D. Jean, J. Baddeley, & J. A. Singer (Eds.), *Handbook of narrative inquiry: Mapping a methodology* (pp. 177–202). Thousand Oaks, CA: Sage Publications.

Bamberg, M. (2004). Considering counter-narratives. In M. Bamberg & M. Andrews (Eds.), *Considering counter-narratives* (pp. 351–371). Amsterdam, Netherlands: Benjamins Publishing.

Bruner, J. (1990). *Acts of meaning*. Cambridge, MA: Harvard University Press.

Campbell, F. (2009). *Contours of ableism: The production of disability and abledness.* New York, NY: Palgrave Macmillan.

Davis, L. (2006). Constructing normalcy. In L. Davis (Ed.), *The disability studies reader* (pp. 9–28). New York, NY: Routledge.

deRoon-Cassini, T. A., de St. Aubin, E., Valvano, A., Hastings, J., & Horn, P. (2009). Psychological well-being after spinal cord injury: Perception of loss and meaning making. *Rehabilitation Psychology, 54*(3), 306–314.

Ferguson, P., Gartner, A., & Lipsky, D. (2000). The experience of disability in families: A synthesis of research and parent narratives. In E. Parens & A. Asch (Eds.), *Prenatal testing and disability rights* (pp. 72–94). Washington, DC: Georgetown University Press.

Fivush, R., & Reese, E. (2002). Reminiscing and relating: The development of parent-child talk about the past. In J. D. Webster & B. K. Haight (Eds.), *Critical advances in reminiscence work: From theory to application* (pp. 109–122). New York, NY: Springer.

Gabel, S. L., & Kotel, K. (2018). Motherhood in the context of normative discourse: Birth stories of mothers of children with Down syndrome. *Journal of Medical Humanities, 39*(2), 179–193.

Galvin, K. (2006). Diversity's impact on defining the family: Discourse-dependence and identity. In L. H. Turner & R. L. West (Eds.), *The family communication sourcebook* (pp. 3–20). Thousand Oaks, CA: Sage Publications.

Huisman, D. (2014). Telling a family culture: Storytelling, family identity, and cultural membership. *Interpersona, 8*(2), 144–158.

Joosse, B. M. (1991). *Mama, do you love me?* San Francisco, CA: Chronicle Books, LLC.

Landsman, G. H. (2009). *Reconstructing motherhood and disability in the age of "perfect" babies.* New York, NY: Routledge.

Linton, S. (1998). *Claiming disability: Knowledge and identity.* New York, NY: New York University Press.

McAdams, D. P., & Adler, J. M. (2010). Autobiographical memory and the construction of a narrative identity: Theory, research, and clinical implications. In J. E. Maddux & J. P. Tangney (Eds.), *Social psychological foundations of clinical psychology* (pp. 36–50). New York, NY: The Guilford Press.

McAdams, D., & Manczak, E. (2015). Personality and the life story. In M. Mikulincer & P. Shaver (Eds.), *APA handbook of personality and social psychology: Personality processes and individual differences* (Vol. 4; pp. 425–446). Washington, DC: American Psychological Association.

McLean, K. C. (2015). *The co-authored self: Family stories and the construction of personal identity.* New York, NY: Oxford University Press.

McLean, K. C., & Morrison-Cohen, S. (2013). "But wait, it gets even weirder…": The meaning of stories. In J. A. Hicks & C. Routledge (Eds.), *The experience of meaning in life: Classical perspectives, emerging themes, and controversies* (pp. 201–212). New York, NY: Springer.

McLean, K. C., Pasupathi, M., & Pals, J. L. (2007). Selves creating stories creating selves: A process model of self-development. *Personality and Social Psychology Review, 11*(3), 262–278.

Oliver, M. (1990). *The politics of disablement: A sociological approach.* New York: NY: St. Martin's Press.

Park, C. L. (2010). Making sense of the meaning literature: An integrative review of meaning making and its effects on adjustment to stressful life events. *Psychological Bulletin, 136*(2), 257–301.

Richey, A. B. (2011). Birth(ing) stories: Combining poetic and paradigmatic approaches to mothers' counter narratives. *Journal of the Motherhood Initiative, 2*(1), 173–187.

Slee, R. (2001). Social justice and the changing directions in educational research: The case of inclusive education. *International Journal of Inclusive Education, 5*(2–3), 167–177.

Ware, L. (2003). Understanding disability and transforming schools. In T. Booth, K. Nes, & M. Strømstad (Eds.), *Developing inclusive teacher education* (pp. 146–165). London: Routledge Falmer.

Contributors

Tammy Bachrach is an Assistant Professor of Special Education at Azusa Pacific University (APU) in Southern California. She received her Ph.D. in Education and Disability Studies from Chapman University. Prior to assuming her position at APU, Tammy was a general and special educator for 18 years, working with both primary and secondary students with disabilities. Tammy grew up in the disability community as the daughter and sister of individuals with intellectual disabilities. Her scholarly work has focused on examining the lived experiences of children raised by parents with intellectual disabilities. In addition, she has a passion for bridging the gap between disability studies, faith communities, and inclusive faith-based schools. Her work has been published in the *Journal of Vocational Rehabilitation* and the *Justice, Spirituality & Education Journal*.

Susan Baglieri began her career in education as a high school special education teacher. She is currently an Associate Professor at Montclair State University, New Jersey. She is coauthor of the book, *Disability Studies and the Inclusive Classroom* (Routledge, 2012 and 2017), with Arthur Shapiro. Other works appear in book chapters related to disability studies in education, as well as in the journals *Harvard Educational Review, Review of Disability Studies, Teachers College Record, International Journal of Inclusive Education, Disability Studies Quarterly, Review of Disability Studies, Investigations in Mathematics Learning*, and the *Journal of Learning Disabilities*. She has served on the board of directors of the Society for Disability Studies and on the advisory board for South Mountain Co-operative. She resides in New Jersey with her husband and two children.

Diane Linder Berman is a high school math teacher at Stafford Technical Center in Rutland Vermont and an adjunct instructor at Hunter College, City University of New York (CUNY) where she teaches classes on including students with disabilities in general education. She holds a Master's Degree in Mathematics Education from New York University. She is the author of two books and numerous articles. She is interested in helping teachers and administrators create inclusive spaces where those with and without disabilities can learn and work together.

María Cioè-Peña earned her Ph.D. in Urban Education from The Graduate Center—City University of New York, where she was also an Advance Research Collaborative Fellow and a Presidential MAGNET Fellow. She is a former elementary school teacher whose passion for social justice in education pushes her to fight for equity and full inclusion for children of diverse backgrounds and abilities. With a B.A. in English and a M.S.Ed. in teaching urban students with disabilities, María's research focuses on bilingual children with dis/abilities, their families, and their ability to access multilingual learning spaces within NYC public schools. Her interests are deeply rooted in language practices and dis/ability awareness within schools and families. María is an Assistant Professor at Montclair State University.

David J. Connor, Ed.D., is a professor in the Special Education Department and in the Instructional Leadership Ed.D. program at Hunter College, City University of New York (CUNY). He is also a faculty member at large in the Urban Education doctoral program at CUNY's Graduate Center. David is the author/editor of several books, the latest of which are *Contemplating Dis/Ability in Schools and Society: A Life in Education* (2018) and the second edition of *Rethinking Disability: A Disability Studies Approach to Inclusive Practices* (2019), co-authored with Jan Valle.

Linnéa Franits is an associate professor of occupational therapy at Utica College in Utica, NY. She has an MA and BS in Occupational Therapy from New York University and is ABD in Disability Studies at Syracuse University. Her scholarly interests are in the area of disability narratives that surround individuals with disabilities as well as their family members. She is particularly interested in interdependency as experienced in families where disability is present, and relies on autoethnographic and arts-based methodologies for her inquiries into these realms.

Elaine Gerber is a medical anthropologist and disability studies scholar at Montclair State University and a former president of the Society for Disability Studies (SDS). Prior to joining the faculty, she served for five years as the Senior Research Associate for the American Foundation for the Blind (AFB) and taught in the graduate program in Disability Studies at the City University of New York. She received her Ph.D. from the University of California, Los Angeles and her B.A. from the University of Michigan (Go Blue!). Her work examines the intersection between culture and the body, initially with a focus on women's reproductive health. More recently, her work has focused on disability, and her current project concentrates on food insecurity and disablement. There are both theoretical contributions and practical applications to her work.

Negin Hosseini Goodrich is an Iranian-American writer, freelance journalist, and disability rights activist. She holds an ABD status in Communications and is currently a Ph.D. candidate in Second Language Studies at Purdue University. Negin has been working for, and with, Iranian disability organizations, including National Paralympic Committee, since 1995. Negin is interested in introducing Iran to the global literature on disability. In addition to authoring four monographs and several articles (in Persian), she published the first Persian resource on disability studies and introduced this academic field to Iran in 2015. Her memoire from Athens' 2004 Paralympic Games was nominated for the International Paralympic Media Awards (Printing Media) in 2005. As a freelance journalist, she strives to promote the rights of Iranians with disabilities. She has published in *Disability Studies Quarterly* and *Review of Disability Studies*

LaChan V. Hannon is the School of Education Certification Officer at The College of New Jersey and Executive Director of Greater Expectations Teaching and Advocacy Center. She is a Ph.D. candidate in Teacher Education and Teacher Development at Montclair State University, researching culturally responsive school practices with particular attention to parent engagement. Her scholarly work is focused on the intersectionality of race, disability, and parent involvement as they relate to the professional development of school educators. Her TED Talk titled *Young, Gifted & Black with Autism* was released in 2016. She has published articles and chapters in academic texts including: *International Handbook of Self-Study of Teaching and Teacher Education Practices* and *Journal of Autism and Developmental Disorders.*

Negar Irani is an Iranian mother and an advocate for families, especially mothers who have a child with autism. She has a bachelor's degree in Industrial Management and resides in Tehran, Iran. As a mother whose son, Ilia, is autistic, Negar is committed to spreading awareness about the positive aspects of life with a child with a disability and sharing accurate information about autism. She uses social media as a platform to share her ideas and answer questions daily. To reach more parents, she has created and managed several public channels on Telegram, including *Practical Points on Autism* and *Negar, Ilia's Mother* (available at: https://telegram.me/joinchat/BDtsqzvmXGHAaQ7TksblQA), which have over 1,345 members (as of January 2019).

Priya Lalvani is an associate professor of inclusive education and a disability studies scholar at Montclair State University. She holds a Ph.D. in Developmental Psychology from the City University of New York (CUNY), an M.A. in Special

Education from Teachers College, Columbia University, and an M.S. in Psychology from University of Bridgeport. Her research is focused on examining the sociopolitical contexts which frame the lived experiences of individuals with disabilities and their families. Additionally, through her work, she seeks to problematize and disrupt ableist practices in schools. She was the recipient of the Emerging Scholar in Disability Studies Award in 2015. Her work is published widely in academic journals including: *Equity and Excellence in Education, Disability Studies Quarterly, Disability and Society,* and *International Journal of Inclusive Education.* She is the co-author, along with Dr. Susan Baglieri, of *Undoing Ableism: Teaching about Disability in K-12 Classrooms* (Routledge, 2019).

Bernadette Macartney is an inclusive education and disability studies in education (DSE) scholar and activist. She has an early childhood teaching, research, and teacher education background. She lives with her family in Wellington, Aotearoa New Zealand. She has a Ph.D. in Education from the University of Canterbury (UC). In her work, she focuses on examining and challenging attitudes and structures that marginalize Disabled people and their families in education and the community. She is a core member of New Zealand's Education for All and Disability Pride Week initiatives and is involved in promoting and making the performing arts accessible to young disabled people. Bernadette was the recipient of the Disability Studies in Education Emerging Scholar Award in 2013.

Erin McCloskey is an associate professor of education at Vassar College. Her primary teaching and research interest is the study of educational injustice: how legal and institutional forces structure the experiences of individuals in special education contexts, how literacy levels are used to disable students in schools, and the overrepresentation of disabled people in carceral facilities. She is the author of the book, *Taking on a Learning Disability: At the Crossroads of Special Education and Adolescent Literacy Learning* (Information Age Press, 2012) and her research has been published in *Disability & Society, International Journal of Inclusive Education, Race Ethnicity and Education,* and *Journal of Childhood Literacy,* among others.

Carol Rogers-Shaw is a Ph.D. candidate in Lifelong Learning and Adult Education at Pennsylvania State University. She earned a B.A. and an M.A. in English, as well as an M.S. in Education with a concentration in Reading from Fordham University. Certified as both a secondary school teacher and supervisor, she taught high school English for over 30 years. Having taught extensively in a program that transitioned learning disabled adolescents, English language learners, and socio-economically disadvantaged students with weak basic skills into mainstream classes, she developed a strong desire to provide increased educational opportunities for marginalized students. Her research interests include expanding access and inclusion in higher education and lifelong learning for learners with disabilities, stigma and disability disclosure, identity development of learners with disabilities, distance education, and Universal Design for Learning.

Laura Castro Santamaría is a mother to three beautiful children, ages 19, 14, and 11. She recently re-entered the workforce after dedicating all of her time and attention over the last 19 years to raising her children. She is an avid believer that, no matter what families endure, the important thing is to keep growing and pushing forward. She is presently a member of her local PTA.

Maria T. Timberlake, Ph.D., is an associate professor in the Foundations and Social Advocacy Department at the State University of New York at Cortland. She is a former general and special educator who now prepares pre-service teachers for inclusive dual certification. Her research focuses on the interpretation of ambiguous policy language (i.e., "access" and "achievement"), how teachers understand the meaning of disability and select pedagogical approaches, and the implications of those decisions for students whose communication, sensory needs, perceived intellect and troubling behavior make them vulnerable to being misunderstood and underestimated. Her work has appeared in academic journals across a spectrum of areas including *Teaching and Teacher Education, Research and Practice in Severe Disabilities, International Journal of Inclusive Education* and *the Journal of Autism and Developmental Disorders.*

Monika Tiwari is a certified special education teacher at Montclair Public Schools in New Jersey. She has a Master's degree in Teaching from Montclair State University. She taught previously in India for many years, which gave her an opportunity to gain valuable experience in teaching to an immensely diverse community. She is the president of the Special Education Parents Advisory Group at Kenilworth Public Schools. Monika is a strong advocate of inclusion for people with disabilities and is very actively involved in changing societal perspective towards people with disabilities. She works extensively to train teachers and parents on inclusive teaching strategies and practices.

Linda Ware was recognized as the 2014 Disability Studies in Education Senior Scholar, following a lengthy academic career at several universities from New Mexico to New York. She has published widely in prestigious national and international academic journals. Her recent books include: *Beginning with Disability: A Primer* (Section Editor w/L.J. Davis, Routledge), *Critical Leaders and the Foundation of Disability Studies in Education* (Co-editor, 5—part series, Brill); and *(Dis) Assemblages: An International Critical Disability Studies Reader* (Editor, Springer). She resides happily near Santa Fe, New Mexico.

Elizabeth A. Wheeler is an associate professor of English and founding director of the Disability Studies Minor at the University of Oregon. Her book *HandiLand: The Crippest Place on Earth* (University of Michigan Press, 2019) examines the public presence and literary representation of children and young adults with disabilities since the worldwide rights laws of the late twentieth and early twenty-first centuries. Her work appears in academic journals such as *Children's Literature Quarterly* and *ISLE: Interdisciplinary Studies in Literature and the Environment* and anthologies such as *Afrofuturism in Time and Space* and *Disability Studies and the Environmental Humanities*. Together with Chloë Hughes, she co-edited a 2018 special issue of *The Journal of Literary and Cultural Disability Studies* on literature for young people. Wheeler is also artistic director of the Shenanigans inclusive theater company in Eugene, Oregon. In 2018–19, she held the Ottilie-Wildermuth Chair Visiting Professorship at the University of Tübingen, Germany. For more information, visit: https://english.uoregon.edu/profile/ewheeler

Disability Studies in Education

GENERAL EDITORS: SUSAN L. GABEL & SCOT DANFORTH

The book series Disability Studies in Education is dedicated to the publication of monographs and edited volumes that integrate the perspectives, methods, and theories of disability studies with the study of issues and problems of education. The series features books that further define, elaborate upon, and extend knowledge in the field of disability studies in education. Special emphasis is given to work that poses solutions to important problems facing contemporary educational theory, policy, and practice.

To order other books in this series, please contact our Customer Service Department:

(800) 770-LANG (within the U.S.)
(212) 647-7706 (outside the U.S.)
(212) 647-7707 FAX

Or browse by series:

WWW.PETERLANG.COM

Made in United States
North Haven, CT
11 July 2024

54647386R00147